TOWARDS LOVING THE PSALMS

TOWARDS
LOVING THE PSALMS

By

C. C. MARTINDALE, S.J.

NEW YORK
SHEED & WARD
1941

DE LICENTIA SUPERIORUM ORDINIS
NIHIL OBSTAT: PATRITIUS MORRIS S.TH.D., S.S.L.
CENSOR DEPUTATUS
IMPRIMATUR: E. MORROGH BERNARD
VIC. GEN.
WESTMONASTERII, DIE 7a FEBRUARII 1940

INTRODUCTION

A note on the genesis of this little book may explain its
character. Its writer was asked, long ago, to make a
meditation-book for Seminarians. He tried, but failed.
Then a translation, or paraphrase of the Breviary Psalms
was suggested; or at least a meditation-book taking each
Psalm in turn. This seemed impracticable. But since,
while saying Office or meditating, he found that certain
verses became " outstanding," or precious, he made notes
on some of these, and finally adapted and amplified them
as below.

Many verses of the Psalms will remain obscure, or not
be to our taste. However, there are few Psalms but contain passages, or at least verses, which thus " stand out ":
they can send their rays, as it were, back and forth; linger
in the memory; make you glad when you come to the
Psalm in which they are, and give " value " to all of it.
Everyone, of course, is bound to have his " favourite "
verses; these may not coincide with those that have here
been chosen. All the better! The author, too, has, naturally,
many others. But, gradually, verse after verse, passage
after passage, becomes luminous. Those that are here
used may suggest ideas quite different from the ideas
that are offered. Again, all the better. The more that is
discovered in the Psalms, the less likely is Office to become
burdensome or an affair of routine, whether among those
who are bound to recite it, or among that increasing
number of the laity who like to say the Little Office of
Our Lady, or Prime and Compline, or to assist at Vespers,
Tenebrae and so forth, and want to make more of the
Psalms than they do.

We have not made use of any definite " method," if only because no one is bound always to pray according to a fixed one. But on the whole we have divided the meditations into three " points," because we are accustomed to that, and because we sometimes wanted first to indicate the " swing " of the whole Psalm, or to mention the Hebrew original if it seemed better than the Latin, though we have tried to clear up obscurities only when they would suffice to occasion a *distraction*. We have not wanted to turn even the material for a meditation (let alone the meditation itself) into a lesson! Hence we have followed no one rule throughout. But on the whole we have tried to indicate the presumably literal sense of the words first—it seemed hardly reverent to seek for " applied," or mystical, or even immediately " practical " considerations *first*, for they include an element of " self " which may well not have been in the mind of the inspired writer at all. Thus, at the one extreme, we have not *forthwith* used definitely Christian interpretations of, e.g. the word " light " : nor, at the other, have we excluded even banal, or far-fetched, or practical notions, if they spontaneously rose into our own mind. Nor have we tried to arrange the meditations in any but the loosest order : nor have we avoided many repetitions—this is not a " book," but a collection of ideas suggested by the Psalms—and after all, the Psalms themselves are full of repetitions.[1]

Should any reader habitually use the Authorised or Revised version, we remind him that the Greek-Latin psalter joins into one the Hebrew Psalms ix and x, and also, cxiv and cxv ; while it divides the Hebrew Psalms

---

[1] We have also here and there added a few detached paragraphs suggested by verses in the psalm from which the main theme for meditation was selected. We recommend : *Psalms and Canticles*, by G. O'Neill, Bruce Publishing Co.; *The Psalms Explained*, by Callan & McHugh, J. Wagner ; *Commentary on the Psalms*, by T. E. Bird, Burns and Oates ; *The Psalms*, P. Boylan, Gill, Dublin.

cxvi and cxlvii into two. Also, the titles of the Psalms are sometimes reckoned as verse 1.

As a sort of " remote " preparation, we have prefixed some papers written originally for the *Homiletic Review*, with the kind permission of the Editor.

CONTENTS

PART ONE
TOWARDS LOVING THE PSALMS

I

IMAGINATION IN THE PSALMS

Pope Pius V, in the document dated 1570 and prefixed to our Missals, says that an emended Missal should correspond to an emended Breviary, and evidently wishes that not only should there be unity of celebrating and unity of singing Office throughout the Latin Church, but that in some sense there should be a harmony between Mass and Office themselves.

One of the remarkable phenomena of our time is the enormous increase in Missals printed *ad usum populi*; and publishers have told us that they cannot keep up with the demand. But again, a very large number of commentaries on the Psalms are appearing, witnessing to the desire of priests themselves to enter more deeply and lovingly into what they recite each day. No doubt, we readily own up to the difficulty we sometimes have when saying Office : we are busy and have to go fast; we are tired, and have nothing but distractions; the Psalms are obscure, and sometimes almost repulsive. Candidly, one may hate *fat*; and as for oil and marrow, not want to be reminded of them. But then : " Mons Dei, mons pinguis : mons coagulatus, mons pinguis! Ut quid suspicamini montes coagulatos ? "—The mountain of God is a fat mountain : a curdled mountain, a fat mountain! Why look askance at the curdled hills ? (Ps. lxvii. 16, 17). And " sicut adipe et pinguedine "—and Aaron whose head was so glossily anointed that the oil trickled down to his beard! One's only chance is not to *imagine* it. But then, if one could when saying the Psalms have one's imagination somewhat in the state of the author's own imagination—if one could acquire his way of looking at things and feeling about things! One would then sympathise, and not be repelled. In what follows, even though we mean to use the Breviary words whenever possible, we would like to get even a tiny way into the Hebrew state of mind, and we begin with the very humblest item—the small picturesque sentences that occur almost unconsciously in the Psalms.

The long Psalm cxviii, for example, is very neutral-tinted, partly because it is so " ethical," and also because it is " alphabetic "—i.e., each group of verses begins with the same letter—and therefore very " consciously " composed, *i.e.*, not able to leave the poet's imagination to run loose. Yet, even it suddenly says : " I am become like a wine-skin in the frost " (v. 83), and this picture is that of the soul pining, hoping against hope, yearning for comfort. And certainly one is, from time to time, all shrivelled and shrunk, snubbed, rebuffed, black and bleak. That is already good, as an image! But when we find that the Hebrew says, " like a wine-skin in the smoke " (hanging there, getting more and more unsightly, yet with the wine maturing within it), and then goes on to say, " Yet I forget not Thy decrees," the image is better still : " I am having a horrible time, but my *content*, my spiritual life, is getting richer and sweeter all the while! " We would never use such a simile on our own account, but, after seeing what it meant to the Psalmist, we can recite it with pleasure and conviction. And again : " They surrounded me like bees, and burned up like fire among thorns " (Ps. cxvii. 12)—we can say that quite heedlessly ; but if one has seen a swarm of Oriental bees, ferocious as hornets, flaring up out of their home that you have disturbed, and the way in which all in a moment dried brambles or even grass blazes furiously up, you realise the poor Psalmist's plight! And you don't wonder that there had to be, even, a pagan "Lord of Flies" (*Baal-Zebub*), so maddening are they, despite the Oriental's power of sitting placidly while green-blue shields of flies cling to his sores and suck them. I imagine that Ochozias (4 Kings, i. 2), after falling down through his window, was stung while unconscious by a poisoned fly, and that is why he sent—to the indignation of Elias—to consult the god of Ekron (Accaron), surnamed the Lord of Flies.

The whole of the quiet Psalm i is really full of images : life is a "way"—a path down which you walk, a road on which here or there you halt, with city-gates, where you sit in groups and talk. Christianity itself was, at first, often enough called a "way" (Acts xix. 23 ; 1 Thess. iii. 11 ; 2 Peter ii. 2, etc., etc.), and Our Lord called Himself *the* "Way" (John xiv. 6). In fact, "way" was a technical term among the Hebrews. The Just Man doesn't go off toward the assembly of the godless ; nor halt where impious men do ; nor sit down where iniquitous men sit. So many branching roads! So many sitting-places! So many groups in which you *could* stand still to talk! The beginning and ending of the Psalm are built up out of these images (cf. xxv. 4). In between, you have the picture of the firm-rooted "tree"—beside the runnels of water—a fruit-bearing tree! Its contrast is "dust," simply swept off from the face of the earth! When reading the Psalm, we ought to have in mind a land depending entirely upon wells, and the vegetation that grows up round about them. The tree near the water, never dropping its leaves, rooted, stable, lasting-out—and the dust, going up in energetic yet expiring eddies. Ah! *that* is the difference between the man rooted in God, in truth, in right —and the Opportunist—the man of the moment, the momentary man! God uproots the wicked ; but I cling firm like an olive-tree (Ps. li. 10), like the palm, like the cedar (Ps. xci. 13).

It would take far too long to collect all the phrases in the Psalms connected with the idea of "way." You

B

walk in it; err from or desert it; run in it; cannot find it; have it shown to you. Psalm cxviii, so "ethical" a Psalm, is naturally full of the metaphor. "O, the happiness of those whose way is stainless; who walk in the Law of the Lord!" (v. 1). "May my ways be made firm unto the keeping of Thy laws!" (v. 5). The "way" is God's Law made known to my conscience: "Look if there be any path of iniquity within me" (Ps. cxxxviii. 24). But it is not I who reveal it to myself: "Thy word is a lantern for my feet" (Ps. cxviii. 105); "Lead me in Thy Way. Send forth Thy Light and Thy Truth, that they may guide me, and lead me to Thy dwelling-place" (Ps. lxxxv. 11; xlii. 3).

All the same, even the right way can be slippery. Mire collects in the hollows. "My feet almost slipped—my footsteps almost stumbled," cries the poor Psalmist, in profound depression when he saw how the wicked prospered. He almost gave up and collapsed into the ditch and stopped there. Sometimes he got into a regular morass: "I am stuck in a deep mire. . . . I have nothing to stand upon. . . . Pull me out of the mire, lest I sink therein!" (Ps. lxviii. 3, 15). And there was always the possibility of a sudden storm in the hills or of melting snows, which liberated a mass of water rushing down a ravine—quickly running itself out, but meanwhile able to sweep away both men and flocks. "The water might well have overwhelmed us: a torrent would have swept over us—an insolent torrent would have gone over us" (Ps. cxxiii. 4, 5).[1] The Lord does pull him out, and forthwith sets his feet on to "solid rock" (Ps. xxvi. 6), and then takes him out into a "wide place" where he can move freely and even run (Ps. cxviii. 32,)[2] And the

---

[1] The Latin interchanges subject and object. In the Hebrew it is the water that goes over the men. We can understand the Latin as meaning: "We should have *vainly tried* to pass through an intractable flood. . . ." There are other references to drowning; but these we omit here.

[2] I think that the Hebrew mind was "all of a piece," and that it was difficult for it to think of "rock" at all without thinking of the immemorial associations that clustered round that word. *Yahweh* was the Rock of Israel—I am sorry

obvious delight of the Psalmist in the sense of "free space" around him (Ps. xvii. 30; xxx. 9; cxviii, 45), where his heart could expand itself and he could draw breath (ibid. 32)—liberation from a sort of spiritual claustrophobia!—is all the more apt if the mud into which he had fallen was at the bottom of one of those cisterns that were often beside the road, and into which the two blind men in the Gospels, trying to lead one another (as in Palestine they constantly did and do, I understand), were likely to slip. In such a cistern Joseph and Jeremias were actually imprisoned. Finally God puts him " in loco pascuae "—in " the lawns of Thy Paradise for ever green" (*Commendatio Animae*) and beside waters of refreshment (Ps. xxii. 2); and even, into His own Tent, on His own Mountain, in the very inmost nook of His Tabernacle (Ps. xxvi. 5, etc.).

But besides the extremely bad roads of Palestine (which account for the whole series of proclamations about " making straight, in the wilderness, a road " for the coming King—they did this so late as for the arrival of the German Emperor before the War), there were dangers both from beasts and men. David, as a boy, had come to grips with lion and bear (1 Kings xvii. 34); and I like to think of the other shepherd, Amos, who so ruefully describes the man who fled from a lion, " but a bear got him!" or escaped into a house and leaned panting on the wall only to have a snake come out from a cranny and bite him; or the herdsman who went to the rescue of one of his beasts, and got back from the lion " two legs or the tip of an ear " (Amos v. 19; iii. 12). The Psalms are full of references to being " snatched, as a lion does " (*e.g.*, Ps. vii. 3; xvi. 12; ix. 29, etc., etc.):

---

that later generations thought it too anthropomorphic to call God " Rock " directly, and made modifications, especially as this mental attitude towards the word is involved in all Messianic passages that use it, and is at the back of the promise to St. Peter. Undoubtedly we have to think of an organic series—God, Messiah, Israel; God, Christ, Church.

but these " lions " are definitely the Psalmist's enemies,
and you collect the picture of rocky roads where in any
shadow an enemy may be lurking—enemies, moreover,
who have the habit of digging holes in the path and
above all of tying cords across it so that in the dusk the
travellers should be tripped and easily set upon. Nothing
delighted the caustic humour of the Hebrew more than
to see his enemies fall into the pit they had dug for *him :*
" He dug a hole, and hollowed it out—and fell into the
very pit that he had made! " (Ps. vii. 16). In Ps. lvi.
5–7, he piles up the metaphors : " He snatched me away
from the midst of the lions' whelps where I was lying
stunned with fear—men, I mean, with teeth like spears and
arrows and tongues like a sharp sword. . . . They had
prepared a trap for my feet . . . and had dug a pit in
my path—but they fell into it themselves! " The references
in Ps. cxxxix. 6, and civ. 14, seem to me to prove that
the Psalmist is thinking not exclusively of hunters after
game : no doubt, he is in the lovely little verse : " Laqueus
contritus est, etc.,"—our life has escaped like a bird
from the net of the fowler (Ps. cxxiii. 7). But his insistence
on the snare being put by the side of the road where he
was walking, or *in* it, suggests a deliberate tripping up. And
Hebrew and general history—right on to modern detective
novels—provide plenty of instances of traps made by strings
or wire. However, one recalls that in the parable of the
Sower, when the grain fell on the hard road and could not
sink into anything, it bounced and rolled about, and birds
had an easy job in picking it up. So birds did haunt the
paths and were liable to be caught there. I still think that all
these passages do not contain only metaphors from hunting.

There is much more that certainly alludes to murderous
assaults, whether these be made upon a man's bodily
life or, so to say, his social life (*e.g.*, by calumny). The
picture here concerns, on the whole, *tongues*, *fangs* and
arrows. Fangs bite into the flesh ; they eat you up.

Tongues are serpents' tongues, with which the ancients easily associated the idea of venom. Arrows came flying suddenly who knew whence, and stuck into you. The enemy "devours my people like bread" (Ps. xiii. 4); he gnashes his teeth till he can eat his prey (Ps. xxxiv. 16, 25); in Ps. lxiii, slanderers whet their tongues into swords, and bend the bow to shoot secretly at the innocent; "they plot iniquity—they exhaust themselves with plotting: men work towards an insolent scheme but—up rises God, and their arrows turn into mere children's playthings!"[1] The metaphor of "vipers" was taken up by both the Baptist and Our Lord in regard of the Pharisees, beneath whose religious-sounding tongue lurked poison, and who certainly, like the "deaf adder that stoppeth her ears, nor listeneth to the voice of the charmer, the skilful snake-charmer!" (Ps. lvii. 5), would not listen to the Gospel. It would be an impertinence to suggest here the equivalents, in our spiritual life, to such enemies; we know our own temptations and the extreme subtlety of their approach. It is enough to recall that the Psalmist *never* excludes the idea of *God* from anything he sings: even when he is most personal, he is indignant with his enemies because in the last resort they are those of the Chosen People, the People chosen by *God*, so that anyone who injures the People or its King, injures—or rather, is attacking—God and God's Plan.

The Psalmist is no pessimist, though he often feels as if all were lost. We, mild in our reactions, must remember the immediate and furious reactions of the Oriental. In bad moments, his soul sticks to the dust (Ps. cxviii. 25); his bones—and the people's—are like clods scattered over the earth (Ps. cxl. 7); he is "like earth without water" (Ps. cxlii. 6; cf. lxii. 1, 2); he opens his mouth and gasps (Ps. cxviii. 131); he vanishes like a shadow

---

[1] I do not suppose that this is very near the original Hebrew; but it is what we read, and the sense, as such, is good.

as it dwindles—he can be shaken off as you shake a locust from your dress (Ps. cxiii. 23); he is flattened down into the dust and his heart is glued to the earth (Ps. xliii. 25). Psalm xxi is naturally full of many mournful metaphors: the Psalmist is a worm; he melts like wax; dogs and lions ssurround him. Needless to recall the great Psalms *Miserere* and *De Profundis*, and the others named " Penitential." Sometimes the Psalmist sees his enemies as merely external, shameless and outrageous; sometimes as external, but due he is afraid, to his own shortcomings; and sometimes as his personal bad tendencies.

But herein precisely is his optimism. The world is halved, in reality, not between sinners and non-sinners, but between sinners who rely on God and those who don't. He sings his songs of repentance, but is all the while sure that God watches over him. He expresses this constantly by alluding to God's " wings." Hebrew poetry very soon struck out its own abiding metaphors. We are here using only the Psalms, or almost only; but the image of God's over-arching, warm, soft and protecting wings can be traced all through the Scriptures. Those wings overshadow him (Ps. xvi. 8; lvi. 2; lx. 3–5; lxii; etc.); and he inherits the Lord's strength. In Ps. cxxxviii. 9, he tries to take the " wings of the dawn "—This means " morning-wings," *i.e.* " if I take wing early ": but in South Africa the sudden plunge upwards of the dawn from behind mountains most spontaneously made me think of wings spreading out, and then settling softly down over a nestling world. And his youth (Ps. cii. 5) is renewed so that it is like that of the eagle. There is here no notion of a phœnix, able to be burnt up and come out of the fire younger than ever (rather like St. John from his boiling oil), but of the strength and yet feathery softness of the eagle, and its power of flying high—right into the Sun! I think, then, that this metaphor of wings hovered between the vision of an eagle and of a hen. Our Lord used the metaphor of the hen, without hesitating. It is a mixture, in the Psalms, of the idea of "soaring" and of "brooding"; and when they told him to "fly away to the mountains like a sparrow" (well, any little bird, Ps. x. 2), he remembered that, even if he *were* like a small bird, he still could find a nest—God's Altar (Ps. lxxxiii. 4); and that his wings were powerful as those of the very wind (Ps. ciii. 3), upon which God was upborne.

One reason for his optimism was the transitoriness of evil, and the Divine Eternity. The whole world changes, as you may change a garment (Ps. ci. 27); evil things shall pass as a dream does when you wake (Ps. lxxii. 20); they tumble as when you push down, with a mere shove, some tottering wall (Ps. lxi. 4); and the very memory of them disappears with a crash (ix. 7); above all, they wither like the weak vegetation of which too Our Lord made a parable. The wicked wither like green grass (Ps. xxxvi. 2; lxxxix. 6; cii. 15); like the grains dropped on flat roofs by birds, which, before you can reap its produce (really before it so much as comes to maturity), dries up; no reaper can fill his folded robe with it; no one can glean it nor make it into sheaves—no one who passes by *those* harvesters would be likely to speak a blessing: "The Lord be with you! Be blessed in the Lord's Name!" (Ps. cxxviii. 6–8; cf. Ruth, ii. 4). On the other hand, the righteous man, his home, his family, are like firm-planted olive-trees, and vines, and palm-trees, not to be rooted up (Ps. xliii. 12; cxxvii. 3; lxxxviii. 7; xci. 8).

But this is not a sort of fatalism merely, for God takes the initiative and *makes* the wicked vanish. His iron rod breaks them like clay pots (Ps. ii. 9; xxx. 13); He smashes those teeth (Ps. iii. 8); He breaks their teeth though they be strong as lions; they flow away like water that runs itself out, like melting wax; fire plunges on them, and before the bramble realises that it has grown into a bush, up it will be burnt (lvii. 8–9; the Hebrew is quite different, but no matter). The Lord wakes up as a man might from a drunken sleep (such is the bold imagery of the Psalmist, by no means unparalleled in the Scriptures, lxxvii. 57); His hands hold a cup full of wine, undiluted with water, but intoxicatingly spiced; He has tilted it this way and that, and made the sinners of the whole world drink of it—yet are its dregs not finished, there is more to come (Ps. lxxiv. 9; cf. lix. 5, where He provides a " wine of staggering " to His own people; and again cf. Zach. xii. 2). He robes them with shame (Ps. cxxxi. 18; cviii. 29; one might reflect on Noe); He whirls them away like chaff or thistledown (Ps. lxxxii. 14); He makes them the " footstool " of His King (Ps. cix. 2).

But for His Faithful He prepares a " cup of rescue " (Ps. cxiv. 13); He invites them to His own abundant banquet (Ps. xxxv. 9; they dwell in His house for ever).

There are many other little pictures that we have no space for : but I cannot omit the vivid one of the shameless enemies that keep on and on returning towards evening, like greedy dogs howling and prowling in the muck-heaps (Ps. lviii. 7, 15). The Jews hated such scavengers, hideous, diseased, and fierce ; the dogs that licked Lazarus's sores were not *friendly*, as though pathetically they helped him when men would not—he was too weak to drive them off. As for God's making man " vanish like a spider " (Ps. xxxviii. 12), I cannot think this means merely a spider's web, so easily destroyed (in Ps. lxxxix. 9, " spider " is not really in the text at all), but either that the dead spider so quickly becomes a mere transparent shell, instantly smashed and vanishing, or because, when dying, its long scampering legs crumple up into a tiny ball—and the great insect *is* no more. Any other metaphor —like the exquisite one of the " weaned child " on its mother's breast, " so is my soul " (Ps. cxxx. 2)—we keep over to deal with in further chapters.

II

NATURE IN THE PSALMS

" Praise the Lord, O Nature ! "

AT Lauds on Sunday we recite the exultant Psalm cxlviii, *Laudate Dominum de caelis,* asking that all creation should praise the Lord—the heavens and their angels, sun, moon, stars and the firmament in which they are fixed ; yes, and the mysterious upper waters that the arching vault holds high above it ; and then the earth with its watery gulfs and the monsters that lurk in them, and all the, phenomena of the atmosphere, lightning, hail, snow, winds ; and then the mountainous earth, fruit-trees and cedars, wild beasts and cattle, things that creep and things that fly, and finally, men, whether kings or judges or simple lads and girls, young no less than old, and supremely Israel, the people of those who come so close to God. We ask that all these should *praise* Him. And all this is magnificently amplified in the *Benedicite omnia opera.*

I am rather sorry that the Hebrew mind didn't appreciate, one would say, *small* things. Job has any amount about the crocodile and the hippopotamus, but nothing about butterflies ; the Psalms say a good deal about sea-monsters, but don't mention kittens or puppies, and I wish they did. True, little birds get a " look-in " : but I fear that small animals are mentioned in the Old Testament chiefly in regard of their ritual cleanness : and while flowers are *noticed*, no Hebrew writer falls into the sort of ecstasy that was Our Lord's when He said that not Solomon in all his glory was arrayed like one of these little field anemones. And there is much about light, but little about colour (save *dyes*).

All the same, we cannot well criticise the Psalms for what they leave out, in view of what *we* leave out. Is it *our* custom, when we see beautiful or even impressive things, to exclaim and beg them *to bless the Lord*? But we very reasonably might do so. I see no reason why the sight of a fine railroad engine, or a delicate operating knife, or a wireless installation, shouldn't make us thank God for its being *so good of its kind*. When God said of the Nature He had made that it was " good," He had been making things very definitely according to " kinds," and the component elements of Nature were not good just anyhow, but according to *their* nature, with *that* sort of goodness ; and as *that* did they compose the external glory of God. Things, really, *are* God's glory ; and when the human or the angelic mind picks up, as it were, each thing, recognises its divine origin, *sees* that it is God's glory—well, these intelligences experience the need to congratulate it, to bid it *speak forth* God's praise ; and thus, they help it to fulfil the end of its existence.

You may say that this is the " pathetic fallacy " ; that insensitive creatures or unintelligent creatures are idly called out to by anybody. Well, in a sense they are. But I would much rather be a man whose soul was wrung by the beauty and sheer reality of things, and who called out to them as if they could sympathise, than a man who knew just what percentage of, say, water went to their composition, and left it at that. Yet maybe the mathematician—especially if he deals with curves, or with forces, or movement—has as many opportunities as anyone for bidding the hyperbola, the pressures, the fountain, to give glory to their Creator!

Moreover, some will of course say that the idea of God involved in this is " anthropomorphic." Who cares? Or rather, of course it is. " He spoke, and they came

into existence : He commanded, and they were made "
(Ps. clxviii. 5 ; xxiii. 2) ; "He gives snowflakes like
wool-fluff : He spreads hoar-frost like ashes : He sends
down His ice in fragments—who can resist His freezing ?
Yet shall He send forth His word—and they thaw : His
wind bloweth, and forth the waters flow!" (Ps. cxlvii.
5-7). "He brings forth clouds from the horizon : He
turns His lightnings into rain : He releases the winds
from their store-houses" (Ps. cxxxiv. 7). I think the
picture is lightning followed so abruptly by torrential
rain that the flame seems downright *turned into* the water,
not extinguished by it (Jeremias says much the same
thing, x. 16 ; li. 16). Of course, there are an amount
of "secondary causes"—but what of it ? At the head
of all, is GOD : it is far truer, and even more scientific,
to eliminate the intermediate than to disregard the Origin.
We are, then, free to exult in our religion without worrying
about the cavillers, and to praise God in His Creation,
and to bid it praise Him "after its kind."

It is certain that the Hebrew had no word for "Nature"
or even the abstract "Creation," but he perfectly well
realised the "world and all that therein is," and knew
that the whole of it depended upon God. And second, he
knew that in the world (apart from Angels, who were
after all, seldom what you might call a practical proposition)
the chief thing was *man*. Man, so small . . . so great!
The supreme expression of this is in Psalm viii (cf. cxxxv.
8-9) : "O Yahweh! O our God! How marvellous is
Thy Name [art Thou] in all the earth! It is from the lips
of those poor little babies that Men are, that Thou hast
decreed that Thy perfect praise should come! When I
look at the sky—moon—stars [and remember what
Palestinian stars *are* /]—O what is *Man* that Thou shouldst
remember or attend to him ? Yet hast Thou made him
but a little lower than God. . . . All is beneath his feet
. . . beasts tame and wild, flying birds, yes, and the

fish that have their goings in the sea!" Therefore it is
God's glory that the heavens forth-tell : His is the handi-
work that the firmament proclaims. " Day unto Day
fountaineth forth its lore ; Night unto Night whispereth
what it knoweth. They need neither words nor language
—no voice of theirs is heard. . . . Yet over all the earth
goeth forth their sounds—to the world's end, their
message." (There is a superb transition in this Psalm
xviii : " Look at the sun! The Sun, coming out from
his chamber like an exultant bridegroom, triumphs to run
his course from one side of the heavens to the other—
not one can hide from his heat. Even so, God's Law,
shining in the hearts of all men "—and the Psalm passes
into the exquisite elegiacs of its second half.)

Now the Hebrew (perhaps because of his sojourn at
the foot of Sinai) was always more impressed by the
terrific phenomena of Nature than by its gentler ones.
Especially he did not like the Sea, apparently so lawless,
any more than the Greek did, who was constantly forced
to go out upon it, and his toil seemed so fruitless, so
" unharvested." The Hebrew kept reminding himself
that God *owned* the Sea (" ipsius est mare," Matins), and
readers will remember the picture at the *back* of every
Semitic mind—the primeval monster, Tiamat (the same
word as Tehom in Genesis that we translate " abyss "),
that the pagan gods had to *conquer*, but which, like everything else, was but the servant, nay, the plaything of God.
The supreme Sea-Psalm (apart from the one in " Jonas ")
from this point of view is surely the ninety-second—
Dominus regnavit (The Lord has taken His seat as King).
" High raised the floods, O Lord ; high raised the floods
their roar ; high raised the floods their waves! Yet, above
the voices of the many waters marvellous—beyond the
upsurgings of the sea—marvellous on high is . . . God."
God, who " fashioned dawn and noon and warmth and
winter " (Ps. lxxiii. 16, 17), collects all these waters " as

in a mere wine-skin " (xxxvii. 7) ; He measures the waters in the hollow of His hand, and the islands are but as a little dust (Is. xl. 12, 15).

It remains that the Hebrews had become accustomed to think of God in terms of storm rather than stillness—which makes the vision granted to Elias all the more extraordinary, when God was *not* in the lightning nor the earthquake, but in the " voice of gentle stillness " (2 Kings xix. 12). Hence we understand how often storms are alluded to in the Psalms.

" The voice of The Lord, over the Waters!
    The Mighty God, thundering!
    The Lord, over the great waters!
The Voice of the Lord, in Might!
The Voice of the Lord, in Splendour!
The Voice of the Lord, smashing the Cedars—
    Yes, smashing the very Cedars of Lebanon! . . .
The Voice of the Lord, slashing across the lightning!
The Voice of the Lord, making the Desert tremble.
    Sweeping away the leaves of the very forests! "
                    (Ps. xxviii. 3–9)

And again Psalm lxxvi. 17–21 :

" The waters saw Thee, O God : the Waters saw Thee and feared.
The Deep was terrified.
Mighty the roar of the Waters! Thunderous the voice of the Clouds!
Yes, Thine arrows pierce through. . . .
The voice of the thunder was in Thy chariot-wheels.
The flashings blazed out over the whole round earth—the Earth shook, and quivered. . . .
Yet, like simple lambs didst Thou lead Thy People home! "

But there are quieter Psalms (though they mostly include Storms!) which take a kind of general view of

"Nature" (as we say) and God's dominance over it. Such is the grateful Psalm ciii. God clothes Himself with Light as with a robe; He domes the sky out into a tent; He treats the winds as winged chariots; His messengers are winds and lightnings; He poises the unshakable earth, even though it were covered with water. But then, He tears apart this robe of water, covering even the hills. Up stand the mountains; down sink the valleys. The leaping of sources in the dells! That is where wild creatures get their drink—above the pools is where the birds can sing! Up springs the grass for the cattle, the vine for man : up spring the corn and the olive. And up rise the great trees where birds can nest; birds and beast are at home there—stork, and wild goat, and poor little hedgehog. . . . And for these night alternates with day. Out creep the beasts in the dark, growling, prowling. The sun rises, and back they shrink. But *Man* goes forth to his work until the sunset—his work on land, and even sea. (The Sea! with its slippery gliding creatures small and large! With its great ultimate sea-monster, that God made to play with. . . .) All of them look to God . . . for their food. But before *sustenance*, they needed their Creation. He sent forth His creative breath—and there they are! He withdraws it—and they die. He sends it forth anew—and " the face of the earth is renovated! "

In Psalm cvi we have the curious *inversion*—" Israel " first, mankind and its necessities second. Israel is created and maintained; *then* you see the fate of mankind as well as of the Chosen People. A superb lyric about a Storm follows : " They rose up to the sky . . . they sank down to the depth . . . they reeled and staggered like drunken men." But up they came,—back they came— and God, who could make fruitful waterful lands into deserts, for *them* did He make the parched land into an irrigated one—orchards, vineyards, habitable cities. The " young ravens " that cried to Him (cxlvi. 9) were not heard more accurately or lovingly than the men who did the same—" according to their kind."

Thus, at long last, the " Promised Land " became—or could have become—what God wanted it to be. In Psalm lxiv. the Hebrew is often different in details from our version. No matter. God, who visits the depths of the sea and sets them astir and sways them into thundering waves, who controls also the earth, who gives joy both to the outgoing of the dawn and to the dusk, who visits the earth and intoxicates it with His presence and enriches it and makes it manifold (not sterile)—" O God ! " the Psalmist cries, " Thou River of Life, so full, so full of life-giving water, prepare food for us (for to this the earth is destined) ; give increase to its buds—its joy is in its budding ; bless the whole circle of the year with Thy bounty ; fill the field with plenty ; cause the desert to grow rich and beautiful ; robe the hills with gladness ! May the valleys stand so thick with corn that they shout and sing !"

It is incredible that the Office, once we isolate even this part of it (not that in the end we wish to isolate anything at all), should not *force* us *efficaciously* to pray for the sprouting of God's Grain, for the burgeoning of God's Vine, in all parts of His earth. (What is that Terrain ? Nothing else, first, save that part of the world in which we individually are.) God dominates the air, the water, the earth. Shall He do less in regard of the floating thoughts that influence men—in the social, heaving environment in which they find themselves, in the actual work and human occupations in which they are involved ? Of course He will not.

When, then, we contemplate " Nature," a fact that neither we nor our Hebrew forebears ever dreamed of offering as *substitute* for God, may we love it, embrace it, make the most of it, take all of it to God ! Then we shall be like the inspired Psalmist, who did exactly that.

III

HUMAN NATURE IN THE PSALMS (i)

IT has often been said that no human emotion has been left without its expression in the Psalms. No doubt this is so, and we easily remember the more violent of such expressions. We shall have to attend to these. But, first, it is as well to recall the quite placid view that the Hebrew was capable of taking of the " right sort of man."

The man who is fit to dwell in God's Tent and on His holy mountain is the one who is honest in thought and word and act, who will not listen to slander, who scorns the malicious, who commits no perjury, who does not lend money at usury, and who accepts no bribes. Such a man is established for ever (Ps. xiv).

Well, one might agree that that is a minimum that could be expected from any decent man! But Psalm xxiii, presumably allied to the former, insists : " The whole world is the Lord's. . . . ' Who then shall dare ascend His mountain—stand in His holy place ? ' ' The clean of hand ; the pure of heart—who sets not his heart on evil, nor swears treacherously.' " Yet, this is not at all a " quiet " Psalm. It is the ecstatic one in which the procession of God's elect is seen sweeping up the steep ascents of Sion while the towering gates lift their heads yet higher to admit God's Ark and the King of Glory. Psalm cxi is also about the man who shall " never be moved," but emphasises the positive side—not only he does not cruelly *take*, but he gives lavishly. As for the long Psalm cxviii, it (like the previously mentioned one) is alphabetical and does not admit of unconscious ardours (as the writer was constantly held up by the necessity of reflecting how to make the next line begin with the proper letter), but it has a sort of intensity about it which lifts it, to my mind, out of the category of what I call " placid " and minimising Psalms. These seem to take no vision further than that of the average " upright " man—and doubtless he is an excellent element in any community, and more stable and stabilising than the fanatic.[1]

However, it is striking how soon, even in quieter Psalms, the passionate element in the Hebrew nature shows itself. In Psalm c David announces that he means to sing of Mercy and of Justice—of the perfect man and the perfect ruler. As for the former, he will just have nothing to do with the wicked : he just " cuts " them. But then the " ruler " becomes roused : he will " pursue " the slanderer ; not only will he keep his house empty of impious men, but from early morning (presumably at the morning court sessions) he will be occupied in slaying the criminals within the land, and destroying evil-doers out of the Lord's City. It is always a certain grief that the exquisite Psalm lxii, *Deus Deus meus*, allows the purity of its yearning for God and its trust in Him to turn into a fierce denunciation of the king's enemies (the sword shall slay them ; unburied, they shall be left to the jackals), and that the last Psalm but one (Ps. cxlix, so beloved by the Roundheads!) should insist that, while the praise of God was on the people's lips, two-edged swords were in their hands, *ad faciendam vindictam*—to take vengeance on the heathen, to bind kings and chieftains with iron fetters, and wreak the destined doom upon them. One cannot but recall that other " purpose " in the *Benedictus*—*ad*

---

[1] The insistence on usury in such Psalms and in many of the prophets, and on the oppression of the poor, is remarkable. Legislation tried to prevent the former, at least within the Chosen People. As facts in social history, and for the formation of a theory about lending-at-interest, all this is important ; but here we are studying what is more subjective—moods, emotions, temperament, and so forth.

dandam scientiam salutis : the Baptist goes forth to teach salvation, forgiveness of sins, and the Heart of Mercy that is God's.

Even the vision of the Messiah was apt to contain this ferocious element. Later on, please God, we shall reflect on Psalm lxxi, which is all of peace, but in Psalm ii the Anointed rules the heathen with an iron sceptre, and shatters them with it like potters' ware (cf. Ps. ci. 33), and his anger can suddenly blaze forth ; in Psalm cix. 6, he executes total vengeance, he lops off head after head, and (if we can trust a reasonable emendation) the heads roll down into the gullies and lap up the water there. The jeering, taunting expression is all too much in keeping with the spirit of that nation which even during the Crucifixion had nothing better to do than to deride the Sufferer.

This ferocious element in the Psalms delights all those who want to maintain that the Old Testament religion was a barbaric, hateful, and contemptible one, and that anyone committed to the Scriptures as a whole is committed to the belief that such a religion was " right." First, it is idle to deny that the revengeful spirit *existed*. The marvellous human pathos of *Super flumina Babylonis* (Ps. cxxxvi) cannot but deeply appeal to one : the exiles hung up their harps on the poplar-trees ; the inquisitive conquerors asked for " a native song " : " How should we sing a Song of Yahweh—in a foreign land ? " But then : " Doomed Daughter of Babel! O the happiness of him who pays thee back in full for thy deeds against *us !* Who seizes thine infants, and smashes them to pieces against the stones! " *That* can sicken! Psalm cviii (6–19) has been quoted as the extreme form of religious vituperation ; but it is at least arguable that this is a long quotation, and should be regarded as what the Psalmist's foes are saying to *him.* I began by thinking that this was only a " way out," but now I think that it is true ; only, it does not help much, because verse 29 is certainly the Psalmist's

—brief, but bitter enough; and I don't believe that the Psalmist foresees (and regretfully states) what God will do to his enemies—he *wants* Him to do it. Besides, there are all too many parallels. When he says, "Let them curse, but do Thou bless," I fear we cannot understand that as meaning, "bless Thou *them;*" but: "*They* curse me; do *Thou* bless me!"

God is continually congratulated on breaking the teeth of sinners (Ps. iii. 8, etc.); He is begged to *come in first,* and trip my enemies up (Ps. xvi. 13): to "discard them while still they live"—so that everyone can see it. God Himself is supposed to become crafty with the traitrous (Ps. xvii. 27), and to enable the Psalmist to pour out his enemies like dust, to scour them away like mud (v. 43); they shall be mere fuel for the furnace of God's anger (Ps. xx. 10); and certain verses recur often in the Psalms almost as traditional. In Psalm xxxiv, *Iudica nocentes me,* you get phrases often repeated and as it were concentrated. In *Deus in adiutorium* (Ps. lxix): "Let them be abashed and shamed . . . driven backwards and abashed. . . . Let them become like dust before the wind. . . . And the Angel of the Lord pursuing them! Let their path be black and slippery. . . . And the Angel of the Lord pursuing them!" (cf. Ps. xxxvi. 15, lvii, 11, where the righteous bathes his hands in blood).

Numbers, xxi. 14, quotes the "Book of the Wars of Yahweh" as one of its "sources." Therefore, we are not surprised to find how large a part War plays in the literature that ensued. Indeed, it is not too much to say that a "war dialect" formed itself, just as a "divine epiphany" one did, and as an eschatological one was stereotyped later on. The ancient Song of Deborah (Judges, v) is frequently echoed in the very mutilated Psalm lxvii. All the historical Psalms recall God's fierce p agues let loose on the Egyptians, and His jealous indignation in regard of "idols" and His wars (cf. also Pss. cxxxiv,

cxxxv, which are but incidentally historical). We can
sum up this section in a line or two—

> Shall I not hate those, Lord, that hate Thee?
> Shall I not loathe Thine enemies?
> With wholehearted hatred do I hate them—
> They are *my* enemies! (Ps. cxxxviii. 21, 22).

The first question seems to be : What did the Hebrews
really think when they sang such words ; and how, in
any case, could they sing them *rightfully?* And second,
how can *we* rightfully recite them ? The former is in
keeping with the tenor of these chapters, which are trying
to study the Psalms as such—that is, Psalms as sung by
the men who composed them. What sort of men were
these ? But then, we did say that *every* human emotion
was expressed in the Psalms—implying, of course, every
emotion not directly sinful like that of lust. In what way
can we Christians experience those emotions ? And express
them in *those* words ? And how could the Hebrew do so ?

At first sight, it is easy to condemn the Psalmist and his
race, and to absolve ourselves. It is easy for us to declare
that we translate the *whole* of the contents of the Psalms
on to a spiritual plane, and think of " sin," hate *that,*
and wish to see it done away with. And indeed that is
simple—*but do we really do this simple thing? We can*
easily recite the words, but we may do so *too* easily ! There
are still private feuds in plenty ; and we could with ad-
vantage meditate on " Forgive us our trespasses *as we*
forgive them who trespass against us." We invite God to
make His absolution of us depend on ours of them ! And
we require to make very sure indeed that we are telling the
truth when we insist that we are hating the sin and not
the sinner ; when we say we are indignant merely with
the grinding of the faces of the poor, and not with such
and such a human millstone engaged in doing it ; that we
loathe the stink of the houses of the poor, yet do not despise

or shirk the poor who live in them ; that we, who have suffered at the hands of another nation, do not dream of showing anything but welcome and affection to a man of that nationality ; that we, conscious of the gulf between white and black, are *seeking* earnestly, for Christ's sake, to bridge it. As a matter of fact, we Catholics are apt to be just as un-Christian and as full of hate (felt and shown) or of bitterness (between individuals, classes, nationalities and races) as almost anyone else is, and far be it from us to criticise the Psalmist.

Again, the Oriental was *intense* in all his reactions, and immeasurably more so than we are. Even when he " lay in wait," plotted, thought his murders out, he did so with an interior passion quite beyond what we, whether on this or that side of the Atlantic, can supply. (I don't forget that New York and Chicago are practically on the same latitude as Naples, and have far more climatic excuse than London has.) The murder (even if calculated) due to personal hatred is surely far more innocent than that due, for example, to exigencies of cold-blooded finance. The only point, here, is that there is plenty in the modern world which makes it impossible for us to crow over the Hebrew. As for that Hebrew, we are also apt to judge him by our own standards, and to suppose that the word " holy," for example, in the Scriptures means everywhere equally what we mean by it. But it really meant " chosen," selected, segregated. David remained the " holy " king even in the hour of his sin ; Jerusalem, even while full of idolatry, remained the " holy " city, and the land was holy-land.

God begins, if we may say so, where He finds people. He found the sons of Abraham possessed of that spark of pure religion that He had always preserved in the world, but smothered by everything else that was Oriental— racially and " nationally," though nations were hardly formed by then. The Hebrew, therefore, carried his temperament with him throughout his history ; and precisely because the Psalms reveal *at least* all that was in the Hebrew, they reveal his passion and his ferocity. It never died out : it might be controlled—he might also become ever so sober and even tender ; but the fierceness was always there— as you see in St. Paul : dare I say, as you see in Our Lord ? " Brood of vipers," " white-washed sepulchres "—not just anyone would say that. Not just anyone could evict the sellers from the enormous temple-court, as Christ did! And read St. John's Apocalypse!

This ferocity of temperament displayed itself among the Hebrews, naturally, when there was but little check upon them ; for example, during the period of the Judges when " every man did that which was right in his own eyes " (Judges xvii. 6), and when the sombre, hag-ridden Saul—or David, still an outlaw—was fighting his way forward. The Psalms are the first to acknowledge the iniquities of such periods. Yet, we must not be too severe even as regards such periods. It is non-Catholic scholars, precisely (like M. Lods), who think that the massacres were far milder than has been reported. And certainly I think that the " war dialect " has to be allowed for. The Israelite *liked to describe* himself as having " hewed " his way into Palestine up to his knees in blood, and prayed against his enemies *in those phrases by preference*. But I expect that a good deal of this *was* " dialect," like that which describes the moon as being turned into blood or the stars as falling out of the sky. This eschatological dialect lasted till the Middle Ages, when it was used about the death of individual important Jews.

We can also say that at least to some extent men *must* be the children of their period. We repeat that the Hebrews were not in the least a perfect race ; they were being led forward in the line of goodness by great men who saw further (under God's illumination) than they did, but (perhaps fortunately) not too much further. It seems to be God's plan to pick up men where they are, and lead them somewhat further, but not all the way. Such was Christ's own method. The goal lay further than His disciples guessed; *their* great work was to carry men further towards it than at first they knew.

Yet, at no stage in the history of the Hebrews do you fail to find forces that made continually for gentleness and peace, not even alone for justice. Yes, these co-exist with the ferocity both of feeling and of word. While an inspired writer is inspired to write as he does, it need not follow that he is inspired to feel, or even to think, as he does, let alone in the ideal way. Hence, a Psalmist may have vituperated his enemies in words that *we* can righteously make use of, but which may have *connoted*, so to say, not a little unregenerate sentiment on his own part. But, even so the *same* writer (or writers) can have entertained, and often did, sentiments of truly sublime kindliness, mercifulness, and the rest, even though these did but shine through his often murky mind; and prognosticate a Future, rather than praise a Present.

But in all this one must still remember that the Hebrew thought of his enemy as primarily *God's* enemy; and so, even if he misinterpreted the *way* in which God meant His enemies to be scattered, that is no more than an instance of what we continually urge—that a man may have a *true* idea of the existence or domination of God, and yet misapply it, or draw deductions from it, in a thousand inadequate or even reprehensible ways.

It matters less from what emotions the Hebrew started than what ideas or emotions were in conflict with, and continuously modifying, his erroneous self. Towards what was the Hebrew mentality growing? Into what did it, at its best, emerge? Into something so sweet and pure that no pagan race has ever had anything to put into serious competition with it. In another chapter we must try to indicate the *conflict* discernible in the Psalms.

IV

HUMAN NATURE IN THE PSALMS (ii)

PHILOSOPHERS are always apt to be rather worried by
words like " temperamental " ; and Scholastic philosophers
do not at all like impressionism or sentiment interfering
with the purity of the syllogism. Yet, I doubt whether
Aristotle would have excluded a man's general make-up
from his attention, if only because in the *Ethics* he describes,
with light yet caustic touch, different *sorts* of men (all of
them " rational animals," but each of them making syl-
logisms with quite different minor premises). And without
Aristotle, Theophrastus wouldn't have written his en-
chanting " Characters " ; and without Theophrastus, there
would have been no La Bruyère—at least, not the one we
know. So the thing has lasted, and if one doesn't attend
to it, one gets into dreadful trouble.

In the last chapter we suggested that climatic conditions
helped to produce different sorts of men ; and that the
Hebrew was a very special sort of man, into whose make-up
the influence of his environment had entered not a little.
So we shall not understand what the Hebrew felt, sang
or wrote unless to some extent we sympathise with the
sort of man that he was because of the world he lived in.
The curious thing seems to be this : the Hebrew, incredibly
narrowed as he was in many ways, yet seems to have
something in him with which *all* sorts of people can more
or less sympathise and which they can understand, whereas
the appeal of the Indian or Chinese is much more restricted.
Hence, the " Catholic Religion " can descend from a
Hebrew ancestry ; but I doubt if it could from a Russian

ancestry. The thing is of practical importance. The Faith is by no means the perquisite of theological professors or northern nuns or business-men or cultured folks. It has to be something that can be used by the fierce Zulu (if Zulus are any more permitted to be fierce), the languorous brown men in some Pacific island, the Edinburgh doctor, the Parisian artist and logician. Hence, when a man hymns pacificism, and says that the great obstacle is not national*ism* but nationali*ty*, and parodies love for one's land by identifying it with what he means by nationalism (love for your land, but hate for other people's lands), he is forgetting all sorts of concrete facts : people *cannot* all of them be just the same as everybody else ; they *must* fall into groups owing to district, climate, customs and history ; they *ought* not to smudge out all these differentiations for the sake of a grey identity, especially if it be only professors or agitators who proclaim it. The Hebrew, then, was (and always will be) very much a Hebrew ; he was right in being so ; we are better able to enter into contact with this immemorial aristocrat in proportion as he *is himself*, and not internationalised into who knows what!

Now, one of the most human attributes of the Hebrew was his liability to suffer violent reactions. In this he was second only to the Russian himself ; the reason being, it seems to me, that the Russian till recently has never had any interior conviction about anything—such, I mean, that his whole intelligence *and will* were committed to it—but has always been a victim (as he still is) to external coercion. The Hebrew had a deep conviction of the Unity and Paramountcy of God, and fully recognised that the Law given through Moses ought to be obeyed. Yet, not only the course of human events did not seem to bear this out, but he felt personally that his own life was not bearing it out. Then down he went into the depths of despondency ; and then up like a cork he came. The Psalm which indicates this most clearly—dare I say, almost amusingly ?[1]—is perhaps the seventy-second. It is one of the great " see-saw " Psalms—Reaction-Psalms. The Psalmist begins with a cry due to the *last* thing he has thought of : " How good is God to Israel! " God is *good* to His chosen. But then he looks back. " Yet . . . I *nearly* slipped. . . . I nearly stumbled. . . . I was *indignant* about the impious, when I saw how everything went peaceably for them! One cannot hope that they will *die*. . . . If they even *suffer*, it doesn't last. . . . They seem exempt from the ordinary troubles of mankind. . . . When others are struck, *they* go scot-free." Hence they get prouder and prouder ; they get fat and sleek ; they stare up to heaven and speak insolently—and they send their haughty words swiftly over the earth. " So even my own people turns towards them—for full days are found there! " They say : " God knows nothing about it. God does not attend to it. It is, precisely, the sinners who prosper."

The Psalmist desponds. " Well, then ; I have kept myself clean, and submitted to all sorts of disabilities, all for nothing! But then . . . but then . . . if I say *that*, I am condemning the whole history of my race! " The Psalmist felt that this would never do! He couldn't abdicate. He couldn't renounce the whole of Israel. He had to make an effort to understand it (*labor est . . .*) —but a hard problem lay before him! Until—until—he went into the Temple, and put his mind to what happened " in the long run." Then he perceives—as a kaleidoscope falls suddenly into a pattern—that wickedness fades like a nightmare, that there is no *permanency* in what is wrong. And " while I was being infuriated, and soured—it was *I* who was not understanding : I was as stupid as any brute-beast. And yet, and yet, it was Thy right hand that all

[1] For I could never deny that the Hebrew expresses himself, even in the Scriptures, with his *own sort* of caustic humour.

the while was guiding me ; it was Thou who wast leading me, and intending, actually, to bring me through into honour! "

Then it is that the Psalmist breaks out into the praise that his first verse echoes : " Ah, what is there for me, in heaven, save Thee ? What could I ask, on earth, save Thee ? . . . To cling close to God—that is my good ! To set my hope upon Yahweh, my God, and to proclaim His praise throughout the Holy City! "

Speaking with extremest reverence (for the Psalm is prophetic and Messianic, and concerned with the Crucifixion), another "reaction-Psalm" is the twenty-first. Its first words : " God, my God, look back towards me! Why hast Thou abandoned me ? " were quoted by Our Lord upon His Cross. It continues with a tragic contrast between God, living serene in heaven, giving every succour to ancient Israel, but forsaking the actual Sufferer whose anguish is related in the most poignant detail.

Yet, as from verse 23, the Psalm turns into a cry of triumph. Not only will the Sufferer be saved—" When I cried to Him, He listened to me," that is, I dare to say, *the* refrain throughout the Book of Psalms—but the succour is to be manifest, public. It shall take place as within a " great assemblage." " All the ends of the earth " —" all the heathen nations "—shall be caught up into this triumph ; generations yet to come shall hear of this ; peoples that the Lord has fashioned shall yet arise and know about it. " All the ends of the earth shall hear of the salvation worked by our God! "

Now, let us speak, maybe, somewhat crudely. *I could not*, if I wished, use the first words of this Psalm and forget or exclude all its other words. I do not think that anyone, conscious of the Psalm as a whole, *could* quote half the first verse, remember the next twenty-one and a half verses, and forget the remaining ten. Therefore, even humanwise, when Our Lord cried His " Eloi " from the

Cross, it *must* have been at least as much a cry of triumph as a cry of desperate anguish. If *I*, because of my mental make-up and my poor northern knowledge of the Psalms, *cannot* but be led by the first words of the Psalm towards all the rest, still less, speaking (as we are) humanwise, could Our Lord have failed so to envisage and be conscious of—in a part-less moment—the *entire Psalm*. Therefore, the "Eloi" of the Cross is *both* a cry of utter distress, *and*—supremely, for triumph is the complete "reaction" of the Psalm—a cry of hope, trust, victory, and "community"-victory. The Psalmist never envisages a private, isolated, self-hugging victory.

We have, then, to expect that in the Psalms there will be a recurrent expression of a mood that the Psalmist *rejects*. We have already seen that in Psalm viii there is a swing-back from the feeling that Man cannot count for anything, to the realisation that he is only a little less than God. Even the melancholy Psalm vi (*Domine, ne in furore*) cheers up, though briefly, at the end. Psalm ix, in its second part, desponds and then reacts: in verse 32, the wicked man is convinced that God forgets, turns His face away, and sees nothing whatsoever; he feels (34) that God will ask no questions. But God *does*, and He has the last word after all. Psalm xii asks God "how long" will He utterly forget me. But then it prays (verses 4 and 5), and returns to trust and even exultation (6). Psalm xxx begins with a strong expression of trust in God, and, assuming it is not an artificially constructed Psalm, built up out of pre-existing fragments, it then passes into expressions of deep melancholy and anxiety, explaining why the need for trust existed, and finally changes into that cry of exultation which indicates that the Psalmist *feels* that God has heard him. Psalm xxxiv again oscillates, even more violently, between one such mood and another, using phrases almost identical with those found elsewhere in the Psalms.

The temperamental character of the Psalmist, reflecting itself in what he sang, seems to me a very good reason for refusing to cut up the Psalms, as we possess them, into fragments allegedly stuck together by some collector of religious verse, simply because the thought does not flow regularly as *we* might expect it to. This pre-occupation with rigorous construction of *thought* seems to me a later product altogether. Not that the Hebrew was unable to arrange his *words* in very elaborate *forms ;* and as for the Apocalypse, its framework is as firmly articulated as that of any human skeleton. Even though we should regard this Book as made up of visions experienced by St. John as different parts of his life, I cannot but feel quite sure that he had the whole plan, its divisions and sub-divisions, before his mind as a complete unit when he wrote it down. But the Psalms are often far more " mood-y " than even the ecstatic Apocalypse ; and once we perceive this abrupt—almost Russian—vibration of mood, and therefore of idea, and therefore of expression, we get a long way towards " understanding " Hebrew literature in all save its purely narrative or statistical parts. Add, that no less violent a swing often occurs between the personalities of the *speakers* within a Psalm. Thus, Psalm ii begins with words spoken by the Psalmist ; then the heathens break in ; then the Psalmist resumes ; then the Messiah abruptly speaks, and finally the Psalmist gives his counsel. Everyone will recall Psalm xxiii (*Quis est iste Rex Gloriae ?*) and its magnificent alternations. However, that Psalm was no doubt *meant* to be sung by alternating choirs, or at least a choir and a soloist. It remains that intense and rapid alternations of mood are to be expected in a Psalmist ; and even Saul himself, now affectionate and now murderous, was but a morbid version of the same thing.

Again, it may be that critics are far too ready to talk of such and such a verse as being " borrowed " from an older Psalm, if only because men, when very excited, are at least as likely to use familiar phrases or even clichés as to strike out very original remarks. A man who would hate to use a threadbare expression like " I've got my back against the wall," might well do so when he was not only obstinate but angry. And, once more, there *was* a sort of " Psalm-dialect," just as there came to be an eschatological one.

But the recognition of these forthright expressions of mood in the Psalms is all the more to be welcomed because the Psalmist expresses certain moods only to reject them. He positively howls with despair ; and having, as we might say, " voided his bosom " thus, he can rise, disburdened, to his *true* conviction of the goodness and reliability of God, and expresses *that*. Indeed, he often *begins* by expressing that in a word or two, and then imaginatively goes back to his state of mind experienced before he " came round," so to say. He relates all his despair, re-feeling it in his very bones, but quite aware that he is going to get out of it, and has indeed already done so.

Inspiration, we know, does not interfere with a man's natural processes. It does not mend his grammar ; if he is a poet, it does not make him into an historian ; it does not equip a tempestuously passionate man with the " apathy " of a Stoic. The Psalmist is therefore moved to express the whole of himself and all of his sentiments, and then—to rebuke himself and discard some of them. I see then no reason why, as we said in a previous chapter, he should not have been allowed to utter sentiments, and display emotions which would fall far short of what Our Lord taught to His Christians : yet in the long run, we can easily recognise that these are not the last word in the Psalms—and even if it was not, of course, one man who wrote all the Psalms, yet the " Psalms " constitute a " book," and did so for the Hebrews no less than for us ; and even if we take only the first part or two of that Book, presumably composed on the whole of the older Psalms, still we find all the elements in these that we find anywhere else, and perceive that Mercy is a crowning one amongst them. The *upshot* of the Psalms, in the impression they make on us, is not war, nor revenge, nor hate. The Psalmists were able to reach a remarkable degree of self-knowledge, of which we may take as symbol the phrase : " Bonum est mihi, quia humiliasti me." They were at heart quite ready to abdicate all that bloodthirsty and materialistic element, and of this we take as symbol : " Hi in curribus, hi in equis, nos autem in Nomine Domini "—" These put their trust in chariots and these in horses : but we in the name of the Lord ! " That really *is* characteristic, and not in the least proper to pagan religious literature.

V

THE INNER SELF IN THE PSALMS

AT school, I think I felt faintly shocked at Ps. cxlvi. 10. "He taketh no pleasure," we sang, "in the strength of a horse, neither rejoiceth He in any man's legs." (Cavalry and infantry are no decisive use, is its real meaning.) Well, even if horse-racing seemed rather a distant affair, the hundred yards and the half-mile were proximate, and one was distinctly supposed to admire anyone whose legs enabled him to set up a record, and to talk about such persons endlessly—and, grotesque though it may seem, I really believe that this verse in the Psalms assisted the general idea that Religion was indifferent to ordinary life, and in fact rather disapproved of it. Religion was the universal snub.

The horse and the man reappeared, rather less contemptuously, in Ps. xxxii. 16, 17. Neither king nor hero are saved by their great armies; and "the horse is deceptive for rescue "; it is not strength nor speed that save. And Psalm xix. 8 exclaims: "These put their trust in chariots, and these in horses: but *we* call on the Name of the Lord."

The Hebrew was both impressed by chariots and horses, and rather easily struck by their relative failure in war. Israel in Egypt must have been profoundly moved imaginatively by the chariots and horses of the ruling people, simply because no one, who possessed neither, could fail to be so; and because even now, when you think of Egyptian wall-paintings, magnificent chariots and horses are one of the first things that rise up in your memory. But then, during the Exodus, chariots and horses had come terribly to grief in the heavy slime of the Red Sea ; and in Palestine itself, it was only when Israel chose to come down to fight in the plains, that they were any good. But even when the Israelites were making a certain number of chariots for themselves, and even had special " cities " for them, I think that the superb stanzas and refrain of the Song of Moses continued to influence their entire poetic imagination ; the prophets constantly denounced those who put their trust in any such thing ; but, by emphasising the fact that the Lord would destroy chariots, they emphasised also their feeling that chariots were certainly things that *needed* to be destroyed divinely, if at all. And, on the whole, they used the picture of " chariot " with a feeling of satisfaction only when they had transferred it to the sky, where God has the clouds for His chariot (Ps. ciii. 3) and drives furiously upon the whirlwind (Jer. iv. 13. Compare " The chariots of Israel and the horsemen thereof! " in the vision of Elias's " Assumption " : 3 Kings ii. 12).

Hence, when we notice (as in the last chapter we recalled that we do) a continual swinging to and fro between the Psalmist's moods, we can be safe in saying that he swings continually back to his *real* self, away from a temporary lower one, and never settles down into the latter. Yet, that real self is real, not by virtue of human nature, not even Israel's nature—on the contrary, Israel was by temperament as pagan as anyone else ; but, because of God's vocation and unceasing presence, because of His blessings and His punishments (which were meant to be the same thing), Israel keeps returning to its " vocational " self, which *is* its real self, just as the Christian's real self has come to be his supernaturalised self.

The Book of Psalms never dreams of disguising the fact of Israel's perversities and " backslidings " ; and when critics heap up instances of the barbaric or idolatrous tendencies of the allegedly " holy " people, we recall

once more that " holy " means primarily " elect," or
" separate," and then that the inspired writers have done
exactly the same thing long before the critics. Of course,
you have purely triumphant hymns about Israel's history,
like Psalm cxxxv, though it too assigns all Israel's triumphs
to *God;* and Psalm cxxxiv is not much more than another
version of the same.

But look at the two Psalms civ, cv! " Remember!
Recollect the Lord and all His promises—and how *He*
kept them, and how *we* did not! " The former half of this
doctrine is expressed in Ps. civ; both parts in the so similar
Psalm which follows. We have sinned exactly as our ancestors did; we have worked unrighteousness, we have
done evil (verse 6). The Psalmist proceeds to the really
astonishing assertion that the People did not " heed "
the miracles that God worked for them in Egypt and
during the Exodus: apparently, this means that they did
not attend to them so as to see the point of them, for
presumably they were aware of the series of disasters that
provided an occasion for their escape, but did not see them
sub specie Divinae Providentiae. One has to be almost
exaggeratedly on one's guard against reading modern
moods or " psychology " into any ancient literature;
but it must be a permanent fact that human nature can
live in the midst of miracles and not " appreciate " them.
Even now, after all these centuries of Christian training,
it is possible for us to " see God's hand " in events or not
to see it. It is, on the one hand, possible to be a pseudo-
mystic, as those people are who, whenever they feel devout
and have a good idea, announce that " Our Lord said to
me. . . ." It is possible to see in every coincidence an
omen. But it is very much easier to disregard God's
guidance altogether. And it is tragically easy to recognise
it, proclaim it, and then forget all about it. The providential
event relapses into the general perspective of the past,
especially when some new uncomfortable thing occurs.

That is what the Israelites (far, far vaguer than we about the theology of " God," His unity, spirituality, goodness) did. When the pursuing Egyptian forces were defeated by the mud and the water, the Israelites gasped—realised they were free from their enslavement, praised God, and " quickly went and forgot what He had done." They could not " wait " for the working-out of His plan for them. On the glaring pebbles and under the furious reverberation of heat from the rock-cliffs in front of them, they wailed for the lush vegetation of the Delta—the onions, leeks and garlic : " Hast thou brought us out that we should perish in this wilderness ? " They would have been glad enough to stay among the idols and the gardens, had they but not been slaves! They revolted again and again : if they *had* to acknowledge the One God, Yahweh, let them at least have Him in visible form as the Egyptians had had their gods. They threw their stolen ornaments into the melting-pot, and " there came out this Bull," said Aaron, almost imbecile with terror of his over-whelming brother, Moses. In verses 32, 33, you would gather (especially if you compare them with the Book of Numbers xi), even Moses was " embittered," spoke savagely ; was angry, you would say, with God ; failed in faith. Anyway, he could not keep them from sharing in the sacrifices of the pagans whom they encountered (the Moabite god ; verse 28) ; from his high rock upon Mount Nebo, he could see the whole of the promised land from which they shrank in terror and loathed the thought of (24 ; and Numbers xiii, etc.), that tilted Land whose snowy Lebanon you can actually see from the southernmost end, but he never entered it.

And when the Israelites did get into the promised land, they fused with the pagan cults they found there. They joined in infant-sacrifice, and, if so, we may be sure that they refrained from no other form of pagan worship they found there. Their " adulteries " were not merely that

" wantoning away from God " that all idolatry is, and as
which, to the end, it was described as being; but they
succumbed to the whole nature-worship of such lands,
and their ritual prostitutions. The Lord, says verse 40,
loathed His inheritance. Yet, He did not forsake them.

As for Psalm lxxv, its definite refrain is : " Et apposuerunt
adhuc peccare ei " (17, 32, 40 sqq., 56). They kept relapsing.
But God's mind was always towards the future, and it is
hardly too much to say that one of the great specialities
of Hebrew religious history is that its eye *was* always
towards the future, and not back towards a mythical golden
age such as pagans nearly always invented. God, says the
Psalmist (verses 5, 6), established His Law in Israel so that
future generations should appreciate it, and *not be like their
ancestors*, a wandering, disobedient, unstable, disloyal race !
They forgot what He had done for them : they sinned all
over again, they sneeringly doubted God, they neither
believed nor hoped in Him. He gave them the manna,
and this strange desert-gum was insipid to them and
sickened them. " This manna ! " They demanded meat ;
the south-west wind blew quails, as it still does, from
Cyprus, and they gorged themselves so disgustingly
that " it came out at their nostrils." Well, He punished
them, and they returned and remembered ; they fawned
on Him with flattering words—*mentiti sunt* is a terse
expression for flattering a man. They kept turning aside,
and God, for His part, kept recollecting that after all man
is but a breath that goes and never comes back. How
be too hard on him ? Men were like an ill-made bow
that cheats the archer : God could not send His human
arrows straight. And even within the Land, they
" tempted " Him—tried to see how far He would go with
His mercy (that is a good human statement, if you
like). They infuriated Him with their idolatrous altars ;
made Him jealous with their co-gods : again and again,
even there, He chastised and almost annihilated them.

Yet after all, after all—He saved them and shepherded them.

This is not a history of the Hebrew People, nor even of the Psalter. So it is no part of my wish to suggest when such Psalms as these were written. It is perverse to assert that either all or that " pauca dumtaxat "—a mere poor minimum—of the Psalms descend from David. But it is quite justifiable to look at the Psalter (or any mass of literature) as a whole ; and that is exactly the way in which one gets the chance of discerning tendencies of thought, continuous flows of feeling. Hence, whether or no these Psalms that I have quoted were written before or after, for example, the Exile, does not matter. That was *always* the way, more or less, in which the Israelite felt about himself. At the back of the whole affair was not a murderous violence but the guidance of God, against which human nature, Israelite included, was always sinning. This went on throughout Jewish history, and unless we are to take Ezekiel's visions as purely symbolical (and why should we ?) we must suppose that hideous idolatries even then went on within the Temple itself. It was only towards the end that Israel had become thoroughly purged of all but its *moral* vices, and moral misconceptions even then discoloured the true notion of the Messiah, even in the minds of the Apostles—nay, speaking reverently, it was from these that the Devil chose his material for the Temptation of Our Lord.

We can then, on the one hand, say that the Scriptures themselves take every atom of wind out of the sails of their critics ; and, on the other, that we should do ourselves a great disservice were we to disregard the very gradual progress of God's revelation, and of the acceptance of that revelation, among the Holy People. The Psalms display this in a very consoling way.

From the very ancient Psalm iii onwards, study the references to " sleep "! There is the sleep that the Psalmist

can freely take, because he trusts in God (iii. 6; and iv. 9 :
" In peace will I lay myself down and forthwith sleep ").
Then there is the terrible stupor that falls on God's enemies·
" They slept their sleep! No haughty hero could find any
of his strength. At Thy rebuke, O God of Jacob, horse
and horseman went numb into sleep " (Ps. lxxv. 6, 7).
Psalm xv. 2 cries out, in the Latin, that God has " no need
of *my* good things "—I can contribute nothing! And in
the Hebrew we read, that I have nothing that can *exceed*
God, rival and outrun Him. Hence, since God, who does
not need him, is yet good to him, both his mind and flesh
can take trustful rest (verse 9).

We have not wanted to stress more than the trust in
God which *essentially* underlay the *national* Hebrew
attitude of " pride " or complacency. Now, if the Israelite
was essentially right in regard of his nation—and no one
denies that he was, if anything, pessimist in regard of the
world at large—it will have been still easier for him to be
right in regard of his individual conscience. The point
always is that, as we saw, he was a mixture (who isn't ?),
and that his mixedness reflects itself in what, under inspiration, he wrote. But in this mixture, one element is more
essential, more characteristic, than the others, and it is in
terms of *that* that we must interpret all the rest; and
it is in that sense that we can wholeheartedly and happily
recite the Psalms.

VI

THE DEEPER SELF IN THE PSALMS

ONE of the most disconcerting facts about Hebrew religion is the extreme slowness with which it achieved any idea of " heaven." Were we not confining ourselves to the Psalms, it would be easy to illustrate this from different books of the Old Testament. No more than any other ancient people, did the Hebrews deny *survival* ; but their notion of survival was that of one which didn't seem worth having. Their conception of *Sheol* cannot have differed much from that of the Assyrian or Babylonian, who thought of it as a dark and dusty place where the " shades " remained practically unconscious. The older Greek conception was much the same. The ghost flits faintly twittering down to the Hidden Land, while " the man himself " remains dead on the battlefield. The ghosts are but strengthless things (ἀμενηνὰ κάρηνα) ; the wits are not in them ; they need to drink some blood before they can understand or speak. The Greeks, uncomfortable about this prospect (as anyone might well be), tried to escape from it by magical formulas and initiations (such as those of the " Mysteries "), but these became shot through with Orphic or Pythagorean doctrines. Either you had what definitely resembled a purgatory and ended up in a " heaven," or were " incurable " and finished up in the fathomless slime of the abyss : or again, you passed through cycle after cycle of existence, till at long last you " flew off from the sorrowful weary wheel." Both for the Greek and for the Roman, the ghost, when it got out from its world (which it did once or twice a year), was on the whole malignant. It envied the " real live man," and had to be cheated with food put outside the houses or at least in the corridors, lest it should come further in and harm the inhabitants. The Roman, always a kindlier creature than the Greek, supplemented his gloomy Ghost-Days by the feast of *Cara Caristia* (or *Cara Cognatio*), when not only the living family buried its feuds and assembled at one table ; not only were the little statues of the household gods invited too, but places were laid for the dead ; ghosts, gods and men all met in friendly union.

The Hebrews did nothing so charming. But, as always, they had their special element. They were supremely distressed because the dead could no more " praise God."

" I am filled with woes. . . . My life is near the Grave : already I am counted as one who has gone down into the pit. No one can help me. . . . I am lonely among the dead (*i.e.*, I am cut off from all real friends) . . . like slain men sleeping in their tomb . . . whom Thou rememberest no more, for they are cut off from Thy hand."

The Psalmist (lxxxvii. 5–13) prays that he may be rescued from death :

" Thou art not likely to work miracles for the dead. . . . Doctors will not raise them back to praise Thee (the Hebrew says : " Or shall the Ghosts rise up to praise Thee ? "). Is anyone, in the grave, likely to tell of Thy mercy—or, in the Lost Land, of Thy faithfulness ? Shall Thy wonders be made known in the darkness, or Thy justice in the Forgotten World ? "

Compare with this Psalm vi. 6 : " In Death there is no one that praiseth Thee : in Sheol, who will give thanks to Thee ? " And Psalm xxix. 10 : " What use is there in my blood, if I go down into the grave ? Shall mere dust praise Thee or announce Thy faithfulness ? " (cf. verse 4).

Psalm cxiii. 25, having said that the heavens belong to
God and the Earth to man, proceeds : " Not the dead shall
praise Thee, Lord—not any of them who go down into
Sheol : but *we* who are still *alive !* " " Their graves are
their homes for ever—their dwellings, for ever and ever.
. . . Like sheep are they swept away—death shepherds
them off into Sheol " (Ps. xlvii. 12, 15). " Let them go
down alive into Sheol! " (Ps. liv. 16) means : " Let them
die in the fullness of life—suddenly, without the rehearsal
of sickness! " Neither princes nor any man can help you :
" when his breath goes forth, he reverts to his original clay :
then come all his schemes to nothing " (Ps. cxlv. 4).

This is part of the Hebrew's conviction of the passing
nature of the world ; it was, compared with God, as
nothing. We are often reminded that a man can draw
false conclusions from perfectly sound major premisses :
" God exists, because otherwise nothing else could : but
several sorts of things exist—fire, earth, trees. Therefore,
there are several sorts of Gods." " God exists and all
depends on Him : but frightful things happen ; therefore
God is cruel and needs to be propitiated by slaughter.
He likes it."

Now, I think that the Hebrew was so smothered (as it
were) by the reality, eternity, supremacy of GOD, that
he hardly was *able* to examine deeply into the nature of the
relative transitoriness of everything else. His imagination
was so profoundly struck by the vanishing of created
things, and his intelligence so possessed by the certainty
of the enduringness of God, that he hardly speculated
whether *man* might not be *lasting* in some exceptional
way.

" Thou hast made my days ' measurable '—easily counted
up from end to end (Hebrew : a mere span) ; what I
consist of is as nothing before Thee : yes, everything is
as nothing—yes, each living man. Yes, like a shadow doth
man pass : idle are his anxious efforts " (Ps. xxxviii. 6, 7).

We are familiar with the splendid Psalm ci, where the Psalmist sees his days like a shadow that lengthens and lengthens, and then suddenly vanishes into the general dark—but he then broadens his vision, and acknowledges that God, at the beginning, made both heavens and earth—the iron heavens; the " too, too solid " earth. Yet, even these shall perish, but God shall still endure. They shall shred themselves away like any garment: God, robed with light as with a garment, yet shall " change " them, and they shall disappear. " But Thou art the self-same, and *Thy* years shall not fail."

St. Paul made superb use of this (Hebrews i); but the next verse provides us with a bridge into a different world, into which the Psalmist's mind kept tending to enter, and did so successfully, at least when God's promises were concerned: there should be an enduring *Israel;* and it would be more than the human soul, the individual soul, could suffer, were it to have no consciousness at all of this.

I think this is the crevice through which the Hebrew mind crawled out into a real, though intermittent, perception of personal, conscious, worshipful, and happy immortality. Certainly, several of the Psalmist's declarations that God will not " leave " him in Sheol are violent expressions that he is " *as good as dead*," but that God will still rescue him. " God rescues me from the hand of hell, when it clutches at me " (Ps. xlviii. 16). All sorts of woes have come upon me, yet " Thou wilt again restore me and pull me forth from the chaos beneath the earth " (Ps. lxx. 20). This answers the question of Psalm lxxxviii. 49 : " What man lives that shall not die ? Who rescues his life from Sheol ? " And in Psalm xv. 10, we read : (I am full of confidence, for) " Thou wilt not abandon me to Sheol, nor permit Thy chosen one to be destroyed." The Biblical Commission, presumably because of the use made of this text in the Acts (among other reasons), has pronounced that we are to recognise in these words a prophecy of Our Lord's Resurrection, and we readily do so if only it is because we, precisely, are those who can see the full meaning of prophetic words, and the same Commission has long ago declared that the prophet *himself* need not have known the prophetic nature of what he said, nor indeed need an inspired writer have known that he was inspired.

However, in Psalm cii we read the following: " As a father pities his children, so pitieth the Lord those that fear Him. . . . He knoweth well what we are made of; He remembereth that we are but dust. Man—his days are like the grass's; the scorching wind sweeps over it, and it remains no more : even so, man's place remembereth him not " (so the Hebrew : the Latin, " man no more remembereth its—or his—place," is less straightforward: Ps. cii. 15, 16). Such sentences, passing as they do into a triumphant declaration of the enduring nature of God's mercy, are among those that make you feel sure that, if the Hebrew had it *put to him* in so many words, " Surely God *will* enable a man to be aware of Him, to praise Him, and be glad in Him, even beyond the grave," he would have assented. Such a victory for God, such loyalty and endless loving-kindness on the part of God, are *more in keeping* with all the other things that the Hebrew believed about God, than the idea of God's forgetting a man once his body had died. That was a sort of unexamined inheritance : he had not looked into it ; he had turned his mind to other ethical problems (such as the apparent success of the wicked) ; his mistake, in so far as it was a mistake, was due to his imagination, stirred by what he saw of *man*, and could hardly have subsisted if he had simply continued to work out the perfectly true things that he essentially was thinking about *God*. He could, without difficulty, have followed what he knew about God's power over death and life, and over nature's *recurrent* life. God sends forth His snow and ice—rivers themselves are immobilised by His frost (Ps. cxlvii. 5–7); but then, He sends forth His word, and it thaws them; His winds, and they make the waters flow anew.

In the magnificent Psalm (ciii) that reviews all creation, everything is seen depending upon God for food and existence itself. When God gives it, they take it; when He hides His face, they are in dismay; when He withdraws His breath (Vulgate: *their* breath), they faint and fall back into their dust. But then, if He sends forth that breath again, life too begins again, and He renews the face of the earth (27–30).

It seems, then, to me impossible that the Hebrew had not in his *inner self* everything necessary for a clear and happy belief in immortality; it was only a step from the recognition that God's spirit gave life and recurrent life to the vegetation that seemed to die, to the perception that He could maintain life in the man who seemed to die. Not only, in this way, would he have had a far clearer vision of the *way* in which justice would be done (and that God did do justice was held very strongly by him); not only would he have been freed from very awkward affirmations (such as, that "I was young, and now I have grown old, but never yet have I seen the righteous man abandoned, nor his children begging for bread"), but he would have been able to develop his sense of "conscience" even further and more swiftly than he did. It is of this very real sense of interior righteousness, and by no means only legal or ritual righteousness, that the next chapter speaks. For even we, even we, can tend to drop back towards the righteousness that consists in obedience to the letter of the law, and turn into those scribes and Pharisees who were *not* the genuine product of the Psalms!

VII

CONSCIENCE

IT has very often been alleged against the Old Testament Scriptures that the "modern conscience" cannot now use them, because the Hebrews thought certain things to be right which we now know to be Christian-wise wrong (angry revenge, for example), and that they keep becoming legalist. Thus we constantly recite the *Miserere*, are struck by its extreme spirituality, observe how God requires and the Psalmist asks for a *new heart*, and indeed that animal sacrifices are rejected. Had they been asked for, the Psalmist would have offered any amount of them : but no—the sacrifice that God wants is a chastened, humbled spirit : "They that worship Him, must worship Him in spirit and in sincerity." *And then*, one may feel, disconcertingly, disappointingly, a ritual conclusion is tacked on : "Wait till Jerusalem be re-built : *then* shall God have the proper sacrifices ; *then* shall they offer Him His due meed of bullocks!"

And in the really lovely Psalm *Caeli enarrant* (xviii), we let ourselves gladly go with the current of the Psalmist's thought, till we are suddenly pulled up by the petition (verse 13) : "Cleanse me from my un-noticed faults." Of course, we can pray that in our own very legitimate sense : "I haven't the slightest doubt that I offend against Thee a thousand times daily and never notice it—so coarse-grained am I, so insensitive, so irresponsive to Thy soft whispers, so religiously *vulgar*, so spiritually fifth-rate. Forgive me ! At least I acknowledge it! I don't even *know* when my Catholic life itself is jarring on You, Lord!" And that is good.

But it seems quite certain that the verse really refers to ritual mistakes and offences against ceremonial cleanness, that one might commit any number of times a day and never advert to it. By the time of Our Lord Jewish religious life had become so officially complicated that ordinary people simply had to give up any serious attempt to observe all the minutiæ that Scribe had declared were all-important, and that Pharisee proclaimed that he, and he only, properly obeyed.

More deeply, the Psalmist asks to be forgiven for the sins of his youth (xxiv. 7), done when—as a man well may feel—he did not have enough experience really to understand what he was doing.

Now we are often told to interpret the Psalms—and this passage among others—in a national sense. The sins of one's " youth " mean the bygone offences of Israel as a whole. This is a very valuable hint, and I think that we ought *also* to do so. But " either . . . or," " wholly . . . not at all," and other sharp dichotomies, are rarely applicable in human history, and hardly ever in the psychological or literary history of the Hebrews. Aristotle himself said that you could not divide hot and cold with an axe ; and human nature vibrates between shivers and panting. What I mean here is, that the Hebrew was extremely conscious of his individual self, but also, and at the same time, of his incorporation with a number of other men (his fellow-Hebrews) and with many generations (all the God-guided Hebrew past). Nothing need make us suppose that David, in this Psalm, was thinking exclusively of his people and not at all of his own moral history. But I certainly do not think that David (or any other typical Hebrew) as a rule thought of himself in isolation and apart from the mass of men (tribe, nation) with which he was incorporated, and which, as in any king's case, he represented. This must have been especially true when he sang and transmitted a hymn which became a popular and perennial possession.

This gives us a hint about the prophetic passages which we try to interpret as of *one thing only*, especially, in the Old Testament, the passages about the " suffering servant " in Isaias. We, Catholics, tend to think that they refer to a definite individual—as a matter of fact, to Our Lord. And we are right. But, then, others come and tell us that they refer to Israel as a whole—though the " individualism " of the passages is such that all feel that *some* one person must be referred to ; and so, to get out of the awkward situation of having to confess that a prophecy was made, critics say that Isaias was referring to himself. But, rather as in the Psalms I think that the Psalmist was usually beginning with himself and what he was personally conscious of, and inevitably went on to think of his people as a whole, so in Isaias the prophet may have begun by thinking of the people as a whole, but have gone on to narrowing his vision down to a definite Messias, and a suffering one at that—exactly what the ordinary Jew could never tolerate to envisage.

And when I say " begun by," " gone on to," even that is inaccurate. The speaker saw one thing beyond (or rather, within) the other *all the time*. I have ventured before now to use a vulgar example : an intelligent woman (yet sufficiently human to look into shop-windows!) can see *both* her own face reflected in the plate-glass, *and* the hat behind it, *and* in the hat a whole symbol of the absurd difference in prices asked from different people, *and* the social problem that this involves, *and* the destined collapse of the present commercial system. The hat may seem to her positively soaked in future blood!

Speaking reverently, and with all due submission to authority, I think this is the sort of mentality that you detect in the writings of St. Paul (when writing about Anti-Christ, especially to the Thessalonians), in St. John, especially in the Apocalypse ; and in Our Lord's own words, when speaking about the siege of Jerusalem and the end of the world; and again, when speaking (John vi) about eternal life and the necessity of feeding on Himself. Is He speaking *only* of Jerusalem? *Only* of the ending of an era? *Only* of the consummation of the ages? No. But of all of them, the one seen within the other, the further pictured within the immediate. The immediate is seen as *true* on its own level; but *truer* on a higher plane, as including far wider, more universal things; as *actually* meant to be a real, concrete symbol of what is Eternal. Is He speaking *only* of the Blessed Sacrament? No. Certainly He is speaking of it; but as within the total idea of our eternal life, achieved by our total incorporation with Himself, which begins by faith and ends with the formation of the perfect Body of Christ—towards which Holy Communion is a supreme-yet-intermediate method. For once, the Way, the Goal, and the Life are identical.

Hence we may easily feel that, in Psalms such as I have quoted, the Psalmist is not to be taken as speaking only of himself, or only of the nation.

Now the sense of need for *interior sincerity* is suggested in the Psalms by their constant reference to *lies*. Such references are too numerous to reckon. Psalm xi is, however, a very good example. *Diminutae sunt veritates*— truth, loyalty, have absolutely vanished from among men. Each tells lies to his neighbour : their lips are liars. *In corde et corde locuti sunt*—they speak with two hearts : they say one thing and mean another. They say : " We shall boast and speak as we please. Our lips belong to us and no one else. Who is our master? " How different are the words of the Lord Himself! *Eloquia casta . . . pura ;* silver tried in the fire, clean from dross, seven times refined!

But the Psalm that shows how deeply the Psalmist felt his personal responsibility for sin and non-sin, is surely the thirty-first. It begins with a positive outburst about the happiness of the man whose sins are forgiven, to whom God imputes no sin, in whose soul there is no cheating. Till he confessed, the Psalmist was miserable: the thorn, says the Latin, was still sticking in him and his wound was festering; he positively writhed in his discomfort. But then he confessed, and was pardoned. And, therefore, let everyone else who has sinned do the same! Don't be obstinate! Don't be like horse or mule —the restive, rearing horse; the stubborn mule with its ears back. . . . *They* have to have force used if you are to manage them. Ah! don't be like that to God!

Nonne Deo subiecta erit anima mea? Though this Psalm (lxi) is directly concerned with confidence, yet the notion of complete submissiveness to God underlies and accompanies it. While a man is wealthy and in high honour, he does not realise his essential littleness finally expressed in his death; he is as dense as the brute beasts (the Hebrew simply says that he does not *abide;* he is no better than the beasts, he dies as they do, *cf.* xlviii 13, 21). But Psalm cxviii says definitely that " it was good for me that Thou didst humble me," that so I might learn Thy law (71); and, " before I suffered, I sinned " (67). Nor is it hard to find the Psalmist so anxious to be interiorly purified that he positively asks for the divine discipline; though, " let us be glad of the days in which Thou didst humble us " (lxxxix. 15), more probably should be: " Make us glad, in compensation for the days of sorrow."

We will allude to three more Psalms which, while not precisely dealing with conscience as such, yet can strengthen the sense of the innermost dependence of man upon God very effectively.

Psalm cxxxviii, *Domine, probasti me :* the Lord tests and tries the Psalmist to the very depths of his being; He knows whether he sits or arises, travels or takes rest; He puts his whole life, says the Hebrew vividly, through a sieve. Not a thought of his but God instantly knows;

E

not a word comes to his lips without God's being aware of it. Impossible to escape, even if one would, from that *all-presence*. If he should climb heaven-high, there is God : should he " make his bed" in Sheol itself, there still is He. Should he speed, as the rapid dawn does, to the extreme horizon (nay, beyond all seas), there would God's hand take hold of him. Nor can darkness hide him : to God darkness is no different from the day. Every part of his body is under God's control ; it was He who formed him even in the womb. God contemplated him while he was still unformed : He wrote down all his days before so much as one of them had dawned! And the Psalmist ends by begging God to examine him yet more closely, and see if there be any track for sin within him, and to put him in the path that leads to everlasting wellbeing.

Psalm lxix has its affinity with what we have just quoted, because in it God proclaims the counterpart to His all-presence—His terrible aloofness. God, in full panoply of thunder and lightning, summons earth and heaven, and His chosen people in particular, to come before Him for instruction. He does not *forbid* their ceaseless sacrifices, but He has no need of them. Nor would He go taking cattle from any herd of theirs :

> " For Mine is every wild beast in the forest—Mine the cattle in the hills. I know every bird of heaven—and Mine is all the beauty of the fields. Were I hungry, I would not need to tell thee—for Mine is the earth and all that therein is. What! do *I* eat the flesh of bulls, or drink the blood of goats? Nay—say *thanks* unto God ; and *so* fulfil thy vows unto the Highest! "

Then terribly He turns to the sinner :

> " Why repeatest *thou* My laws, and takest My covenant up upon thy tongue ? And all the while thou hatest My

instruction, and castest My words behind thee. If thou
seest a thief, thou runnest off with him ; and throwest in
thy lot with the adulterers."

And God concludes by re-emphasising the only true
sacrifice—that of the heart's praise.

This Psalm certainly probes deeply. So terribly, in
fact, does it stir the conscience that—almost for the sake
of our own pacification—we end by alluding to Psalm
cii, perhaps the loveliest in the Psalter. Yes, we sin ; yes,
even we who are of His chosen people, with whom He
has struck a covenant better than that to which He was
so faithful with faithless Israel—we sin. But He pardons
all these our sins . . . healing all our sicknesses . . .
not requiting us accurately because of our wrongdoing
nor paying us back for our impiety. High as the heaven
is built above the earth, so firm, so widely over-arching
has He established His loving-kindness over those who
worship Him. Far as dawn is from dusk, so far He sets
our sins from us. Yes, as a father pities his weak little
children, so God pities us. Even though this Psalm may
not start from a sense of individual gratitude and trust
(though I think it does), it *provokes* them. How could
a man sing this hymn, without his deepest heart awakening
and giving itself wholly to its God ?

VIII

" CAELESTIS URBS "

In these chapters we have wanted to detect what is *lovable*
in the Psalms, and so we began with what to us *is* lovable
—their frank, alert humanity and keen appreciation of
Nature. But, human nature being mixed, it is probable
that we should find elements in the Psalms that we do not
like, and certainly what is exterior in Hebrew human
nature was not always likable. So we tried to look more
deeply into that nature, and to see how marvellous was the
innermost element within it. We found that neither in
regard to the world, nor to the nation, nor to self, could
the Hebrew eradicate from himself an ever purer perception
of God, who, he knew for super-certain, was at the back
of all things and on whom all depended.

Now we return outwards. We said that, if the Greek
attitude to life could be summed up in the word " fatalism "
(all summings up in single words are rash, but I think
this one is not unjustifiable), the Hebrew attitude could
be called " vocation " and the sense of it. To what, towards
what, was the Hebrew " called " ? In the most material
sense—towards Jerusalem.

We cannot but be right in meditating on this name
Jerusalem, as it appears in the Psalms, if only because it
has entered from the outset so deeply into Christian
thought, emotion, imagery, and liturgy. We should want
its total connotation to be so rich that, the moment it
resounds, all the depths within us should be stirred. After
all, Our Lord loved Jerusalem passionately—the actual
town, the very stones at which the Apostles cried out in

wonderment. Our Lord *wept* over it, and surely not only over some spiritual notion that it stood for, but over the very city so soon to be demolished. Yet, of course its appalling sin—sins committed, and the supreme sin of which it was about to be guilty—tortured His heart most of all : " Thou that *killest* the prophets! " And this wrung from Him one of those very few sentences that we can call " bitter " : " It is impossible that any prophet should perish *outside* Jerusalem."

It was, however, St. John who, by means of his Apocalypse, placed the Heavenly Jerusalem—even more than St. Paul did—at the head of an imperishable literature. The Bride of Christ descended from heaven and clothed the earth with her beauty. All the earth became God's Holy Hill. From the throne of God and of the Lamb at its summit— that temple-throne that no more needed ever-burning lamps, because They were the light thereof—proceeded the Holy Spirit, the Living Water long ago promised by Christ, and it went cascading from one jewelled terrace to another, through the Grove of Life whose leaves were for the healing of the nations. Hence one of the sublimest hymns in our Breviary, *Caelestis Urbs ;* and hence the countless variations on that theme, made not least by those in pain or imprisonment—all the versions of " Hierusalem, my happie home," and the poignant cry suddenly breaking into the poet's description : " Ah God, that I were there! "

Soon enough, the city summoned pilgrim after pilgrim. No one can understand the Crusades, unless he first realises what Jerusalem stood for to the Middle Ages. Upon the lips of how many dying Saints have lingered the words : " Laetatus sum in his quae dicta sunt mihi "! Their feet were already standing in heaven's " outer courts " but not yet, not quite yet, had they entered God's Holy House. " *Sicut cervus. . . . Quam dilecta. . . .*" The Church has without intermission breathed those words. And, until we feel all that we ought about Jerusalem, we shall not be able to be fully at ease with the Church's symbolism that identifies Mary with the City of the King.

There are the quiet passages in which " Sion " is named almost technically, as in doxologies (*e.g.*, Ps. cxlv. 10); there are allusions to God who is King in Sion (ix. 12) and who shall be hymned there (15), and petitions that rescue may come thence (xiii. 7; the same as lii. 7). All this, as it were, takes the name for granted and hardly insists on it. But " sentiment " is soon aroused. It is from Sion that God proceeds in " beauty "—Sion is the " crown " of His beauty (xlix. 2); the people are told to examine the place (xlvii)—pilgrims, doubtless, who had not seen it yet, or to whom, as (one might think) to the Apostles, it was a new place every time they *did* see it. " Great must be the praise of God—in His own City, on His Holy Mountain : firm founded is it, the pride of the whole earth! Mount Sion, on its north side—the City of the Great King! "[1] God is manifested in its very dwellings—so does He protect them! The splendour of Jerusalem quite demoralises (as we should say) even its grandest visitors from the remotest lands. Then the pilgrims break out : " As we had heard, so now we see —we, actually *in* the City of the Lord! " And they upraise their own hymn of exultation. And the City's guide, so to call him, resumes (13) : " Walk around Sion! Take it all in! Tell how many its towers are! Put your attention to its strength : measure [Hebrew : walk through] its mansions, that you may tell it to those who shall come after you that *God* is here—*Our* God, for ever and ever. *He* is our king forever! " We might compare the far more mystical Psalm lxxxvi, *Fundamenta eius* (see below) : also Isaias xxxiii. 20, and what follows.

There are many Psalms definitely intended, I suppose,

---

[1] I venture to think that there is nothing here, however remotely, mythological, but simply a statement that the Temple was on the northward part of the rock on the rest of which the city stood.

for worship, alluding to the pilgrims' entry into the Temple and the Holy City : the simple little *Quis habitabit ?* (xiv), and the supremely grand *Quis ascendit ?* (xxii), with its double outcry to the gates that they should lift themselves up tall so that the towering glory of the Lord might enter. The Hebrews loved *public praise*. High Mass (provided everybody sang it, with mere occasional alternations from the choir) would have been much more to their taste than Low Masses " heard " individualistically —not to say Low Masses heard, no doubt collectively, but with a silent congregation, each intent (if on anything) upon a private prayerbook. " I will praise Thee in the Great Assembly," is almost a refrain, and occurs in a most personal Psalm, *Deus Deus meus :* an essential part of the sufferer's rescue was that he should proclaim God's goodness to as many people as possible. Modern reticence and cultured undertones would have seemed unintelligible to him (cf. also xxxix. 10). Not that he *could* not isolate himself and brood, especially when puzzled. I think that " donec intrem in sanctuarium " (lxxii. 17) really does mean that the Psalmist was so overwhelmed by the prosperity of the impious and the trend of the Holy People towards materialism, as we should say, that he ended up by going into the Temple, sitting down in a quiet nook, and thinking it all over. Then he saw the solution, and felt what a fool he had been.

The Temple, moreover, was the starting-place of God's triumphs and of those of His Anointed King. It was from Sion that the Sceptre should proceed that was to rule from horizon to horizon. So the Messianic Psalms ii and cix. 2. As for Psalm lxvii, I doubt if anyone has been able to make adequate sense of its very corrupt verses ; none the less, verses 16–19 must allude to Sion. I fancy that there is an allusion to other mountains, either as important in heathen worship or as all of them as belonging to the true God, and an inquiry as to why in either case they should look superciliously at the crag of Sion, which no doubt, was not so very large, but at any rate was God's chosen place, and rich with every imaginable blessing. But I confess that, when reading this Psalm, I have to occupy myself with general ideas rather than with anything directly suggested by the words. Anyhow it asks (29) that God shall send forth His might from Jerusalem, give permanence to what He has already done there, and bring the defeated nations suppliantly thitherwards. And both in the liturgy and in history, the opening words have had an enormous effect : *Exurgat Deus, et dissipentur inimici eius*. Other ritual hymns are notably Psalms cxiii and cvii ; but they are more hymns sung *within* Sion than *about* Sion.

But, for all that, Jerusalem was several times destroyed. Temple after Temple perished. Here something much more human enters the vision of the Psalmist—and, we may say, something yet more sublime ; for, in the midst of the City's seemingly irreparable disasters, his *faith* survived.

Few Psalms are more enthralling than the eighty-eighth. The Psalmist, true to a very frequent impulse of his soul, begins by praising God *whatever* has happened. From the first verse to the thirty-eighth, there is a magnificent panegyric, a rehearsal of God's promises to David and His eternal Covenant, a Covenant to which He will be loyal even though the people sin, and though He have to punish them. But *then* . . . " Thou hast Thyself broken Thy word. . . . The Anointed is cast off . . . the Shrine is ruined . . . the walls are broken down. . . . David is become a mockery ; his enemies exult over him and pillage him ; he had hardly begun to grow up, before he is slain ! " Then follows the enduring cry : " How long . . . ? Oh Lord, wilt Thou for ever turn away ? . . . Where are Thine ancient graces. . . . Thine *oaths* ? " Give heed to the disgrace of Thy servants, coming from so many sides, and all of which I keep within my own heart—the contempt in which Thine Anointed is held !

That is tragic in all conscience; but how pitiful is the Psalm (lxxix) about the Vine—the Nation, the entire Nation, transplanted out of Egypt and tended so carefully till it filled all the land, and gave shadow to the very hills, and twined itself round the very cedars, the huge northern cedars. "And then, Thou hast broken down its fence; any passer-by can ravage it; every beast can trample it; fire destroys what is left." "Oh God of Hosts," the refrain implores, "look down again from heaven. Behold this Thy Vine and visit it—establish us once more!"

Psalm lxxviii is another such hymn of misery because of the devastations wrought in God's Land. "Oh Lord, the pagans have invaded Thine inheritance, have defiled Thy Temple, have turned Jerusalem into a mere hovel!" The City had been so devastated that it was like those lonely little shacks such as men crouched in while they kept watch over field or flock at night.

Psalms ii and lxxxii picture the heathen rioting unitedly and making common cause against the Holy Land; but Psalm lxxiii is perhaps the most vivid of this set of Psalms. "God, why dost Thou utterly reject us; why enrage Thy wrath against Thine own pasture's flock? Remember Thy People, that Thou didst purchase long ago, didst acquire it as the land to be Thine own—the Mount of Sion, in which Thou hast Thy dwelling! . . . What wicked evil the enemy has wrought within Thy Sanctuary! They that hate Thee, boast in their heart of Thy holy shrine, and in their blind insolence have set up their standards, their images, over the very entrance! Like men hacking down trees with axes in the woods, so have they hewn down Thy gates utterly: with axe and pickaxe have they ruined it. They burned down Thy tabernacle to the very ground! All of them, all of them, said in their hearts: 'Let us silence every festival of God from the land!' And indeed, our holy symbols see we no more; we have no more any prophet; God heeds us not any more."

Such may be tolerated as a paraphrase of these verses, as the Latin offers them to us to-day. It is not denied that even the Hebrew is here and there obscure; certainly the picture would very well suit the tragic period of the Maccabees; but I see nothing that forces us to relegate the Psalm to so late a time. I can imagine nothing more likely than that the Psalm is ancient, but was made instinctively much of by the Maccabean period, for the Psalms were ever upon Israel's lips and constantly modified in details of expression, as we see when a Psalm exists in the Psalter itself in more than one form (*Deus in adiutorium*, etc.) or appears also in the Books of Kings. Thus, when Antiochus put his image as sun-god in the holy place, an earlier expression meaning that the invader had planted his *signa* (standards, military symbols) as trophies on the top of the walls, would easily receive a new and yet more horrible significance.

How often must the initial words of these Psalms have been upon the lips of priests of late years in Mexico, Russia, Spain! With what added intensity must they not have repeated them when they had just *seen* their own churches burnt: when effigies of Lenin replaced icons of immemorial holiness over the gates of Russian cities! To the Jew, the presence of a pagan symbol of any sort in that Temple where every figure of God was so strictly prohibited must have seemed no less appalling. Even the shields that Pontius Pilate caused to be hung up in the temple precincts nearly occasioned a revolt, and so did the Roman eagles. And we in England must often sigh, when we repeat *Deus venerunt gentes*, and recall that not one of our ancient Cathedrals is any more Catholic, nor contains an Altar. May we *always* recognise, as the Psalms invariably urge us to, that it is when *we* have sinned that God chastises us: "Be no more mindful of our iniquities of yore!"

IX

DUC NOS QUO TENDIMUS

There are too many Psalms about Jerusalem—too many beautiful and significant ones—for us to have discussed them all within one chapter. And the great object of the Breviary is, not to give us right and interesting ideas about the Hebrew people, but to inspire us with holy desires.

" One thing have I begged from the Lord—I long for it—to live in the Lord's House all my days ; and watch the beauty of the Lord, and to be ever present in His temple " (Ps. xxvi. 4). I think that this legitimately suggests that you could, as it were, take lodgings within the temple precincts ; and I should like to find a *background* for the tradition that Our Lady, in her childhood, was put to live there for at least part of the time—a distant, and therefore traditional, background.[1]

This yearning for God's City is expressed still more strongly in Psalm xli: " The stag cries aloud for the running stream—even so, my soul, for Thee, O my God. . . . When shall I come and actually stand before my God ? " The Psalmist, distant from Jerusalem, is mocked

[1] The Psalm (xlv. 5) containing the verse, " Fluminis impetus lætificat civitatem Dei," is regularly applied by the Church to Our Lady. The Hebrew has : " A river—its divisions rejoice the city of God." That has been explained s if the very encirclement of hostile armies gave pleasure to the impregnable itizens. I cannot believe this, despite the habit of the Hebrew to exaggerate nd to taunt. It must be connected surely with phrases like " Flumen Dei epletum est aquis." The great beneficent stream of God's goodness encircles nd clasps the City : " El Elyon," continues the Psalm, " keeps His dwelling-place inviolate." *Deus in medio eius.* God is within her and without. Here s alike the picture offered by the Psalm, and the ground for its application o the Immaculate Mother of God.

by his foes: " Where is *now* thy God ? " He brood
over old days, when indeed he used to journey to Jerusalem
and the Temple (the Latin puts this in the future—h
trusts that the day will come). Still, he rebukes himse
for this despondency; and in the second part of th
Psalm (xlii) he feels certain that God's loyal light wi
lead him back—God, who gave such joy to his youth
will not refuse it to his later years.

" How dear is Thy dwelling, Lord! " (Ps. lxxxiii)
Here undoubtedly is the song of a man who has pilgrimage
to God's House, and has achieved his goal. The bird ha
" homed " : the dove is back into its ark and nests ther
—*altaria tua !* Happy they who can always live there
but happy, too, is he whom God has helped, who has place
the steep journey in his heart and has passed throug
dreadful gorges right into the place that he had set befor
him! One day in those courts was better than a thousan
even in his home. What that he could live even as a servan
in God's house, rather than among sinners!

But everyone must acknowledge the extreme beaut
of the Psalms of which most are grouped as " Gradual '
Psalms. No one is sure why they are *called* that. Wer
they return-from-exile songs, or simply pilgrim or carava
songs ? Surely they were not " step " songs, so-calle
either because they were sung on the Temple steps, o
because here and there they contain a sort of rhythmica
progression. Why they are *grouped together* is fairl
obvious. They and a few others have a " family likeness '
of a most definite sort. Not only are they concerned wit
absence from Jerusalem, desire to return to it, the rout
thither, and the arrival there; but there is a pathos,
childlike tone in them, seldom seen elsewhere.

There is the comparatively quiet little Psalm cxix
rather the song of one kept afar through commerc
than through enslavement. He is surrounded by cheat
ing and insult, rather than by cruelty. ' Alas tha

my sojourn is [not 'prolonged,' but] in 'Meshekh'
—roughly, the north of the Black Sea: and that I dwell
in Kedar—nomadic Arabia." His journeyings took him
far to north and south. "Too long have I sojourned amid
men who hate peace. *I* am a man of peace; but when I
speak to them, they gratuitously insult me!" How naïve
is that! But there are, too, black depths of woe: "De
profundis!" (cxxix), "Super flumina Babylonis" (cxxxvi).
There is the desperately sad slaves' song, "Ad Te levavi"
(cxxii): "*Too much* has our soul been glutted with the
insults of the rich, and the contempt of the proud!"
Then they begin to come home. Surely, Psalm cxx *is* a
caravan song, in which one voice answers another, as still
you can hear in the East—interminable "conversations"
in which each singer picks up the clue just offered him.
"I strain my eyes towards the hills (of home)! Whence
shall help come to me?" "From *The Lord* is my help!"
"May thy Guardian not slumber!" "Nay, neither
slumbereth He nor sleepeth—Israel's Guardian." "He is
at thy right hand—sun shall not smite thee by day, nor
moon by night. *He* guardeth thy coming home, even as
He did thy forth-going, henceforward, and for ever!"[1]

Psalms cxxiii and cxxv may also belong to this cycle of
thought. Had not the Lord been with us, we should
have been swallowed up alive: we should have been
overwhelmed by the torrents! But no. "We were rescued,
like a bird, from the snare of the fowler: snapped was
the mesh, and we—we are set free!" "When the Lord
reversed Sion's enslavement, we were like men [not
'who were consoled,' but] who dream! We could not
believe it true! Even the heathen marvelled and said that

---

[1] "Thy right hand," because the left arm carried the shield. The right side
was inevitably exposed. In ancient battles, the whole line used to edge right-
wards, each man trying to get a little under the shelter of his neighbour's shield.
Sunstroke is at once intelligible: but the moon? Perhaps because it *blanched*
everything; it brought white leprosy to the imagination, and was thought
to cause it. And, "moonstruck," "lunatic."

our God had done great things for us. But may the Lord
change even our present life, as a dried-up ravine in the
South becomes changed (when the rains send water
tumbling down it)! Harvest shall come! They that sow
in tears, shall reap in joy, yea, return rejoicing, carrying
their sheaves."[1]

Anyway, they reached home. " Oh my joy, when
they said to me : ' We are going into the House of the
Lord. Our feet are actually standing in thy gates, Jerusalem
—Jerusalem, thou City so firm-built, so strongly interknit!' (To thee all Israel made pilgrimage : in thee they
found Justice!) Pray for Jerusalem! Peace to thy walls!
Prosperity in thy towers! . . . For the sake of the House
of God, I pray good things for thee! ''[2]

Psalm cxxvii is the happy song of men who are home
again—who live, not on doles, but on the produce of
their own plot of land : who have a *home*, with wife (like
a vine within its enclosure) and sons (like olive-boughs) :
may this endure! And not only a home, but a community
of fellow-minded men. " Ecce quam bonum et iucundum,
habitare fratres in unum!" (Ps. cxxxii). But work
is still to be done! They realised (Ps. cxxiv) that men
who trust in the Lord are like Mount Sion, immovable
for-ever, ever-enduring : even as the hills are eternally
round Jerusalem, so is God about His People. Still,
there are pagans in the land ; God will not allow that to
last forever. Only . . . let men be upright in heart!

[1] Even now I cannot feel sure that this Psalm is, as some think and as is
suggested above, and as Ps. cxxiv. may be, an expression of gratitude for rescue,
yet of distress that the Israelites, returned to their desolate city, were still stunned
both by their bewildering release and by the blankness of the outlook. The prayer
that their fate may be changed, as a torrent channel is, can be a request that
their future may be as different from the *past* (not the present) as a life-giving
stream is from a dried-up chasm.

[2] Again I cannot feel sure that this Psalm is not due to returning exiles. It
is said that they would *not* have seen the City as " built," but demolished. But
unless they arrived over the Mount of Olives, what they would *mostly* have
seen were the crag and the undemolished walls. Besides, it is a song, poetry ;
not an archaeological statement. They sang of what they felt—joy in return
—and of what they visioned—Jerusalem as they wanted it to be.

Those who turn aside into entanglements—for example, by marrying with the pagans—will be led away along with them—to *their* destiny! Turn rather to the rebuilding of Jerusalem. Yet do so, not in pride: not through presumptuous nationalism. " Unless it be the *Lord* who build the House, they labour in vain, who build it. Unless it be the Lord who sentinel the City, the watchman waketh but in vain." Not—ah! had not Israel learnt *that* lesson?—not by human effort will the divine thing be done. " Idle, to rise before the dawn, and so late seek rest, you who eat bread earned by grievous toil! To His beloved, God gives all *that*, even while they sleep! " (Ps. cxxvi).

It may be that Psalm cxxviii belongs here. Terrible oppression had Israel endured even from her youth—sinners had ploughed their furrows long upon her; but the Lord had cut the ropes that harnessed their oxen. May those bad old times vanish utterly—like grass sprung from seeds dropped by birds on the flat roofs; before it can be picked (or comes even to the perfect blade), it withers up. Not from *that* shall a reaper fill his hand, nor find enough to carry in his robe: not because of *that* shall any passer-by exclaim: " God's blessing on you! " Grüss Gott!—as was the happy custom in those Jewish harvest-fields—may it still be so in the southern German and the Austrian hills!

Yes, the Lord had chosen Sion, so sings the superb commemorative Psalm cxxxi: " This is My abiding-place forever: here will I dwell, for I have desired it . . . and *there* will I make My Messiah to arise " (cf. lxxvii, as from verse 60). When she was beaten down, God answered the prayer: " Rise up, and have pity upon Sion; for it is time to have pity on her—yea, the time is come " (Ps. ci. 14). Well might Jerusalem be bidden " Praise the Lord " (Ps. cxlvii); the winter was over and gone, God had sent the breath of His " second spring," the rivers flowed anew.

Our spirits may always rise when these pure but pathetic
little Psalms come round in the Breviary : but Psalm lxxxvi,
" Fundamenta eius," is surely one that can never go stale,
but must always thrill one : *Fundamenta eius*. We have
already, I think, quoted it in these pages : but it must
never be wearisome, so perfect a prophecy is it of the
true Jerusalem, which is the Catholic Church.

(*The Psalmist sings*)
God's firm-founded dwelling is on the holy hills—
  The Lord loves Sion's gates beyond all the homes of
    Israel!
Magnificent things must be said of Thee—
  God's City!

(*God speaks*)
I shall make mention of Egypt and of Babylon,
  As among them that know Me!
See—the Philistine, the Tyrian, the Ethiopian folk—
  All these came into being there!

(*The Psalmist speaks again*)
Then of Sion must we say:
" Every, every man was born there!
    The Most High Himself must have founded her! "
In His books the Lord makes register
    Of the Peoples and the Princes
        That were born there!

They that dwell in Thee
    Do sing and dance—are *happy !*

It is a stupefying prophecy, perhaps only to be equalled
by a passage or two in Isaias and especially Ezekiel. But
let us keep to the Psalms, and to this Psalm. It begins
with the most uncompromising statement that God's
enduring Home is Mount Sion : that He loves Sion beyond
all the rest of the Holy Land. Magnificent things must,

then, be proclaimed concerning this, God's, City. But then, suddenly God declares that the hereditary foes of Israel—the enormous foes that Egypt (Rahab) and Babylonia were, and the nearer though smaller foes, the Philistine (*alienigena*) and the Arab—find their true existence *there* (*fuerunt :* came into existence, were born, obtained therefore their true citizenship—*there*). All-inclusive True-Jerusalem! No wonder that the Psalmist, almost aghast, exclaims that, if *that* be so, " this one and that one "—*every one*—was born there ! (Man's true and complete Self is to be found only within the Church.) God reads through His records, and notes the names of peoples and their governors. Yes ; not one is excluded. Ah! Jerusalem has become Man's one true home : elsewhere he is always homesick, *there* happy.

" Thy Kingdom come on earth—as it exists in Heaven! " Oh, be the vision verified! Putting aside all those earthly loves, parodies of the divine one—all those earthly " unities," " circles premature," attempts at finishing-off everything here in this world of mere analogy, this two-dimensional outline of the *Res Catholica*—or rather catching up all our plans for personal good behaviour (social amelioration, peace between nations, universal brotherhood), let us subordinate them to, incorporate them into, the " beata pacis visio "—the blest vision of peace—which is what *God* intends, what God sees the world *really* to be, what the world is meant to be and is (despite all weary appearances) becoming. Let us labour for that ; sacrifice ourselves and all our individualisms for that, for by no other road save sacrifice will the vision " hurry to its consummation." The Lamb was " slain since the foundation of the world," but, though slain, He is standing. Death " hath no more dominion over Him." " Having died to Sin once," He liveth " unto God " forever.

F

X

VENIET ET NON TARDABIT

It would indeed be strange should we say anything about the Psalms and nothing about the "Messianic" ones. Yet, I mean to say but little, for, though I recognise fully the "prophetic and Messianic" character of certain Psalms, I am not *attracted* by the picture of the Messiah such as they put it before us. It seems idle to revert to the Psalms for *that*, when we possess the Gospels; we have constantly to correct or amplify what we read about the "Messiah," which is not necessary when the Psalms are directly expressing the movements of the human soul, our own included.

Thus, Psalm ii is certainly Messianic and certainly magnificent. The promise that the rage of the heathen and their rebellions will at the last be futile, is consoling. The dramatic alternations of personages speaking is fine. But I am not *attracted* by the picture of God's mocking the heathen, and speaking merely in terms of wrath, nor of promising the whole world to His Anointed that he may proceed to rule them with an iron sceptre and shatter them like so much crockery. Moreover, one is haunted by the memory of the uncertainty of the Hebrew original towards the end.

As for Psalm xv, would anyone suppose it *was* Messianic till the last verse was reached, which was forthwith interpreted by the Apostles as applying to Our Lord (nor may we hold that it does not)? "Thou wilt not suffer Thy Holy One to see corruption." The Psalm is a charming one, but it foretells a fact rather than portrays a

person, save, perhaps, one who is habitually grateful and
trusting.

The Royal Marriage poem, Psalm xliv, moves me by
one or two of its lines, and the image of the marriage
between God and the soul, God and Israel, or Christ and
His Church, is one which Christianity itself has endeared
to us ; but perhaps we detest sacred *orgies*, which
appear perfectly unfitted to this or any Sacrament, and I
wish that Christian marriages were blessed very early at
some quiet Mass, and *habitually* consecrated by Holy
Communion. Have as decorative a " house-warming "
as you please and as your conscience permits on the
return from the honeymoon! But leave the Sacrament
alone, and don't embed it so deeply into a pantomime
that no one even notices it!

Therefore, a " marriage pageant " may be distasteful
at the outset. The poet bestows on the bridegroom praises
that are familiar anywhere in the Orient ; and it seems
all very well to talk of " veritas et mansuetudo,"—truth
and gentleness—when the king's campaigns are described
in terms of slaughter. I know how all this has to be
interpreted : but this Psalm is so exceptionally pictorial
and vivid that the picture tends to take precedence of the
idea. Verses 7 and 8 have a critical problem at the back of
them ; and however definitely we may recognise them as
Messianic, I rather shrink from supposing the Psalm to
have addressed the Messiah directly as *God*. In fact, the
strong contrast between God and the Messiah in verse 8
makes it difficult to suppose that, even if the word " Deus "
be right and a vocative in verse 7, it is addressed to the
Messiah at all. But when we are praying—and these are
chapters concerned chiefly with the Breviary and those who
recite it—we do not want to get mixed up with criticism,
apologetics, and controversy. In the rest of the Psalm,
" Audi filia . . . obliviscere, etc.," and " Adducentur "
to the end, have nothing to do with the Messiah.

Psalm cix has in it, again, some wonderful lines : but the significance of some of these (*sacerdos in aeternum*, etc.) is due largely to the use we ourselves have made of them, about ourselves, for so long. I hardly expect that we, when praying, experience much inner reaction to the name " Melchisedech " as such, or in its application to the priesthood of Our Lord. In fact, presumably the direct meaning of the Psalmist was that the Messiah was to exercise his rule from Sion, even as Melchisedech the Priest-King once did, and so the Messiah inherits the whole of that ancient hero's prerogative, priesthood as well as kinghood. But the rest of the Psalm, so far as one can make sure of the text and even accepting it just as it stands in Latin, is so bloodthirsty that the affections it stirs in us, when gentle, are due to its being used so much at Christmas. The vision of Bethlehem comes *through* it, and, for me at least, dominates almost in spite of it.

Psalm xxi stands all by itself, because of Our Lord's having used its first words on His Cross. In fact, each time it recurs in the Breviary those first words quite eclipse what immediately follows, into which, it seems to me, we have deliberately to *put* the idea of vicarious suffering, of Christ having been " made sin " for us, because we know, independently, in what sense alone sin can be connected with Our Lord. Still the Psalm can be dear, partly because of the verses describing the mockery of the Sufferer and the distribution of His very garments, and the piercing of hands and feet, but even more, because taking it as a whole, it is Our Lord's personal triumph, and then His glorification in His Church, that are all the while rising like a dawn throughout the murk. Yet, for personal consolation, it is the exquisite prophecy of Isaias that I would prefer to read.

Hence, it is clear that what I am saying is (1) that it would seem wrong to me to omit reference to the Messianic Psalms in these pages, and yet (2) that I cannot include

them with conscious enthusiasm. It is an affair of sentiment, alas—not of idea. Wholeheartedly, I accept the
Biblical Commission's answer to Dubium viii. It declares
that several Psalms (without enumerating which—they
are doubtless more numerous than these, but these will
certainly be among them) " vaticinated " the advent,
reign, priesthood, passion, death and resurrection of the
future Messiah. It continues to declare that these oracles
concerning Christ are not to be confined to a prediction
of the future fate of the Chosen People, *and nothing else*
—" ad futurum *tantum* sortem populi electi." This
certainly implies that they refer to it in part—and I should
add, to its present and even its past—because Christ was
" in solidum " with the Chosen People as truly—if not
altogether in the same way—as He is with His Church.
St. John in the Apocalypse makes that quite clear. The
Prophets join with the Apostles in making one continuous
and splendid company. The immense majority of ancient
commentators (and of modern ones too, I think) see in
the Woman that gave birth to the Man-Child, the Jewish
Church. Not the Jewish Church, *exclusively*, no doubt
—Mary too, and the Christian Church also, which all
the while is giving new birth to Christ in Christians. In
short, there is One Body; and Christ is " All in all,"
or at least is straining to become so.

Hence it is impossible to find anything inappropriate
even in the strangest prophecies whose *apex* (or innermost
circle, or most spiritual plane) is the Messiah in person.
The Kingdom was not thinkable, to the Jew, without its
King; nor the King without His Kingdom. Hence the
error of those who struggle to interpret the visions of
Daniel as wholly concerned with nations, or wholly with
persons; or, again, the " Suffering Servant " in Isaias
as exclusively the Nation Israel, or exclusively the Messiah.
Not even, I am ready to admit, is the person of the Prophet
excluded, any more than the personal condition of the

Psalmist is in many of the Messianic Psalms. The Psalmist was a concrete prophecy of the Messiah; Israel itself was one substantial prolonged prophetic fact. Here surely is the true " *indoles*," both prophetic and Messianic, not only of the Psalms, but of prophecy as a whole, and notably of the eschatologists. The inspired writer can quite well begin from one contemporary fact—himself, maybe, or some event tragic or glorious; in it he sees the whole history of Israel, and in *that*, here and there like a sunlit snowy peak emerging for a moment from the mists, the Figure of the Messiah.

Thus, the really beautiful Psalm lxxi, though its title undoubtedly seems to mean " about " or " for " Solomon, cannot possibly be other than Messianic. Here is another feature of Hebrew literature—it asserts where others imagine or aspire. I mean, plenty of Oriental writings adulate their kings, but this Psalm is not flavoured with adulation. Many a poet has idealised even living persons, but this goes far beyond idealisation. Pagan literature *hopes*, though more often it laments and puts the good time in the past. But Hebrew literature *asserts*, on a basis of *promise*. I hold that this can be proved, and is not merely an affair of literary taste. In fact, the Fourth— " Messianic "—Eclogue of Vergil caused such a commotion less, I think, because of the isolated sentences in it (such as " iam redit et Virgo," and the mysterious child it speaks of) than because of a quite special flavour in the poem, which I cannot but call " Hebrew." This surely accounts in part for the zeal displayed by scholars in proving that Vergil could perfectly well have access to Hebrew or Hebraised literature (*e.g.*, the Sibylline books); whether he did or didn't, and though the Eclogue is transfused with the golden haze that illuminates all Vergil's poems, I maintain that in it there is a Hebrew flavour which almost by itself would justify the poem being called—nicknamed, if you will—" Messianic."

After all, there is nothing novel in the doctrine that the *whole* of Jewish history, and therefore of Jewish literature, is " prophetic." In proportion as we see it as expanding and contracting in its scope, or somehow like a globe of glass illuminated from its centre (with the light waxing strong and again waning so that now we see into the very heart of the dense mass, and now only a faint interior diffused radiance, or any other imagery you please), the more we appreciate the totality of the inspiration and the prophecy. Then, the individual verses that definitely predict Our Lord, His Nature, Life and Death and Glory, cease to appear isolated, astonishingly and disconnectedly stuck out at you, encountered—to use a somewhat coarse comparison—like currants in a massive, doughy bun.

It remains that the Messianic Psalms are not calculated to make one *love* the Messiah; and indeed, when the Jews obtained their Messiah, and a Messiah whom they could not—one would have thought—*but* love, they were so unprepared to love Him, so disappointed that He was not the victorious, noisy Messiah they had wanted, that they fulfilled their own prophecies and killed Him.

Perhaps it may be said that if the doctrine of God—who was wholly God and nothing else—developed slowly (in the way of purification or spiritualisation) among the Hebrews, that of the Messiah, who was thought of as human, cannot but have developed much more slowly still, yet must have followed the same direction. For the Messiah was God's beloved and wholly pleasing Son, and therefore can hardly have been thought of otherwise, ethically, than as God was being thought of. Now, there is a real element of lovableness in the Hebrew thought of God, as shown in the Psalms (and of course elsewhere). No doubt, the consecrated past is always present in the Hebrew mind: always the primeval dragon stirs in the slime under their terrifying ocean; the Red Sea pours its waters into all their memories of deliverance; the thunders of Sinai never cease to echo. Hence the magnificent descriptions of the divine theophanies—God's advents—in the Psalms. Psalm xvii is, so to say, a classical description of such an advent; clouds and darkness are about Him; fire goes before Him; the mountains melt like wax at His approach (cf. Pss. xvii, lxvi, etc.). But always there is, interwoven with the terrific *mise-en-scène*, the idea of Right and Righteousness: always the earth rejoices at that Coming (see especially Ps. xcv. 11–13). So not only Righteousness is never absent from the thought of the Messiah and *His* rule; but it makes for happiness, and happiness of the sort that *God* brings. Now, that happiness is not only the exultation of the victorious warrior, but one of tenderness and trust. We have already quoted the exquisite Psalm cii; hardly less beautiful is *Qui habitat* (Ps. xc). But we may be allowed to finish by referring to the childlike simplicity of Ps. cxxx:

"Lord, my heart is not haughty, my eyes not proud. My path is not amid great things—things too wonderful for me. Indeed, indeed, my thoughts are humble; I have *silenced* my soul (Hebrew). As a weaned child rests back upon its mother, even so is my soul within me" (that is, it leans back in perfect peace upon its Lord).

Such, I feel sure, is the meaning of the Psalm: and, if so, we are approaching the days when the Messiah too should be thus lovable and beloved, and John could lean back upon the Sacred Heart.

XI

THE PSALMS OF THE NEW TESTAMENT

It hardly seems out of place to meditate for a moment on the three great Psalms of the New Testament—the *Benedictus*, the *Magnificat*, and the *Nunc Dimittis*—especially as they too occur, and daily, in our Office, and are able to give a " colour" to the whole Hour to which they belong.

By " colour," or " flavour," I mean something of the sort of what the hymns for Terce, Sext and None provide. It cannot be frivolous to seek for anything that " enlivens " the Office on days of spiritual dullness, and many come with delight to Terce and None because of their hymns. They are, thank God, singularly uninjured by the vulgarity of the Renaissance—true, in Compline, *pro tua clementia* has replaced *solita clementia*, and thus an idea, and a comforting one at that, has been expunged for the sake of a "quantity." The Benedictines keep *solita*, I think; and their *O felix Roma* still continues *quae tantorum principum*, and has not undergone the impoverishing change into *duorum*.

Nunc Sancte nobis Spiritus brings with it a real pentecostal thrill : the Holy Spirit absolutely floods the priest, and a key-word seems to me to be *refusus*. I fear it may suggest a " refusal," and not, as the Latin does, a pouring forth and, if I dare so speak, a kind of backwash. I remember seeing the African dawn welling liquidly up over the Inyanga Mountains, of which the top seems (50 miles away) as flat as though you had ruled it with a ruler. The light welled up, and then literally poured over, illuminating every intervening ridge, and then streamed *back* from these, reflecting itself on the shadowy westward-facing slopes. An incandescent tide! It helped towards saying

Terce better ever since. *Rector potens* seems to me rather chill : it is grand, but stiff, like good Roman architecture with little save size and " order " to recommend it. But the hymn for None catches hold of you—*tenax vigor !* Rare, perhaps, for an Ambrosian hymn to address God by means of abstracts ; still, we have often had *artifex*, *auctor*, and here we have the preservative force of God holding the world together, even when it begins to tilt towards its eventide, as we do towards *our own*. Impossible not to feel this innermost immovable power of God, setting all nature vibrating, on its side, with energy.

It may not be difficult to feel Vespers somewhat similarly pervaded by the *Magnificat*, and therefore by Our Lady. Save on her feasts, she enters Office as hardly more than part of a framework—the initial Ave and the concluding Canticle. But Vespers are always said in a Marian atmosphere. Having caught this idea, it is not difficult to allow the other two Psalms, *Benedictus* and *Nunc Dimittis*, to do something the same for their respective Hours.

All these hymns are so thoroughly in the spirit as well as the language of the Psalms that it is out of the question that they could have been invented by anyone who was not steeped in the Old Testament hymnology, or even who had grown up in a non-Palestinian air, at a distance from the events or from those who had played a primary part in them. We must not allow—even on critical grounds —anyone to say that St. Luke himself invented them. We see, in the Acts, that when he is reporting what the early Apostles did before he was in active companionship with St. Paul, his language is notably closer to that which he uses in his Gospel, though I should regard it as critically certain that one and the same man wrote the Gospel and the whole of the Acts. It is then not surprising to find that the diction of the Magnificat is altogether that which prevails in the Old Testament, not least, of course, in the Canticle of Anna (1 Kings ii) and Psalm cxii, *Laudate pueri*. Yet, how great are the differences of *feeling*! Much of Anna's song is pathetic, and befits the occasion : but how much is in that vindictive, contemptuous tone of which there is so much in that older world! Our Lady in two brief lines makes the contrast between the overthrow of the haughty and the exaltation of the humble in their estate, between the satisfaction of the hungry and the sending away empty of the rich. You feel that Anna is thinking a great deal of those who had sneered at her : it was for her, now, to exult over them. Had anyone sneered at Mary? Well, even if they had, she would not have remembered it ; nor at such a moment does she thrill with exultation and gratitude towards any save God, in view of the wonderful destiny that He had accorded to her lowliness. In a word, the elaborately composed Canticle of Anna[1] may be regarded as suitable to a woman who has long been miserable because she was sterile, and now exults over her critics ; whereas Mary's has nothing of that about it—virginity is different from barrenness, and *that* fresh loveliness of hers God did not diminish, even when His most high power overshadowed her and made her mother of His Son. If Mary had an " ancestress " when singing her *Magnificat*, it may surely have been she who wrote Psalm cxii—for why should no Psalm have been written by a woman? We cherish the Psalm of Debora, and Miriam and her maidens sang the refrain for Moses and for Aaron when the Red Sea was passed.

It is hardly too much to say that Our Lady has a lien on dawn and dusk. This must be because we think of her, not as Sun, but Star. Even so, the *Stella Matutina*, heralding daybreak, seems to have yielded to the attraction of the selfsame star at evening. The evening Angelus has won popular affection that the midday one never has—not at all because of Millet's lovely picture, for that was a symptom,

[1] It falls very easily into a scheme—two halves, each composed of two stanzas themselves composed of three distichs, and separated by a little stanza of two distichs.

not an origin. In the evening children are tired, and turn naturally towards their mother. *Sicut ablactatus*. . . . The poor little weaned child is, in a sense, in discomfort; yet it knows its mother, and with a weary little sigh nestles back on to her breast. Southern Europeans have loved to gather at sunset round Mary's statue and to sing her simple hymns. *Laeva mea sub capite eius, et dextera mea amplexabitur eam*. Like the picture of Our Lady of Good Counsel! Her baby puts one arm round her neck, and the other round her breast. So may the soul become a small child in the evening, and nestle up to Mary—which (save for great Saints, I imagine) is harder to do in full day-time.

As for the *Benedictus*, we can safely say that it obtains its full meaning only if we remember that it was sung when Zachary and his wife had already been visited by Mary. It is not till halfway through that the old man turns to his own child. John's position was to be lofty enough; still, he was but the preparer of a path; the path would have been no good had not the Messiah been about to travel by it. The tremendous fact was that Salvation was already begun: Mary had conceived her child, and *therefore* John was great. The whole first part of the *Benedictus* is Messianic. In fact, it is difficult not to feel the change in the character of his emotion when Zachary turns towards his son: " And thou thyself, little child. . . ." One should not indulge in weak sentiment; still, it is impossible not to let the mind pass rapidly from this baby—so soft and tiny in his mother's arms and surrounded by all the sympathising relatives—to the grown Baptist of thirty years later, haggard with fasting, blackened by the ferocious sun, a man of long loneliness and even lonelier when the crowds were all about him, resigning even his friends to Jesus when He came, and passing from the brief joys of the Baptism almost straight to the frightful obliteration of his dungeon and the imminent axe. Yet, the *Benedictus* is nothing but tenderness: to appreciate that, one has but to hear it sung at a graveside.

For the man, especially, who has died " in Christ," it is because of the mercy of the heart of God that a dawn has risen in the skies—" to give the light to them that crouch in darkness—in the dark of death—and to make straight their ways along the path of peace." Still, at Lauds it is not of death, even as portal into fuller life, that we are thinking, so much as of a beginning of a new day. And the priest praises God because he knows himself— child as he is, poor weakling as he is—to be called, as the Baptist was, to prepare a way for Christ into every heart. Terrible thought, that by my worldliness, my boorishness, selfishness, offhandedness, inaccessibility, conceit, bullying autocracy, I may be shutting up Christ's paths, making the way rough not smooth, tortuous not straight! But let us rather start our day with exhilaration if we can, always remembering that " our sufficiency is from God," and indeed it is very apt to go straight from Lauds to Terce, if only to follow up the tremendous stimulus of the *Benedictus*, and its suggestion of *great* things, *much* work, by a heartfelt invocation of the Holy Spirit, that He may give the only true efficacity to " *os lingua*," to lips and tongue, to thought and feeling; the only true power to our energy—for how much human energy we can expend without its being of the slightest spiritual use to anyone! *Non in multiloquio . . . non in dialectico . . . unum necessarium.*

We learn that the *Nunc Dimittis* was sung at nightfall from the earliest days of the Church, nor is there the least reason to labour its appropriateness. It is one of the loveliest little poems in existence, and was certainly sung by a man full of the spirit, not so much of the Psalms this time, as of Isaias (*e.g.*, xlix. 6) and of his rapturous visions of the Light in which the heathen too should walk. It may seem almost unkind to contrast the ecstasy of aged Simeon with the joy of Jacob (Gen. xlvi. 30) when he felt he could die happy now that he had once more seen Joseph, for the patriarch too was a prophet. But how pale are those ancient verses foretelling the tribal destiny of his sons, however truly they may contain the vision of an ultimate Messiah! And anyhow, their interpretation is so obscure as not to help us much. But here we have not only a superb prophetic rapture, but also the intimate pathos of this old man who, like the best and holiest among the Jews, could do little save wait and watch himself growing older, and yet the vision tarried. He loved his people, which was God's people, and yet he could not share in their nationalist, materialist desires. His was the immemorial cry of the Saints : " How long ? " " The Lord delayeth His coming," and he too had been told to " wait yet a little while." But how long the " little while " had seemed while it lasted, though now that everything had happened, for him as for the aged generally I suppose the many years all shut themselves up into one brief " yesterday."

Simeon received his revelation directly from God : evidently Mary and Joseph had told him nothing. He caught the Child from their arms and broke into his hymn, and they stood amazed. But after his first cry of gratitude and praise he passed into prophecy, and exclaimed—not that this Child should be merely, like John, the prophet of the Highest, a herald, preparing the Messianic paths, but—

> A Light, to be a revelation for the Gentiles,
> Yea, a glory for Thy chosen People, Israel.

It is remarkable how he puts the Gentiles actually before the Jews : perhaps, once more, the aged are more able to see near-by things in their true perspective, shrunken somewhat. After all, the things I so prized count for very little compared with the great things of God : I fought for human triumphs ; I see that even if I caught up with my hope and got my desire, I should have ceased to want to have it. That is a much greater tragedy than just not getting what you thought you wanted. But there is nothing tragic about Simeon, nor was the " peace of Israel " nothing but a human hope. It is rather that

Simeon sees the world but as enveloped in the Light that streams from Israel. Israel possessed henceforward that which she might give, and with true delicacy of soul Simeon is even more glad in the gladness of the receivers of the gift than proud that it is his nation who gives it.

This is perhaps the right way for us to go to sleep. The day is over, and one is tired enough and only too ready to tumble into bed and relinquish everything for a while. It was a wholesome devotion of our ancestors to lay themselves down in company with Christ upon His Cross and as though in their own grave, thinking they might never awake to this light again. But one relinquishes everything, not so as to let either the past day or the future ones slip and slide into a "nowhere." " In manus tuas "—into God's hands one puts one's most unconsummated work. If, please God, we have sown, by all means let it be others who do the reaping, if but the heavenly granaries be filled.

It is not exacted of all priests that they be erudite in the Scriptures, and still less that they should apply what knowledge they have picked up, while they are actually saying Office. But if we were right in suggesting that the Psalms mean infinitely more when we can say them somewhat in the spirit and with the mind with which they were written, so it is quite possible that even these New Testament ones can be better appreciated if we link them vitally up with that Old Testament from which their singers were after all by no means disconnected. Indeed, the Church never has been and never can be dissevered from her Hebrew past, because it was a divine past, and Christ belonged to the old as truly as He does to us. We would like every part of the inspired Scriptures to be *dear* to us, so that we *prefer* God's own word to any other " literature " whatsoever, however devout. And it may become so, partly, if it be linked up with those who anyway—please God—are dear to us, not least all those who surrounded Our Lord during His holy childhood.

XII

SHALL WE SAVE THE PSALMS?

It is clear from the New Testament that the Apostles, St. Paul included, were steeped in the Psalms (cf. the magnificent exordium to "Hebrews"). The Psalms were at once incorporated into the Liturgy; if the New Testament provided the first Christians with the image of the Shepherd and the Lamb, it was the Psalms which handed on that of the Stag eagerly seeking the living water. The *Acta Martyrum* are full of instances which show Martyrs, even quite young boys, desperately (or rather *naturally*) repeating verses from the Psalms while they were being tortured. St. Ambrose says that people talked in church when other parts of the Scriptures were read, but, when the Psalms were recited, all were dumb; and that a man should blush if he did not begin the day with a Psalm, since even the birds devoutly sing at morning and at dusk (a St. Francis before his time!). The very classic-minded Sidonius Apollinaris says that the river banks re-echo with the bargemen's "psalm-songs"; and Paula and Eustochius wrote from Bethlehem to Marcella that the ploughman, the reaper, and the vinedresser sang the Psalms to lighten their work. St. Gregory Nazianzen, while still a pagan, dreamed that he was singing *Laetatus sum in his* and the dream haunted him, and he came thus to baptism. When St. Monica died, the whole of her son's companions sang the Psalm *Misericordiam* (Ps. c) to console him; and he died with the Penitential Psalms written up large before his bed. Marcella, mentioned above, actually gathered a group of women around her, studied

Hebrew so as to sing the Psalms properly (and Greek, so as fitly to read the Gospels), learned the entire Psalter by heart, and apparently recited the whole of it daily. Paula died with the Psalms *Quam dilecta* and *Domine dilexi* on her lips; and round her dead body Psalms were sung in Greek, Latin, Hebrew and Syriac for three whole days.

As for St. Jerome, who in a sense controlled these ladies, we know how continuously he worked at the Psalter: to my mind, it is disastrous that his Psalter according to the Hebrews (*i.e.*, taken from the Hebrew text) was so offensive to both clergy and laity that they refused to accept it, and our Breviary Psalms are far harder than they need be, being no more than his second revision of the previous Latin translation of the Septuagint. But at least it shows how much the faithful valued the Psalms. They did not want one customary word altered. I do not know that our modern laity would feel upset, were some word or other of our Liturgy changed—a really grave consideration. And what, even, about our clergy ?

The election of St. Martin as Bishop of Tours was decided by an " accidental " quotation, by a layman, from Psalm viii. Everyone knows how in East and West monastic life was practically regulated by the Psalms. When Ambrose rebuked Theodosius, he could say, " You have copied David in your crime: copy him in your repentance," and be understood; for when Theodosius did penance, he is said to have done so in the words of Psalm cxviii. 25.

It is impossible to follow the Psalms through history: enough, perhaps, to say that Pope John VIII granted the request of SS. Cyril and Methodius that the Scriptures might be translated into a Slav tongue in the words: " Let everything that hath breath, praise the Lord "; that St. Patrick is said to have gained a unique victory over the Druids (equipped with chariots) by his recitation of *Hi in curribus*, etc.; that St. Columba could recite the Psalms by heart though he *read* only the alphabet; and the exquisite story of his death is interwoven with that of his writing out the Psalter.

In Welsh monastic institutions it was arranged that the Psalms should be sung day and night without inter-mission. You may say that not one of the Saints who taught the Faith in England failed (as the records show) to love and use the Psalms in all circumstances: St. Dunstan died with Psalm cx. 4–5 upon his lips. So did St. Thomas Becket; so did men so similar, yet so different, as Charlemagne and Hildebrand. Charlemagne, savage as he was, liked even to be nicknamed " David " by his friends, so did he love the Psalms.

We have mentioned pilgrimages and the Crusades and St. Bernard. As for St. Francis, he trod with loving awe on the very stones, remembering those words: *Posuisti pedes meos super firmam petram*. St. Louis of France never took his seat as judge without repeating (from Ps. cv.): *Beati qui custodiunt iudicium, et faciunt iustitiam in omni tempore*. And he too died repeating a Psalm.

We pass gradually into the revolutionary period, which, oddly enough, may definitely be called a Psalm-period. On the Protestant side, this seems to me to have been due to the desire (1) to quote Scripture, and (2) to behave militaristically. I am quite sure that, were you to analyse the use made of the Psalms by Catholics and by Protestants during this period, you would find more penitential and loving Psalms on Catholic lips, more blood-thirsty verses upon Protestant ones. St. Thomas More repeated his favourite Psalm, the *Miserere*, actually on the scaffold; St. John Fisher wrote a treatise on the Penitential Psalms, and he too died repeating verse after verse from Psalms. So, almost at the same time, did St. Francis Xavier. So did St. Teresa. So did St. Francis de Sales. St. Vincent de Paul escaped from imprisonment in Africa by means of a Psalm.

I do not wish to minimise the religious piety of Protestants when they used the Psalms. Many of them used them as devoutly and resignedly as Catholics did. The French Protestants, forbidden to use their own versions of the Psalms, used a Catholic version rather than not use any. And it would be easy to show how great a part the Psalms played in the lives of the great Protestant social reformers.

We do not here discuss either the virtues or the horrible brutalities of the Pilgrim Fathers. But I am sure that it would be interesting to work out the theme of Psalm-singing, from the psychological point of view, in connection with that emigration and its results. It appears that Francis Higginson, the first duly appointed teacher at Salem, decided to leave England for the New World because of the prohibition upon " singing Psalms " and praying without the official prayer-book. Almost every great name—Wilberforce, Stanley, Humboldt, Howard (prison reform), Henry Martyn, Havelock in India—that we associate in the sub-modern period with philanthropic or social enterprise or self-sacrificing public service can be linked up with a love for the Psalms.

But I do not know that our modern statesmen, politicians, economists, diplomats, or even philanthropists derive their inspiration or courage from the Psalms. In fact, they obviously don't. That is part and parcel of the modern cross between theism, agnosticism and materialism that surrounds us. *Transeat !*

But *we ?* We have never, in theory, abdicated our birthright. Far from us to suggest that *most* priests, *most* nuns, do not love their Office, heavy though they may find its burden in the stress of necessary duties. We know only too well how desperate we feel when the day is ended, letters are unanswered, and Office is unfinished. We may even know what it is for Office to become the theme of nightmares. You dream that you are saying

Office—and lo, you have no book, or are saying it in English, or without moving your lips—just thinking it, as some busy man did get leave from some Pope to do, so they say!

But the test is, whether one *ever* likes saying the Psalms. Whether (on a holiday, for example, and at leisure) one is glad to have the chance of saying Office slowly, savouring it. Whether anything from the Psalms rises spontaneously to one's lips : " O Domine, quia ego servus tuus et filius ancillae tuae. Omne desiderium meum ante te et gemitus meus non est absconditus a te. Sub umbra alarum tuarum. . . . Adiutorium nostrum. . . ." If it doesn't, what is becoming of the Psalms ? If they are not kneaded into *our* mind, into whose will they be ? Yet, the laity themselves have three great echoes from the Psalms as part and parcel of their religious life—that is, if they ever are asked to take part in Vespers or in Compline ; go to funerals, they must. For the *Magnificat*, the *Nunc Dimittis*, and the *Benedictus* are nothing else but Christian Psalms ; and how terrible it would be, were what Our Lady said to be quite without interest or appeal for her own children!

May we hope for three things. First, that in all seminaries the Psalms should be explained in a human and not too eruditional a way. To be frank, not every student can cope comfortably even with Latin, let alone Greek or Hebrew! And heaven knows that these pages lie open to every charge of unscholarliness. But every human creature can assimilate what is human—and the Psalms are one of the most human collection of songs ever put together. May they then be so exhibited to our students that every priest says his Breviary with delight! I say " to our students," because, once a man is a priest, he may well have no time to develop his *study* of the Psalms. I do not quite believe that, for if a priest took one Psalm per week, he would be well acquainted with the Psalter in five years

—I say "five," because some Psalms take a great deal of time to be understood. On the other hand, some are very simple—the first, for example, or *Laudate Dominum*. But we may hope that most priests will live many sets of five years.

Secondly, may nuns be helped to manage their Office —whether the Little Office of Our Lady or the full Office, if they say it—more happily. I know that to recite *anything* (the Hebrew alphabet) to the glory of God, if you are told to do so, is a meritorious act ; but it is not the best possible sort of act, and it is a very tiring one, and we ought not to pile fatigue on to the exhausted shoulders of our teaching or nursing nuns. " I will pray *also* with my intelligence."

Thirdly, is there any way of helping the laity to know, love and be glad to use the Psalms ? Certainly there is, if one is determined to do so, and takes the laity a few at a time. Study groups, Psalm study groups, may attract very few, out of a *parish ;* but the few would make a nucleus. They could hand the stuff on. Here in England it is the custom to sing *Laudate Dominum* at the end of Benediction. What does the laity make of it ? Very little or nothing, I should suppose. But how easy it would be to teach them what each word means ! How easy to turn it into an impassioned missionary prayer ! Catholic England and America and Ireland are developing so rapidly their " foreign " missionary enterprise. How much faster would it develop, were every soul that says the *Laudate* to mean it *really* as a missionary prayer ! Just as were each person present at Mass to say, and *mean*, " et cum spiritu tuo," how rapidly would the spiritual life of each priest advance ! How could the Lord resist such a con-vinced and collective and sevenfold (if not nine-fold) prayer !

These chapters are now finished. Their writer knows that plenty of mistakes in detail will have been discovered in them by students. But then, he did not wish to write learned disquisitions. He has tried, all his priestly life, to make the most of his duty of saying Office : he knows that it is a *prayer*, and that he ought to try to *pray* it. He has found it very difficult. He has often wished he hadn't got to do it. But he has found that if he could de-Oxfordise, de-Anglicise, de-Europeanise, de-Modernise himself, he could do it better. He could say the Psalms happily if he could get into the " Psalm-atmosphere," and pray the Psalms in the mood in which they were written. But then, the wheel ran back. He found that the more you were in David's mind, the more you were in your own mind : the more you were in any man's *deep* mind. It is the deep mind, the inside mind, one's unsuspected mind, that matters : with it, I am sure that the Psalms will always rhyme.

PART TWO

MEDITATIONS UPON VERSES FROM THE PSALMS.

MEDITATIONS UPON VERSES FROM
THE PSALMS

IT may help if we again recall that these are not " meditations on the Psalms," so much as meditations suggested by certain verses in the Psalms—and indeed, on verses such as we find them in the Latin translation of the Psalter, which itself was derived from the Greek translation of the Hebrew. It does not follow that it was less meaningful or even less true to the original because of that. And we allude to the Hebrew original, so far as it is known, only when we think it can help us.

It is not always easy to be sure what it was—apart from the fact that any document, in course of time, becomes to some extent " corrupt," as they say, and requires " emendation." One source of difficulties is this—the Hebrew did not write down the vowels of a word, but only its consonants, so only the obviously necessary sense, or a strong tradition, could make a reader feel sure what a word *must* be, when there was an option—rather as though we, on reading NT, had to make up our minds whether that stood for *net*, or *not*, or *nut*. Another point is, that Hebrew tenses did not represent so much an action in the past, the present, or the future, as a decisive, momentary action as contrasted with a prolonged one—whether in past, or present, or future. This has its real importance when Prophecy is concerned : the same word *can* be translated as referring to the future, when perhaps it represents some long enduring action or state in the present or even past. And again, Hebrew had not so many conjunctions as we have, and liked to put sentences simply side by side, or to link them with a quite vague particle, so that it is not always clear whether *e.g.* the author meant that " this " happened in order that something else might happen, or, with the consequence that something else happened. These are, so to say, mechanical reasons why it is not always easy to be sure of what the original Hebrew, even if it can be reached, shall mean.

A more literary source of misunderstanding may be this—Hebrew poetry did not rhyme, or " scan," as ours does, but it was full of " assonances "—rather as if we wrote : " Thy red blood that was shed for me, quite washes to whiteness black sins." Such " interior echoes " can seldom be reproduced in English. And again, not only were Hebrew poems often written in elaborate stanzas, full of " echoes," but usually they fall into groups of two lines, the second of which repeats in slightly different forms, or amplifies, or contradicts, the previous one : " What is Man, that Thou rememberest him ?—Yes, human man, that Thou approachest him ? " We must not at once try to find a completely new idea in such " second lines."

We must, too, be prepared for the dramatic, vivacious, exclamatory temperament of the Hebrew. The Psalmist, having begun with some quite passionate declaration, can pass at once into a serene recollection of the past ; then, without warning, address himself to the listener, and then to God, and then, also without " stage direction," so to say, put the next words into the mouth of the People, or again of God. He questions : he asserts : he quotes.

Finally, he has his own special psychology which affects his language. He is absolutely " concrete," and does not say that this is " like " that, but that this *is* that : " The moon was turned to blood," or sackcloth. He does not say that a " phase of history was finished," but that the stars fell from heaven. He can say " I am prayer," for " I pray earnestly " : " My cup is overflow," for " my brimming cup." He does not timidly say that he interprets God as intending—as meaning. He quotes Him as *saying* this or that : and, further, everything is more than merely *within the mind ;* it is practical and efficacious. " Thoughts " are plans, plots, and carried out into action unless defeated by some other " thought " : if God " remembers " a man, He does so in order forthwith to do something to him : His " verdicts " are not mere ethical decisions that such or such an act is right or wrong, but issue forthwith into reward or punishment : in short, processes are " telescoped " ; the consequence of an action is seen *in* the action and vice versa—toil and wages involve one another almost as certainly as father and son do : and since everything was seen as under God's Providence and therefore Will (for He does not sleep, nor act erratically), events are described as happening in *order that* something else might happen. This creates, at times, moral difficulties for us, especially since the Hebrew is apt to omit all intermediary causes and assign the ultimate result of some complicated process (involving, for example, man's free will) directly to God : " Speak to them in parables in order that they may not understand." *We* would ask : " But then, why speak to them at all ? " The Hebrew would say, simply, that God " hardened their hearts," disregarding not only our question, but any consideration such as that they hardened their own hearts, and that God did not interfere with free will but allowed them to do so, *with the result* that they would not be obedient or *let* themselves understand. Hebrew methods of expression are not, therefore, merely due to the nature of the Hebrew language, but to that of Hebrew thought. We shall not, then, fully appreciate the Psalms or any other part of the Old Testament unless we to some extent learn to think like a Hebrew. But we hope that while these considerations may be of use for those who read this book, the little meditations may serve their turn even without reference to this Note.

I

PRAISE THE LORD, FOR HE IS GOOD

THE ultimate reason why Creation should exist, is the Glory of God. Inanimate creation " gives " Him this glory by merely existing. Man, being intelligent and able to choose, must do this also consciously and deliberately. When we men do this, the expression of our " giving glory " is, first, living as we ought to, but also, the direct offering of " Praise " to God.

But joyous triumphant Praise is a climax, a peak to which we may not be all the time attaining. The first step—the " beginning of wisdom "—is the " fear of God "—not, being frightened of God ; but, having awe for God. This is an experience or attitude not too familiar to our generation, which has been schooled to regard the world as simply upon its own level if not beneath it. God is not attended to. This makes men much shallower than they were, and unfit for the very noble exercise of humility—indeed self-humiliation—in the presence of God. No doubt such humility displays itself often in the simple endeavour to avoid sin, as displeasing to God : but it continues to mount by way of prayer expressive of man's need for help, and of gratitude for help or blessings received. This is worship—a positive homage, and not all-but negative like the *avoidance* of sin. But worship can mount higher still, to the level of joyous Praise, and ecstatic Adoration. All these levels of worship will be found in the Psalms. As always, the " meditations " will single out only a very few of the possible texts. We may hope, however, that they may school our souls—give them a bent, a tendency,

towards recognising gladly any invitation to Praise that
a Psalm may offer, so that we may forthwith and " naturally " respond to that suggestion, and indeed " Praise the
Lord " alike in His works and in Himself.

FEAR UNAFRAID

*Initium sapientiae, Timor Domini. The beginning of
Wisdom is : Awe for God.—Psalm cx. 10. Sunday ;
Vesp. ; 2.*

1. Pius XI, in the wake of his predecessors, pointed out
again and again that men were responsible for the chaos
of human affairs because they excluded God from their
enterprises or attempted construction of States ; and still
less did they begin from Him. For a successful course, we
need starting-point, path, and goal. Naturally, if we
disregard both starting-point and end, we cannot be right
about what lies between—we shall, as St. John often says,
merely " wander," not " walk."

2. But we must not take up just any attitude towards
God. We have not to decide what God shall be allowed
to command us ; nor pick and choose among His undoubted
commands. Our attitude must be, from the very outset,
one of *awe*. Even though under the light of the Christian
revelation, we know that God loves us, we have to beware
of off-handedness, familiarity, frivolity, indolence. May
God, from time to time, *overwhelm* us with a sense of His
Majesty and Holiness.

3. It is when we have become quite " small " in the
presence of God, that we can advance with complete
serenity and simplicity. Such was the " little way " of St.
Thérèse of Lisieux. Man's " nothingness " as compared
with God was the profound perception of St. John of the
Cross ; and it was because she had assimilated this so well,
that his daughter, the little Carmelite, was able to take

her way restfully, never "fretting"—knowing that God
meant to ask very great things from her, precisely because
He knew she would assign none of them to her own merits
or talents.[1]

    .   .   .   .   .

    Such, too, was Our Lady. When the Angel appeared
to her, she "feared." She did not "rationalise" her
experience. Still less did it occur to her that she was, by
grace and in vocation, higher than any Angel. When
Gabriel explained his message, she did not hastily yield
to it—" Quomodo fiet istud?" How should this be?
It did not *seem* in accordance with God's will as hitherto
known to her. The Angel explained further, and she
answered : " Behold the handmaid of the Lord, be it done
unto me according to thy word." She was perfectly ready
to reverse all her expectations or plans, once she saw God's
Will. Awe, then, with its consequence of absolute self-
surrender. And *then*, the Magnificat ! Exultant Praise!
" Sanctum et terribile Nomen eius " (verse 9*b*, " Holy
and awe-ful is His Name," are words echoed in her own :
" And Holy is His Name! " (she left out " terrible.")
Magnificat ! Fecit mihi magna ! My soul—all that is
within me—attributes Greatness to God—and to me, in
me, God hath done *great* things and through me shall do
them! The Psalmist could announce this (verse 1) in full
public : Mary, modest and retiring maiden, could not do
that : but at least she had to share her joy with St. Elizabeth.
Read this Psalm for the sake of the notion of Greatness
that it emphasises : *great* are God's works, and for ever
enduring. He hath sent Ransom to His People—yea,
for ever doth His Covenant endure. In the face of Infinity
and Eternity man must bow in awe : no wonder that " awe "
is the " essential," the wholly necessary element, in true
wisdom, and in that sense its " beginning."

---

[1] *Initium* probably means the essential, chief and in that sense "starting-
point " of any true understanding of life. See Prov., i. 7 ; ix, 10.

Compare Zachary's hymn : " That without fear, rescued from the hands of our enemies we might serve Him " (Luke i. 74) : and St. John's : " Perfect love casteth out fear " (1 John iv. 18). Of what am I afraid ?

HOLY IS HIS NAME

Quoniam sanctum est ! Holy is He !—Psalm xcviii. 3. Fri. Lauds ; 1.

1. The refrain of these stanzas is disguised in the Latin : " Let them extol Thy Name, for it is great and worshipful —Holy is He! (3) : Exalt the Lord, our God, and worship at His footstool—Holy is He! " (5) : " Exalt the Lord, our God, and worship at His holy Hill—for the Lord, our God, is Holy! " (9). To grow accustomed to such refrains, guiding words, governing ideas, construes and also diversifies the Psalms, and makes their recitation easier : the " sense " is set free and shines through and around the words.

2. It is good to meditate on the Holiness of God, even though at times, and *for* a time, it may set Him aloof from us. Only Moses was allowed to climb the holy Mountain. St. John (Apoc. iv. 6 ; cf. xv. 2) saw Him fenced off from all creation by a " sea of glass "—even the Redeemed could but set foot on it : they could not so cross it as to become identified with God. Only the High Priest could enter the Holy of Holies. And yet, by virtue of His Omnipresence, God is within us and within all that is, which is enough to make us regard any created thing, any person (even unheeding, even sinful), with awestruck reverence.

3. At Mass we join in the immemorial hymn of the Thrice Holy. May we never say that part of Mass lightly. But, being Christians, without letting go of anything that we have learnt about God's Holiness, we pass at once to

" Him who is coming in the Name of the Lord "—Jesus
Christ, our fellow-man: we carry the Sanctus forward
into the Benedictus: and further still, into the Agnus Dei.
So deep, so near! " Yes, to a death upon a Cross! "
" *That* is why God hath given Him the Name at which
every knee should kneel! "

.   .   .   .   .

Irascantur (1) should mean: " tremble; shudder."
Honor regis (4) can mean: " It is to the King's honour
that he should love justice—Thou hast established right
order (in his kingdom). *Ulciscens* (5). God was merciful,
but punished their (evil) doings.

Verse 4 (*honor regis*) may reasonably be translated:
" The glorious King loveth justice," somewhat as " length
of days " means " long life." The sublime austerity of the
first two stanzas might be disheartening: but the Psalmist
reminds us that God is not only merciful, but has willed
to show also His accessibility to human prayer, and has
even appointed men whose office and duty it is to pray,
and again, raises up men who *do* pray—for Samuel is not
numbered among priests as Aaron and, in a true sense,
Moses were. Remember the exquisite passage in which
Abraham pleads with God for the Cities of the Plain
(Gen. xviii. 22–33): and the prayer of Moses (Exod.
xvii. 10) and that of Samuel (1 Kings iii. 4): and again the
terrible passage in Jeremias xv. 1: " Though Moses and
Samuel stood before Me (to intercede) yet would My heart
not turn to this people ! " We see at once the tremendous
efficacy of the Prayer of the Saints ; and also, the obligation
of all priests, and of all who feel the *call* to prayer, to intercede earnestly for the whole world—not forgetting the
" next " world of Purgatory.

.   .   .   .   .

Among simple people, both sanctity and accursedness
are apt to provoke the notion of " intangibility." The

un-consecrated must not touch what is holy : the accursed makes him who touches it unclean. Our Lord has " broken down the dividing wall" between us and God : we have free access, free speech, with our Father, thanks to Him. Yet here and there we too preserve the " intangibility " of what is sacred—the chalice, for example. This ought not to make the laity ashamed, or think of themselves as somehow not holy, nor called to holiness : on the other hand, it ought from time to time to recall to the priest how he *has* been " consecrated," set aside. But again we know that physical contact with what is morally unclean, even mental contact (if we are humbly prudent) cannot directly produce in the Christian any taint of any sort. The fountain of Christian vitality and purity is within—God's grace: nay, we should be able, thanks to the forth-streaming of that interior grace, to purify.

THE NEW SONG

Cantate Domino canticum novum ; cantate Domino, omnis terra ! Sing unto the Lord a New Song ; sing to the Lord, all thou whole world !—Psalm xcvi 1. Tues., Lauds, 1 : and see Psalm xcvii., 1 ; Thurs., Lauds, 1, and many others, e.g., Psalms xciv ; xcviii ; xcix ; and all the Hallelu-Jah Psalms, cxlvi–cl.

1. Though these Psalms contain isolated verses well worthy of meditation, perhaps they provide, rather, attitudes of mind, one of which is the " praising " one. One whole part of the Office consists of Lauds. We, and all Creation, are meant to " praise " the Lord. Each single thing should reflect, in its very being, a limited part of the greatness, goodness and beauty of God : it should, as Our Lady said of herself, " magnify " the Lord—we can use that word even in our customary sense : make God seem greater than ever He did before. And again, each created

thing should correspond to *that* " in " God which God meant it to. That already is God's Praise. But spiritual creatures, like the angels or ourselves, must not only be and act as God wishes us to, but consciously, deliberately, show forth His glory—and we, just because we have voices, also vocally.

2. We were created *in order* that we might do this. So when we are doing so, we have the joy of knowing we are doing exactly what we were created for. We can praise God *for* inanimate nature : St. Francis's Canticle of the Sun—" Blessed be Thou *for* our brother Sun, our sister Water . . . " : but the Psalms (*e.g.* cxlviii, and the *Benedicite*) boldly call on nature itself to praise God : " Praise Him, sun and moon! " Nature by its very existence is God's Praise : but we can pick it up, incorporate it into ourselves, give it a voice, and create a better harmony throughout the universe.

3. But the Psalms go further, and constantly call on the Gentiles and their kings to " praise God " : let us praise God also in the name of the Un-believer, and fashion yet another " New Song " in the world.

· · · · ·

The whole of this Psalm is a paean of praise and quite straightforward. It may help us if we realise that the Hebrew *all-but* visualised the " Attributes " of God as majestic spiritual Beings standing in His presence or accompanying Him. " Praise and Majesty stand before Him : Strength and Grandeur are in His Sanctuary " (6) : Justice and Mercy form part of His procession.—As for the other Psalms alluded to :—In xciv, the call to Praise is followed by a sorrowful recollection of the doom of those who *refuse* their homage : verse 9 means : " Harden not your hearts as (ye did) at Meribah (" Striving "), as on the day of Massah (" Trying, or Testing, *i.e.* of God) in the desert. See Exod. xvii. 1–7 ; Num. xx. 1–13 : cf.

Deut. xxxiii ; Ps. lxxx. 8. In Ps. xcvi. 1, we again find an appeal to the whole earth to rejoice—to " the many islands " to exult. The Hebrews disliked the sea, and its islands stood for distant and pagan places. Undoubtedly the Psalm foresees God as King of the World : we must pray it with " large " hearts, able to sustain the highest hopes. Ps. xcviii is alluded to elsewhere ; and so are the Hallelu-Jah Psalms. Even if, in our meditations, we reach no further than the first words—" Praise ye *the Lord* " —we shall have made a good and lofty prayer.

MANIFOLD PRAISE

Laudate eum secundum multitudinem magnitudinis eius ! Praise him according to the multitude of His greatness !—Psalm cli. 2 Sat., Lauds, 5.

1. How can we do this ? We cannot. We recognise that there is no proportion of any sort between ourselves and God. We can " give Thee thanks *because of* Thy great Glory " ; but not so as to reach up to it and praise it as it deserves to be praised.

2. But the verse means rather : " Praise Him according to the manifestations of His greatness "—the ever-expanding manifestations of that Glory, increasingly made known to us. This can be symbolised by the Psalmist's piling up of all sorts of musical instruments, as though each were suitable to some variety of divine acclaim. And indeed, the *quality* of the music of bugle, violin, harp, of the thunderous drum differs in each case. We are told to praise God " in virtutibus suis," in His " Powers," His powerful acts, the manifold expression of His power. It is well within the psychology of the Psalmist, and should be in ours, to take a different sort of delight in butterfly, and storm : in a violet and a cataract. Nor need we fear any discovery of science. Each reveals something more

for which God is powerfully responsible, and for which
we can praise Him.

3. Yet the Christian can, after all, praise God worthily,
because of his incorporation with Christ. Let us unite
ourselves in all these final Praise-psalms with Our Lord,
and sing them with His Heart and voice. It is thus that we
can say, at the " little Elevation " (which is, really, by far
the greater one)—" Through Him, together with Him,
and *in* Him, there *is* unto Thee, O God, *all* honour and
glory! " Not only " may there be " ; but " there *is*."
What we cannot give, Christ can ; and we, in Him, can.

· · · · ·

Perhaps it is a duty for each generation to praise God
for what is special to it—its new discoveries, for example.
There are two ways in which this is *not* done—first, clearly,
when they are mis-used, as the cinema, broadcasting, the
press, rapidity of transit, high explosives, can be. Lies,
as well as truth, can be given far wider, far swifter publicity
than of old. Pius XI said to those who were reluctant to
admit " innovations "—" Make good use of what so many
use for evil." It is a dreadful thought that the gifts of God
(for so they are, though we put them down to some human
inventive genius—he discovers what *is there ;* he does not
make it) should be used against God. But further, we may
just forget God in our excitement and thrill, or just because
the new facilities are so convenient. In hours of spiritual
weariness, or indeed of bodily fatigue, why not just sit back,
look around you, see what you value, and then explicitly
thank God for it ? " Thank you, my God " is not a tiring
prayer to say ; yet it can mean so much! The Hebrew words
for " praise " hover between the direct sense of praising,
and the indirect sense of thanking—after all, thanking still
includes a certain amount of " I " ; I thank for the gift to
me : but pure praise forgets self. Still, it is in His manifold
gifts that the richness of God's being is made known to us.

OUR LADY'S HYMN

Quis sicut Dominus Deus noster . . . qui in altis habitat, et humilia respicit in caelo et in terra? Who is like to our God, who liveth in the highest, and yet looketh back unto all humble things, alike in heaven and on earth? —Psalm cxii. 5. 6. Sunday, Vesp., 4.

1. Surely this Psalm was in Our Lady's mind when she sang the Magnificat? Try to say not only the Magnificat but this Psalm, and any other Psalm that lends itself, *with the mind of Our Lady*. It is good practice to try to guess what she would have thought, when praying these ancestral words or reading the Old Testament.

2. God is not " too high " to be aware of all that passes upon earth ; but His verdicts and estimates often turn those of earth upside down. Yet I must beware of judging even what I think wrong, in a sour sort of way. It is in mercy and loving-kindness that He looks at " humble " things ; it is from the proud that He " turns His face away ", and they perish. The Incarnation has taught us that there is nothing towards which God does not look lovingly ; only if an obstinate proud will perseveres to the end, must He reject it.

3. There are then " humble things " also in heaven. All that is created, is immeasurably below God. The highest archangel depends wholly on Him for his very being. Yet certain angels rebelled. " We will not serve! " Perhaps they saw that human nature, in the Word Incarnate, had been exalted higher than they ; and that Our Lady herself is Queen of Angels. To-day, men are being *taught* to rebel against God. All the more may we linger over acts of pure Adoration—an act that *can* be offered only to God. " Quis sicut Dominus Deus noster ? Quis ut Deus ? " " Who is like unto God ? " This is the very name of St. Michael—

God's servant, however much he too is " in authority,"
saying to his fellow-angels : " Go," and they go—" Come,"
and they come.

THE ANGELS' HYMN

*In conspectu angelorum psallam tibi. In the presence
of the Angels will I sing praise to Thee.*—Psalm cxxxvii.
1. *Thurs.*, *Vesp.*, 5.

1. The Psalm, so opposite in spirit to the despondent
cxxxvi, " by the waters of Babylon," testifies to Israel's
sense that the People is delivered, or about to be. Therefore,
praise shall be sung to the True God in the very face
of the false ones. For " angels " is, as often, substituted
in the Greek and Latin versions for the Hebrew " gods."
But we will meditate on that word " angels," lest we tend
to forget their existence. The Church does not wish us to.
In the Creed at Mass she reminds us that God is Creator
of " things invisible " as well as of the visible universe :
in the Preface, she wishes us to unite ourselves with all
those heavenly Beings which, grade above grade in glory,
rise high above our poor mortality.

2. It is good to reflect that we are, as it were, only on the
fringe of the world of Intelligence. Men are poor little
things compared with those mighty spirits. Yet they,
too, need to be humble ! They, too, have to worship the
Word Incarnate, in whom *our* nature is united with the
divine one. It is held by many that the " fall " of the Angels
consisted in their refusing thus to worship what was
" beneath " them, though as to this, there is no Catholic
dogma.

3. But (verse 6), the Lord is *so* exalted, that *all* created
things are immeasurably inferior to Himself : when human
men—like the strong enemies of weak Israel—puff themselves up, He " regardeth it from afar " ; (cf. cxii. 5, 6)
almost as though He could not be interested in *that* ; it

deserves no close examination. The paradox is true—the humbler we are, the nearer we come to God; and if we would consort with Angels, we must be as humble, as truly " servants," as they.

THE CHURCH'S HYMN

Beatus, cuius Deus Iacob adiutor eius. Happy is he who hath the God of Israel for his help !—Psalm xlv. 4. Wed., Lauds., 5.

1. This is the first of the five Hallelu-Jah (Praise ye Yahweh!) Psalms with which the Psalter closes. Only for two verses (3, 4) does the Psalmist turn aside from God Himself, as worthy of all praise, to remind us that we are *not* to put our trust in princes, nor indeed in any human man—*they* cannot save : their breath leaves them ; they return to their own dust ; on that very day their schemes come to naught. The contrast serves but to render more glorious the vision of GOD all-praise-worthy.

2. Can I be said to be "enthusiastic" about God ? Do I spontaneously "praise" Him—if not with great shouts of "Alleluia," at least in *some* way more suited to my temperament, personal, national, or racial ? Is there any element in my life which I can describe as spontaneous praise ? The Psalms constantly make me ask this challenging question.

3. This Psalm, however, does not keep to praising God for what He is, but also praises Him for what He does. "The Lord it is who gives food to the hungry—who looseth the prisoners—raiseth up the prostrate—giveth light to the blind—guardeth the immigrant—taketh care of the orphan and the widow." Compare Isaias xxix. 18 ; lxi. 1 ; and Our Lord's own credentials, sent to the Baptist in prison. Seeing then that this is the " character " assigned to God, and to the Messias both in prophecy and fact, we

cannot but examine whether we are in any sense " praise-
worthy " for that sort of reason. Is there a " family-
likeness " between ourselves, Our Lord, and our Heavenly
Father ?

THE HEATHEN'S HYMN

*Laudate Dominum, omnes Gentes ! Praise the Lord,
all ye Peoples !—Psalm cxvi.* 1. *Mon., Lauds,* 5.

1. The Psalm is familiar because of Benediction. But
do we give full value to its verses ? " Praise *the Lord*,
all ye Pagans! *Him* praise ye, all ye Peoples! For it is
upon *us* that His mercy is established ; yes, the loyalty of
the Lord endureth for evermore! " (*Veritas* means " truth "
in the sense of being " true " to someone, or to one's
given word.)

2. We acknowledge then that God has given to us what
He has not given to all—His Mercy is in a special way
shown to *us*, promised to us, stamped and sealed upon us,
nor will God ever be unfaithful to it. But His Covenant
was made with the Jewish People, not with each individual
Jew : so, too, His promise is made to the imperishable
Church—not to each individual Catholic. I still retain
my prerogative, therefore, with a certain anxious awe,
praying earnestly for perseverance.

3. But this is essentially a Missionary Psalm. The Jew
speaks directly to the non-Jew. On our lips, the Psalm
speaks to all non-Catholics throughout the world. After
Benediction, received and assimilated by us, it is very
right that we shall call upon, challenge, summon, lovingly
convoke the entire non-Catholic world towards Praise of
the Only True God.

OUR MORNING HYMN

Ad Te orabo Domine mane. . . . Mane astabo tibi et videbo. . . . Introibo in Domum tuam. In the morning will I pray to Thee, O Lord. . . . In the morning will I present myself to Thee and look for Thee. . . . Through the multitude of Thy mercies will I enter Thy House and worship towards Thy holy Temple.—Ps. v. 4, 5, 8. Mon., Lauds, 3.

1. We can develop the habit of making our thoughts go at once to God when we wake—maybe in a confused, clogged manner if we find it hard to wake up, but enough to give to God, as He deserves, the first-fruits of our consciousness. If we follow this up with the Sign of the Cross, that is good. Our first deliberate action will have been His, and Christ's. We *start* our day as Christians, under the " shield of His good will " (13). Much of the Psalm is occupied with the thought of " enemies." We certainly need every kind of divine protection against unseen, unguessed, or semi-guessed foes. Foes, too, who attack us under the semblance of good, which they undoubtedly will do just in proportion as we try to act aright.

2. Priests are accustomed to people's leaving out their morning prayers much oftener than they do their evening ones. They are in a hurry—but then, in the evening we are tired—or else they feel less " spiritual " at first than they do later on. We *must* preach and practise the consecration of the day at its outset. A *serious* " Morning Oblation."

3. Of course Daily Mass is the ideal. Short of this, it is good to go to Mass at least sometimes when we are not obliged to. This shows good will, an appreciation of the supreme value of Mass, and a recognition that it is through God's *goodness* that Mass so much as exists and that it is through His *favour* that I am allowed to go to it.

II

PRAISE HIM IN HIS WONDROUS WORKS

We know much about God, but we do not see Him. Few even are they who " sustain the Invisible *as though* they saw Him " (see Hebrews xi. 27 : " He endured, as seeing Him that is invisible "). But we do see God as " by means of a mirror," dimly, *i.e.*, reflected in His works : therefore in them we see enough of God to warrant our praising Him *in them*. We do not, then, wish to be unaware of Creation : no ascetical renunciation demands that of us : provided only we do not turn the created thing into an idol, and substitute it for God, the more we attend to the whole hierarchy of " Nature," the better. The Psalmist can fall into a sort of ecstasy over inanimate creation itself : he does not fail to attend—any more than God does!— to animate, yet not human-wise living things. But naturally he sees God's greatest self-revelation in Man— and, since the Incarnation, we can see Him there incalculably better. Thus men can become, as it were, Priests in regard of all that is; for they can see in anything that is, somewhat that is God-like and fit to be offered to God. This offering they can make all the day long : and thus turn even non-living things into a conscious Gift, a living Praise. Not only is this what God " deserves," but also, it is an apostolic thing to do, for, the more we recognise God in our fellow-men, the more reverently and loving we order ourselves towards them, and the more we win their hearts—and that is good, provided we do not wish to *keep for ourselves* human respect or affection, but " hand it on " to Him who alone fully deserves it.

GOD'S CREATIVE WORD

Velociter currit sermo eius. Swiftly speedeth His word.
—Psalm cxlviii. 4. Fri., Lauds, 5.

1. This Nature-Psalm does not regard Nature directly as " praising God," but as offering a term of comparison with God's own action. God sends His snow like wool-fluff; He scatters His hoar-frost like infinitesimal innumerable white ash—He pours forth great lumps of hail (possibly, bits of ice tumbling down from Lebanon by way of Jordan)—and who can stand up against His cold? Then suddenly He speaks, and melts them: He breathes, and forth flow the waters once again.

2. This shows to our eyes what we know with our minds but often hardly realise—the instantaneous, irresistible efficacy of His decree. He sends forth His decree —swiftly speedeth His word. . . . And in particular— His decree about His Holy City is irresistible: He has established Jerusalem; to Israel has He entrusted His Law—not so has He done for every nation! Nor shall His Word return to Him void (Isa. lv. 11).

3. St. Augustine says that we attend to miracles because we are too accustomed to the far greater miracles that go on all the time. He says it is less marvellous to make many loaves out of a few, than even one grain from which all the crops proceed—from which all the bread in the world is made—from nothing! So it is not to the glory of God if we let ourselves get accustomed to Nature and do not notice it. May we then never get thus accustomed! May we always be astonished by the beauty of the world, and never lessen it. If you attend to a plant, a sunset, you are attending to the very thing to which God Himself is attending. Happy the man who is doing, even in his poor way, just what God is doing, in His!

GOD FEEDS BOTH BEASTS AND BIRDS

Qui dat iumentis escam ipsorum, et pullis corvorum invocantibus eum. God gives their food to the cattle ; yes, and to the ravens' little ones that call to Him.— Psalm cxlvi. 9. Thurs., Lauds, 5.

1. Never must we allow ourselves to be confused by that "science" which excludes attention to the *direct action* of God in nature. Of course an immense interplay of created forces issues into any material result in our universe. But not only is God the origin of all this series, but God is at all points preserving those forces that are acting, and that on which they are acting. The action of God is right *up* to us. The First Cause is not *long ago !* We are absolutely right in saying that God thus feeds all living animals : "Not one sparrow falls to earth, without your Father" (Matt. x. 29).

2. We are often rebuked for saying that "animals have no rights." We are not "meditating" upon that ; but we well may remember that *God* has. All things belong to Him. However much He created what is lower than man *for* man, He remains sovereign Lord of all that is. I dare not wantonly injure or misuse *any* of His manifold creation. The more I "appreciate" God, the more shall I reverence His creation.

3. I am then not likely to succumb to the absurd idolatries of decadent races, which actually worshipped beasts and plants : nor yet to the sentimentalism which perverts all order, and may attend more even to a pet animal than to a child : or again which issues into the "spoiling"—horrible and accurate word—of a child. That means that I treat the child more as though it existed for *my* entertainment than for God's glory, or even, for its own temporal and eternal well-being and happiness.

Read Job xxxviii, and see verse 41. " Who provideth his food for the raven when his young ones cry to God, and stray (or call out) for lack of food ? "—In this Psalm, then, we see how tenderly God cares for the helpless beasts ; but will not help those who trust in themselves —in their cavalry or infantry!

THE GREATNESS AND THE LITTLENESS OF MAN

Quid est homo, quod memor es eius ? aut filius hominis, quoniam visitas eum ? What is man, that Thou rememberest him ? yes, human man, that Thou dost visit him ?—Psalm viii, 5. Sunday, Matins, ii. 1.

1. This glorious Psalm is happily so familiar, that just to recite it can do all for us that a " set " meditation can. It simply *is* a majestic hymn of praise ; and in praising God man is fulfilling the primary purpose of his existence.

2. The littleness and the greatness of mankind! Man is so small, that even the immensity of the universe abashes him—and yet he is so great, being created by God and having received intelligence to *know* that universe, to appreciate its beauty, and to see God in it, that by praising God on its account he can as it were endow even inanimate things with a voice and cause all created things to join in his own hymn.

3. However low his estate—though he be but as a babe and an infant compared, for example, with the Angels— let alone with God—yet when he lifts up his voice to praise, he justifies his existence and that of God's handi-work. Nay, when he *uses* anything as God meant it to be used, he is praising God, for, God created it so to be used and again its existence is justified. And by uniting ourselves with Our Lord, we can praise God with *His* gratitude and love—He who Himself exclaimed over the loveliness of the wild flowers, and thanked His Father

that He had revealed more to the innocent and simple than to those who were self-sufficient and "wise in their own conceit" (see St. Matt. xi. 25). In 8b, the beasts of the field are *wild* beasts, as contrasted with the sheep and the oxen.

GOD GLORIOUSLY ENTHRONED

Dominus regnavit. The Lord hath enthroned Himself. —*Psalm xcvi.* 1. *Wed., Lauds,* 1.

1. This expression, with which other psalms begin, means more than "is King"—it implies that the Lord has in some special way proclaimed Himself as King, taken His throne as King. Moreover, He does so *manifestly :* doubtless the terrific phenomena of Sinai had for ever impressed the imagination of Hebrew poets. One of the oldest pieces of Hebrew literature is the Song of Debora (see Judges v. 4–5) : in it, the tremendous Advent of God is described already in terms that became almost stereotyped, like those in which the Last Day was described. The Hebrews thought of God more in terms of Power than *e.g.,* of Love.

2. Contrast, therefore, the marvellous vision of Elias (3 Kings xix) where every violent natural phenomenon was displayed—but God was not in them. He spoke as in a *whisper.*

3. Contrast, too, the Coming of Our Lord—in how much of His Life, in the Passion, in the Blessed Sacrament, His Divinity "hides itself." "Vere tu es Deus absconditus," says the Vulgate. Certainly our Enthronement of the Sacred Heart in our families—certainly our festival of Christ-King—imply many hidden, quiet virtues! None the less, the key-note of this vehement Psalm is "happiness." Study how often that notion recurs! The Coming of God is *meant* to make us happy, by whatever road He reaches us.

STORM AND STILLNESS

Vox Domini intercidentis flammam ignis! The voice of the Lord, cleaving the fiery flame!—Psalm xxviii. 7; Mon., Lauds, 3.

The Latin version of this Psalm is obscure. The first verse should probably be simply: "Ascribe unto the Lord, O ye mighty men—ascribe unto the Lord glory and honour!" Verse 6; the advent of the Lord makes the very mountains quiver like frightened beasts: verse 8; the Lord, *i.e.*, His storm, causes the hinds to bring forth their young prematurely, and strips the forests bare (*condensa* can be compared with our "thickets"). The essence of the Psalm is the self-revelation of the Lord in a storm.

1. The Hebrew loved to assign all that happened to its First Cause. It is far truer to say that "God sends the rain" than to say that rain is due to the condensation of moisture in the atmosphere, and forget God. I will accustom myself to seeing God's *action* in all that is— for it is His present power that keeps all things in existence. God's activity is adorable all around me, and also, in my soul.

2. Though an earthquake, a storm or a volcanic eruption is a small thing in the world at large, let alone in history, yet it is great for men, and for me, because physically we, too, are very small, and such events are "great" in proportion to me. I ought not to be "un-impressionable." I ought to be able to stand in awe of natural phenomena and certainly not have a kind of cult of venerating nothing.

3. Yet I am right, especially as a Christian, to see and hear God in very small things too—quiet and un-advertised things, and especially in the beauties of character that will escape my notice if I am not alert to them. And, as a

priest, I shall not need to shout or be rhetorical in the pulpit or on the platform. Conviction, and a simple faith that God is speaking through me, and a true love for the Faithful, will work the changes of heart that emotionalism, denunciation of a violent sort, or sensational turns of phrasing never will.

GOD GREATER THAN THE SEAS

Mirabiles elationes maris : mirabilis in altis Dominus. Marvellous are the surgings of the waters : (yet more) marvellous on high is God! Psalm xcii. 4. Sunday, Lauds, 1.

1. " The LORD hath enthroned Himself! " Magnificently is the Sovereignty of God proclaimed, and His eternal Throne, high above the tumult of the world. The Sea, and Rivers generally, stood to the Hebrew as chaotic, or, as symbolic of Nations. Palestine lay helpless between the Euphrates (Babylon :—) and the Nile (Egypt). But stronger than these was *God*. *A vocibus* denotes a comparison. " High raised the floods, O Lord—high raised the floods their voices ; high raised the water-floods their waves! Yet beyond the voices of the waters, marvellous and manifold, beyond the surgings of the sea—more marvellous on high is GOD! " Such is the sense of this glorious Psalm.

2. It acted as a sort of preface to the " theocratic " Psalms, sung (in the Second Temple at any rate) on Fridays, when the " earth had been established and populated "—the day before the Sabbath Rest. There is no more solid basis for our piety than reflection on this dogma of God's Sovereignty. " We must obey God rather than men " (Acts v. 29). The Feast of Christ's Kingship itself may lose part of its value because we think of " kings " in modern terms—constitutional

monarchs : " democratic " kings : kings by the will of their subjects. This is not true of God or of His Christ. They are raised eternal and absolute above all earthly limitations, changes, and upheavals and reverses or revolutions. Similarly our obedience has to be as loving as indeed They deserve, but, *absolute*.

ENRAPTURED WITH CREATION

Delectasti me Domine in factura tua. Thou hast enraptured me, Lord, with what Thou hast made !—Psalm xci. 5. Sat., Lauds, 2.

1. The verse continues : " And I exult in the works of Thy hands! " The theme of the Psalm is, in reality, God's action, government, in regard of the Just and the Unjust —only a fool, says the Psalmist, should fail to recognise it. But we apply it forthwith to inanimate creation—or at least we will not exclude but concentrate on that. Alas, that so many, lest they forget God, have to shut out created beauty from their eyes and mind : and that those who do attend to it, so often quite forget God and do not praise *Him*.

2. The Book of Wisdom so thoroughly acknowledges the greatness and beauty of, for example, the stars, that it agrees that it is not *surprising* if, among pagans, human homage stopped there, and if men practically treated such marvels as divine. But then, it says : " They ought to have reflected on their Creator, and realised how yet *more* strong and beautiful must *He* be." After all, there are those who, no sooner are they struck by beauty of colour, form, or music, find themselves *unable* to do anything *but* thank God for it. *Their* difficulty would be to forget God.

3. Yet, in order to praise Him, they do not have to exclude from their minds either the beauties or, alas, the ugliness of creation. When a Saint went into ecstasy over

i

a flower, she did not have to *argue* : " How much *more* beautiful must its Creator be! " and forthwith give the flower the go-by. When St. Ignatius stood on his balcony and looked at the stars, and exclaimed : " How base earth seems to me, when I see the sky! " he was able to perceive God, and His glorious work, and also the worth and yet the poverty of created things, and of human character and work, all in *one* vision. May we thus become *wholly—God's—men* !

GOD'S ROBE OF BEAUTY

Decorem induisti. Thou hast robed Thyself in beauty.—Psalm ciii. 2. Sat., Sext.

1. " Creation " is a better word than " Nature," which is spiritually meaningless : Creation involves God : if we remember that, we *cannot* be idolators : and if we remember (as *Genesis*—so closely followed in this Psalm—reiterates) that God saw all His creation to be "good," we shall also feel free to offer His due homage to God in all created things. The Psalm begins and ends with an ecstatic praise of God, who, invisible, robes Himself in visible beauty by means of His works.

2. God clothes Himself in light ; He stretches out the heavens beneath the upper waters hard ; the clouds are His chariot ; the winds, His wings ; storm and lightning, His messengers.—He forms the solid earth, but waters still cover it. He speaks—the waters yield ; the hills rise up ; the valleys sink : there shall be no more Flood! But the valleys contain springs ; streams flow down the mountain ravines : thither come all wild beasts to drink ; and above them, the birds twitter from the rock-crannies. That water, running down from the heights, makes the soil fertile—food for beasts ; food for men—wheat and wine for man, strengthening and delighting.—Trees too appear—lesser trees in the plain ; mighty cedars upon

Lebanon. And in them, birds nest: the House of the Heron is their Chieftain! As for the mountains, the stag gallops over them; in their crevices the coney makes his refuge. . . . In all ways God cares for them: the sun knows when to sink; the moon has her hours: in the dark, the moonlight, out come the beasts; they roar; they forage; they ask their food from God. Then up comes the sun—back they gather again; they all of them go to rest—and forth comes man, at his own labour till the evening. . . . But more! Here is the sea! It teems with creatures great and small, and over it sail the ships. All—why even the great Dragon in the Depths, created by God to be His plaything—await their timely food from God. When He gives, they take, and are filled with His goodness. He turns aside—they are in dismay: He takes their breath from them—they perish; they fall back into nothingness: again He sends forth His breath, new life arises, earth herself is renewed.

3. Enjoy this Psalm! experience its zest! And add a prayer, as the Psalmist does, that the *one* flaw, *man's* sin, may be removed.

THE TREES OF GOD

Then shall all the trees of the woods exult, before the face of the Lord for He is come!—Psalm xcv. 12; Tues., Lauds, 1.

1. We are glad that the Hebrew poets so much liked the trees and felt that they responded to the presence and power of God. In Isaias lv. 12 they " clap their hands " at His advent: in Isaias xliv. 24 the mountains and the forest-trees upon them break out into shouts of joy. We can allow our fancy to perceive this response not only in the rushing sound heard when the wind plunges on to them, but in the strong upleap of fir-trees, the sort of incandescent haze—first of bronze, then of an incomparable

green—when the larches begin to bud, and in the great golden orange and crimson orchestra of autumn. May we ourselves respond to such things and pass our praises on to God!

2. The History of the Tree! The Tree of Paradise, that must have looked lovely, and been fragrant, and its fruit seemed sweet. But we took wrongly hold of that sweetness and it became bitter and the fruit poisonous and the tree was stripped of its leafage till there stood, descended from it, the stripped Tree of the Cross. *Ipse lignum tunc notavit damna ut ligni solveret*: God "marked e'en the this Tree, the ruin of the first Tree to redeem": "that he who in the wood had conquered, might, in the Tree too, be defeated." (Preface for the Cross). And finally, the Grove of Life on the slopes of the Hill of the New Jerusalem, "whose leaves were for the healing of the nations" (Apoc. xxii. 2). It rose green and glorious on either side of the River of Life that went cascading down the terraces of the Mountain-City—the Christian People, full of grace, *vegetati*, given sap and springing vitality to by the Holy Ghost who proceedeth from the Father and the Lamb. Thus is the soul led to "the lawns of Thy Paradise for ever green"—*semper virentia*—and takes its rest by the waters of refreshment that make their way not only through the forests in great waterfalls, but quietly, through green pastures.

III

EXPERIENCE: GRATITUDE AND TRUST

"*Sentite de Domino in bonitate*," say the Scriptures.
Let your thoughts about God be good-will thoughts:
"think of God in terms of goodness": let your "reaction
to God be that of good will corresponding to good will
. . ." God is good; He is good to you and means well
to you: make, then, a return "in kind"—briefly: love
Him because He first loves you. Somehow thus must we
paraphrase the simple words. We wish, then, a deep
realisation of the goodness of God, with its consequences,
gratitude and trust, to anticipate any sense and instinct
of abashment, humiliation, even sorrow, let alone terror
to fly from before His face. We prefix, therefore, meditations upon verses calculated to inspire us with those
feelings of gratitude and trust which both flow from and
increase our perception of God's goodness. This does
not mean that we forget our sins. On the contrary, God's
incredible goodness is manifested "most chiefly," says
the Liturgy (10th S. Pent), in sparing and showing pity.
Indeed, we might hardly dare to contemplate our sins until
we were well established in the conviction that God loves
us "with an everlasting love" (Jer. xxxi. 3); He loves
us in spite of our sins and even while we were committing
them—if He did not, why should He seek so earnestly
to bring us to repentance, and have redeemed us at the
cost of the death of His own Son? Moreover, if we are
clear beyond any shadow of doubting that God loves us,
we shall reach without any difficulty the supreme motive
for being sorry, which is, precisely, the Love of God.

Not even the Hebrew trod exclusively, or even chiefly, the road of fear : it is a precarious one, and leads to despondency almost as easily as to contrition, and beats the soul down rather than encourages it ; and the motive of fear has anyhow to be corrected afterwards by that of love, whereas if we love aright we shall hardly need to use the motive of fear at all, for " perfect love casteth out fear " (1 John iv. 18) : we *do* need to " fear," simply because our love is so very far from perfect. But at no time is it good to concentrate chiefly upon self : God and His goodness always come first, and are infinitely more powerful and life-giving than self and sins.

The Hebrew did not arrive at any of his conclusions about God by pure speculation but by intuition, experience and the direct Gift of God. Certainly he was taught by law-giver and by prophet : " The Lord, thy God, is One God, and Him only shalt thou serve." But his innermost soul " reacted " passionately to this and re-affirmed it over and over again, ever more spiritually and ever more intensely. We know that we Christians are not to *base* our religion upon private opinion or subjective sentiment : yet it is matter for anxiety if that religion does not " mean " anything to us, and if purely human events strike out more response from our souls and even our emotions than our faith does. It is but right that sometimes we should *feel* sorry, grateful, enthusiastic, peaceful. In his *Exercises* St. Ignatius is very anxious that we should " experience " the truths on which we meditate ; and he gives many hints as to how we should interpret our experiences and what we ought to think about ourselves if we habitually, or during crises, experience nothing at all.

The Hebrew, however, was very far from having only personal experiences. He always saw himself as the member of a race—incorporate with the whole of its history, so that he could draw his experience from all the past—and that past included many a divine promise as to the future. To him, the People was, quite simply, God's servant, God's elect, God's son, preserved through violent and tragic centuries in view of " the Day of the Lord." Hence the whole People and its history were not only an incarnate prophecy; but the very source of gratitude and trust: at any given moment, the Psalmist could feel the whole of that long past flowing into him, and could perceive himself as moving forward toward an absolutely ascertained triumph.

It was, we think, this element that gave stability to the very "temperamental" Hebrew, as we should say. We have already referred (p. 23) to his violent alternation of moods. There was also in him a certain shallowness—the Psalms insist on the ease with which he forgot even the greatest miracles; he gave no heed to them; he did not understand them and apply their meaning to his life. He was too often the exact opposite to Our Lady who " preserved " all that was said and happened: pondered it; " put it together " in her mind; never lost any of it and continuously saw deeper into it. Finally, God had, we may say, to achieve His triumphs in a people which hardly *wanted* Him to. They would have preferred to join in the worships of the nations round about, with their savage and licentious rites. It is enormously impressive to see, in the history of the Hebrews, how, left to themselves, they would infallibly have gravitated towards those other nations and have perished along with them. The Psalmist therefore wishes that " experience " should be also the fruit of reflection, and in particular issue into gratitude, trust, repentance, and determination to do great things for God, as God had done for His People.

THE SWEETNESS OF THE LORD

Gustate et videte quoniam suavis est Dominus. Taste and see that the Lord is sweet.—Psalm xxxiii. 9. Wed., Compline, 1, 2.

1. The word translated " sweet " means, rather, " good," kindly, generous. St. Peter (1 Ep. ii. 3) applies this to Our Lord, which is another example of the unhesitating application to Our Lord of titles or expressions used, in the Old Testament, of the One God. We need not, anyhow, fear to think of God in terms of sweetness ; God wishes us at least sometimes to feel the sweetness of His service : and if we find our sense of God's holiness, justice, infinity and so forth taking the sweetness out of our relations with Him, we must correct that, preferably by reading about Our Lord in the Gospels, and especially in St. John's.

2. There may be, however, a certain cloying lusciousness about certain " devotional " books, or prayers. This has never suited the English character, which was happy and at its ease with God, but not given to that exuberance or exaggeration which sounds quite acceptable when read in a foreign language. I need not, therefore, use such prayers if they do not suit me : again, if I do like the very emotional prayers, I had better test myself to see whether their intense expressions of love, desire for union and so forth are balanced by the charity of my ordinary behaviour among others. It is possible to make a fervid Communion or " visit," and forthwith to show ill-temper or selfishness at home.

3. The more we accustom ourselves to the Church's own Prayer, which is in the Missal and the Breviary, the more we shall strengthen our devotion. Nothing can be more deep, convinced, sincere, reverent, awe-struck and

yet trustful than the great Collects of the Church. It might almost be argued that the more a soul loves, the less the tongue talks.

．　　．　　．　　．　　．　　．

None the less, we may hope that we shall not be insensitive also to the gentler and " sweeter " elements of our Faith, which can create in us every *kind* of love— save, of course, its wholly sensual caricatures. After the Great War, our younger generation was proud of having discarded sentimentalism—that was to the good—but also sentiment—that was bad, and did not in the least do away with emotionalism or even check hysteria. " Thrills " were sought as much as ever : if, once upon a time, people talked too easily of the " heart," and made too little use of their intelligence, there was no improvement when the centre of gravity was transferred to the nerves. May then the beauty, the tenderness, the gentleness, the " dearness " of God reveal themselves to us and evoke their due response : it is well to remember that the Church's Liturgy itself contains prayers for the " Gift of Tears," and there is nothing to applaud in being merely " hard." God says that He will " take away the heart of stone and give you a heart of flesh " (Ez. xxxvi. 26). Those who are trying to give up their will to God may be conscious that there is in the midst of their soul, as it were a pebble that will not dissolve. One little nucleus of obstinate unregenerate *will*. " *That*, I *will* not." Only, half the time one does not know and will not let oneself know what the " that " is.

In verse 6, we have the beautiful image that when God " looks on us," all our world grows sunlit : when He turns His face away, all is dark. The Hebrew, in v. 11, says that " the young lions "—for all their strength, are famished : however weak we know *ourselves* to be, yet God will feed us.

DIRECT EXPERIENCE

Ego cognovi. I—I know!—*Psalm cxxxiv.* 5. *Tues.,*
Lauds, 5.

1. The words are quoted from Exodus xviii. 11 :
Jethro, the pagan priest who was father-in-law to Moses,
heard how God had rescued the Hebrews from Egypt,
and exclaimed : " *Now* I *know* that Yahweh is greater
than all gods! " He did not deny the existence of other,
national, gods ; but he had had proof that the God of
Israel was greater than they. And this is in tune with
the whole of this Psalm. Albeit we do not *base* our religious
belief upon feeling, yet the Psalmist is constantly appealing
to the fact that he *does* experience the power, the goodness,
the *reality* of God. And the Christian who is honestly trying
to live according to God and Our Lord, is almost certain
to experience the same from time to time. It is idle to try
to force God's hand, and it leads to every illusion if we
try to think we experience the " touch " or presence of
God : but if we do not, and are not conscious of wilful
sin, we can, like the Psalmist, expostulate humbly with
Him : for after all, how strong is the contrast in this
very Psalm between the un-seeing, un-hearing, un-heeding
idols and the Living God, who is always *acting upon*
us ?

2. The Psalmist prays that worshippers of idols may be
made as sense-less as *they* are. We, not so : we will pray
that eyes and ears may be opened by God's grace : but
so far as we are to be ministers of that Grace, we shall
be of no avail unless we use the only solvent of hardened
hearts, which is love.

3. Psalm cxxxv (Thurs., Vesp., 2, 3) is made up largely
of phrases from cxxxiv ; but it has a refrain, and just
because it *is* a refrain, it (i) is meant to be emphatic, and

(ii) is easily slipped over. "For His goodness endureth
for ever." If we can be sure of that, and thank Him for
it, in hours of "desolation," we shall indeed be profiting
by them!

In verse 3, "for it is sweet," refers presumably to the
Name of God, not to the act of praising it. But we may
wish to find sweetness also in our acts of worship, not
least when they are obligatory.

RELATE GOD'S WONDER-WORKS!

*Narrate omnia mirabilia eius. Tell of all His wondrous
works!—Psalm civ. 2; Sat., Noct., i. 1.*

1. The "historical" psalms are not to everybody's
taste. The details of the Plagues or the Exodus may
weary us. But the Israelites could not detach their minds
from the wonderful things that God had done for them,
and felt that others, too, should be impressed by their
recital (cf. Ps. cv. 2; civ. 1).

2. We ourselves could know the Old Testament better.
The Liturgy is always using it; so are the New Testament
Scriptures. Our Christian Faith is not severed from the
history of the Hebrews: and our view of our religion
can be wide—we may know all that the Church now
teaches—yet not deep, in that we know nothing, or only
patches, of her history. But then, I cannot tell *others*
God's marvellous works in past times, whether for, or
through, the Church.

3. I would do well to "deepen" my knowledge, by
learning what God has done for His Church in the past:
and the Psalm encourages me to reflect, too, upon my
own history, until I am full of awe and gratitude. For even
if I cannot see that God has done specially great *material*
things for me during my life, there are the tremendous
all-embracing facts of my pre-destination, vocation,

redemption, and destined glorification. And certainly, my having been constantly forgiven by God when I sinned, and been patiently treated by Him while I was obtuse and could not see His hand in events. Thus, the history of the Israelites is in many ways my own, " writ large." I ought to be able—especially if I am, or am preparing to be, a priest—to reach the Preface at Mass *genuinely* full of gratitude; to appreciate why Mass was first and convincedly called the Eucharist; and to say with all my heart—*Vere* dignum et iustum est! *Truly* is it right and just that we to Thee at all times and in all places should give *thanks!*

FORGOTTEN SINS

Peccavimus cum patribus nostris; iniuste egimus; iniquitatem fecimus. Patres nostri in Aegypto non intellexerunt mirabilia tua. . . . Cito fecerunt; obliti sunt operum eius. We have sinned along with our fathers; we have done wrong; we have worked iniquity. Our fathers in Egypt did not understand Thy marvels. . . . Quickly, quickly did they forget His works!—Psalm cv. 6, 7, 14. Sat., Matins, ii.

1. The Psalmist is fully frank in his confession of his and the People's sins: in Psalm lxxvii (Fri., Noct., i, 2) there is a definite refrain. " In spite of all this, they continued to sin yet further!" In that Psalm, its whole purpose is defined (verses 10, 11): the preventing the actual generation from being like its ancestors—a generation which despite God's goodness to it, constantly sinned, professed repentance, and relapsed—in Psalm cv. we have details of the savage idolatries of the Israelites —they sacrificed their sons and daughters to the heathen gods of Canaan. No critic of the Hebrew race is as severe as its own self-reproach.

2. Before we rebuke anti-Catholics, we should at least repent our own sins—that may be worse than theirs, since we possess revelation and unequalled motives for right-doing, and surpassing graces. We must not acknowledge this out of a spurious broad-mindedness, a snobbish show of "tolerance"—but for our own sakes, so that we weep blood over our sins, alike ancestral and personal, which have prevented, and prevent, so much good.

3. The strongest argument against the Church consists in bad Catholics. And again, in Catholics who do not sin gravely, but melt into their environment and have just the same ideals as the "respectable pagan" as to money, social position, business-methods, pleasure and the other illusions of this world's "passing pageant." It is possible to live in a world of marvels (as indeed we do!—a world of Grace) and "give no heed" to them; not understand them; even forget what God specially does for us almost as soon as it has happened. But what He has done is meant to be a pledge of what He will do, if but we remember, thank, and trust.

RECALL—FORGET—RECALL

Non recordati sunt. . . . Et rememorati sunt. . . .
They did not recollect, . . . Then they remembered.—
Psalm lxxvii. 42, 35. Fri., Matins, Noct. i. 2.

In the last meditation we saw that the Israelites "did not understand" (gave no heed to . . .) God's works for them. This implies a wrong will. (See St. Luke xviii. Our Lord had told the apostles in the clearest possible way about His Passion. But "they understood nothing of these things; His meaning was hidden from them: no, they did not understand what was being said." This was because their minds simply *would* not admit the notion of a defeated and dying Messias.) But here we may see a certain "frivolity." God did marvellous things for them and almost immediately they forgot. Then disaster befell them, and they remembered and repented. But then it began all over again.

2. The Hebrews had a "tradition"—so have we! But on the whole they remembered only what they liked of it. Then God "hacked" at them by His Prophets. The Old Testament is right—psychologically, socially and historically when it says that God visits the sins of the forefathers upon the children even to the third and fourth generation. What we do, and even what we omit, *alters us*, and on what we are depends our influence; and on our influence depends our environment. No one lives to and for himself alone. I fling my stone into the water and the circles widen out for ever.

3. Men seem to learn but little. After a war, they do yet again what led up to that war. May we often look back upon the world's history and on ours. It will show that precisely in so far as men have disregarded God and the spirit, they have suffered: and that if the Church has suffered, that may well be because even within her "the charity of many hath waxed cold."

.   .   .   .   .

We have the expressions: "It made a very deep impression on me": "I wasn't impressed." The latter is our rather supercilious way of saying that on the whole we thought poorly, meanly, of whatever it was. But we seldom comment on that fluidity of spirit, invertebrateness of mind, which may be responsible for our not retaining impressions that we ought to have retained. A word, a sermon, a meditation which do make a "dint" in our consciousness may be able to make nothing permanent or operative. This is unfortunate: we do not assimilate such experiences and become nourished by means of them. The Israelites could not but have been "impressed" by the plagues of Egypt and their escape : but soon enough they were wishing to be back, and worse, were worshipping the golden calf. And again, we may be unable even at the outset to "take" an impression. We see no distance into a thing. Life runs by as a mere series of happenings. Finally, we may be impressed by disasters foreseen or feared, so as to be obsessed by them, but uselessly : fear of War can reduce people to a state of nerves, but it is just those very people who seem least willing to undertake any serious persevering work. Probably it is because they have never attempted to do anything continuous and also unselfish, that when the need arises, they are quite helpless. The history of Israel may help us to pray for developments in character about which we might otherwise have never thought. Deep understanding : lasting convictions : loyalty to ideal : unconquerable resolve.

O THANK THE LORD!

Benedic, anima mea, Domino ; et omnia quae intra me sunt, nomini sancto eius. Bless the Lord, O my soul ; yea, all that is within me, bless His holy Name !— Psalm cii. 1. Sat., Compline, 2, 3.

1. The Psalm is a meditation in itself, and its own "colloquy." Bless, thank, the Lord! *All* that is within me. . . . "But there is evil within me ! How can *it* praise Him?" Somehow, it can! We, who want to be "good," may see, with surprise perhaps, that God does not mean to make us so all of a sudden. The blind man began by seeing men, but vaguely—like trees, only walking. He took time to be cured. Meanwhile, though sin does not praise God, sins can provide us with material for God's ultimate praise.

2. God shows Himself merciful to our iniquities—all

of them. That is the "negative" beginning. He draws
us out of our pit. Then He proceeds to crown us with
pity and "tender mercies." He full-fills all our desire
—even our half-hearted desire to be "better." This is
the Lord's "way." God gave light to Moses and the
People—yet they slipped—they hankered after sin—they
actually sinned. But God is a "long-suffering" God.
He can be described as waiting, as hoping. Endlessly
patient. Even if He is angry—that will not last for ever
unless we force it to. Hardly worth while cataloguing
our sins and assessing them! God does not act "in
proportion to them." There is no "keeping accounts"
with Him; for, though He is strictly just, He is so,
"according to His goodness"—not as a human judge is.
In Him, mercy and justice are mysteriously one.

3. High as the heavens arch over the earth, so high, so
firm, does He establish the sheltering vault of His mercy
over us. Far as sunrise is from sunset, so far does He
cast our sins from us. As a father pities his children, so
God pities us—a Father knows his own son! Yes—
He knows whereof we are made ; He remembers that we
are but dust; a withering grass; a fast-fading flower.
Life sojourns for a space within us, but cannot hold out :
it passes, and forgets where once it was. Not so the Lord!
He lasts ; His Mercy endures. He has promised. Even
if we forget Him, He desires but to re-establish us : So,
bless the Lord, all you Universe! you Angels, powerful
Spirits, whose power is none the less best shown in your
faithful service! Yes, bless the Lord, my Soul! Bless
Him for what you are ; but range throughout creation,
and wherever you find yourself, collect what is around
you, and *make* it praise the Lord!

O TRUST IN GOD!

Qui habitat in adiutorio Altissimi. . . . He that dwelleth in the shelter of the Most High. Psalm xc. 1. Sunday, Compline, 2.

1. So simple, yet so sublime is this Psalm, that it may be best to read and re-read it without singling out special verses. The Hebrews loved to picture God as sheltering His People beneath His wings (Exod. xix. 4; Deut. xxxii. 11; Ps. xxxv. 8; even Our Lord uses the expression, Matt. xxiii. 37). Night, for a primitive people, had special terrors: the " arrows " of noon were perilous: pestilence stole forth in the mist and dark: deadly diabolic storms raged out at midday. But none of this nor any other evil should harm the trusting soul: why, God has given a special charge to the Angels themselves that they should support, uplift and carry him over the rough places of its pilgrimage.

2. The Latin has two striking expressions that we can adapt for our own consolation. *Negotium perambulans in tenebris*—the Thing that goes moving about in the dark —the undefinable, undecipherable, vaguely evil things that haunt us and are worse than any known dangers; few but have experienced these anxieties that they cannot tie down properly to any cause and are all the worse for that: and again, the *daemonium meridianum*—the noonday devil; the lowering of spiritual life that comes in lethargic hours: and if in England the noon is not violent or leaden and exhausting like the oriental one, any " hour " will serve to symbolise those moments in which we feel semi-stupefied; as if all spring, zest, vitality of belief, hope or zeal have left us. Nor need we fear to apply this to middle-life, when a change may come, and we " settle down " to routine if not apathy, and " fervour " seems

K

a thing proper to a youth that is lost. Our crass or insipid or " heavy " moods are worse than open temptation.

.   .   .   .   .

3. See how gloriously the Psalm ends with a change of speaker—*God* speaks. The Hebrew delighted in these dramatic changes: but here, how appropriate! It is as though God could not but answer the trustful cry of verses 2 and 9a. God indeed gives charge over us to His Angels: when the road grows too rough, they carry us. But more—He acts directly we call; He is not far off—He hears: all the time of our need, He is *with* us: He not only rescues us, but will " glorify " us; will grant us a happy immortality of Salvation. Thus the Christian will amplify the sense of the last verses. To " know God's Name " means much more than being aware of the only true religion: it means to know *Him*, and so, to serve Him—for Hebrew " knowledge " was meant to be forthwith to issue into action.

HOW CAN YOU BID ME FLEE?

In Domino confido : Quomodo dicitis animae meae—Transmigra in montem sicut passer? In the Lord have I taken refuge—so how say ye to my soul—" Fly off, like a bird, to the mountain?"—Psalm x. 1. Sunday; Matins, Noct. iii. 3.

1. The little bird flies off to the mountains—to thickets and crannies in the rocks: who could ever find it there? And indeed the Israelites more than once during their harassed history had to take refuge in the caves; and Our Lord represents men, at the Last Day, crying out to the mountains to hide them and to the rocks to cover them.

2. But David says that it is with the Lord that he has taken refuge: hence he lives serene. This sense of trust

in God, repose in God—in His arms, under His wings—is constantly expressing itself in the Psalms. If I attend to it, after a while I shall not need to reflect separately on the texts which contain it; they will give forth their serenity like a fragrance and this will have a direct effect upon my soul.

3. Verse 5 is: "His eyelids question the sons of men (*i.e.* men)." The Hebrew says: "His are the eyes that see—His eyelids try mankind." The eyelids contract, to focus the gaze. The scrutiny of God must not alarm me. He reaches to the very truth of things and need not, like a human judge, sift evidence, or listen to partisan speeches or himself, possibly, be confused and mistaken. I would *prefer* that God should see me thoroughly, my sins included. Even among our fellow-men there are those who seem to look deep into you, and read the "back of your mind." I may fear, or resent that: but not the gaze of God.

THE LORD SPEAKS PEACE

Audiam quid loquatur in me Dominus Deus, quoniam loquetur pacem in plebem suam. I will listen to what the Lord, even God, speaketh within me—for He shall speak peace unto His people.—Psalm lxxxiv. 9; Fri., Lauds, 3.

1. A Psalm of deep gratitude. God rescues the People: God speaks to, and within, each soul (so the Latin). We pray—we speak to God so much—and we listen so little! What God has to say to us is infinitely more important than what we say to Him! "But I cannot *hear* what He says!" You will not, with your ear: you may not even in your thoughts. But God speaks in *His* way, deeper still: His Word is "creative." It makes a change in what it reaches: later on, you may indeed observe that God *has* spoken. "Speak, Lord, for Thy servant is listening!" (1 Kings iii. 10).

2. Sometimes we feel that we are such poor creatures that even if God does not cast us completely off, He cannot have anything special to say to us. And yet, on the one hand, we do not want Him to leave us quite un-spoken-to, nor yet, on the other, do we want Him to " condone " our sins and pretend that they were or are not. The Psalm joyously says that *in Him* " mercy and truth " have *met*; they have encountered one another and are in perfect harmony : yes, Justice and Peace have kissed one another : God is Just, and yet there is peace between Him and us. The mystery can be solved only by reflecting on Our Lord, who " broke down the dividing wall," and " made the twain to be one " (Eph. xi. 14).

3. Forthwith, the whole earth, and each soul, responds to, corresponds with, Heaven. Truth, loyalty, rightness with God, rise up like a golden harvest from the earth : Justice looks down from heaven and does not repudiate earth's produce—yes, the Lord grants His good grace, and our earth gives, in return, fruits for ever well-pleasing to the Lord.

LED TO THE GOODLY LAND

Spiritus tuus bonus deducet me in terram rectam. Thy good Spirit shall lead me into a right land.—Psalm cxlii, 10. *Fri. Lauds,* 3.

1. Compare Psalm lxii. In both, the soul gasps to God, faint for lack of water in its desert land. Here it goes deeper still, into the dust of " Sheol " where only the Dead dwell. " My enemy has put me to dwell in dark places, like men dead very long ago. . . . Turn not Thy Face from me, lest I become no better than them that go down to the Pit."

2. But God, who in-breathed life into Adam so that he " became a living soul " (Gen. ii. 7), and even to the Dead Bones (Ezek. xxxvii) gave new life, sending His

Winds from the four corners of creation, can re-vivify my soul even when it feels itself at the last gasp. In ancient symbolism, the Holy Spirit is also called *Digitus Paternae Dexterae*—the Finger, the Touch of our Father's Hand: and again in Psalm lxii. 9 we read that His right hand hath " lifted me up."

3. But the " parched wilderness " recalls that other symbol for the Holy Spirit, used by our Lord Himself: the Living Water (" this spake He of the Spirit that He should give them "; John. vii. 38). Our Lord *wants* us to be refreshed among so much monotony, barrenness, dull dustiness of life. In the Apocalypse (xxii. 1) St. John sees the Holy Spirit as a river of Life, cascading down from the Throne of God and the Lamb, and by its cool nurture causing the Trees of Life to spring up all around it, " whose leaves were for the healing of the nations." *Riga quod est aridum : in aestu temperies.* Cool in the scorching heat : moisture for parched-up soil.

THE SPACIOUS LAND

Exaudivit me in latitudine Deus. God hath widely listened to me.—Psalm cxvii. 5. Sunday ; Prime, 1 (usually).

1. An exultant Psalm, very suited to the Catholic idea of Sunday, which is meant to be a day of freedom, of rest, of joy and of unselfish gladness because of the Resurrection. (*Is* that our feeling about Sunday when it comes round ? It is not meant to be a day entirely occupied with religious services : but it ought to be suffused, as it were, with the sentiment of *Christian* joy : paschal joy. Sunday, spiritually speaking, is not over once we have fulfilled our " obligation " of going to Mass.) The quoted verse may indeed mean that God has rescued me and *put* me in a wide free space instead of a prison : but let us

often remember that God does things " largely," on a
grand scale, and let us try to attune our life to that.

2. The Psalm is " picturesque." My enemies roar up
round me like a cloud of oriental hornets : they flare
up with the ferocity of brambles blazing in a sun-
scorched land. I was hit so hard that I staggered and
was about to fall—but the Lord put His hand beneath
me. " I shall not die, but live, and will relate the Deeds
of God."

3. The pagan Greeks used to make much of the " reversal
of fortune " in their tragedies : but this meant as a rule
the fall from a height into an abyss. Here, the stone
which the builders rejected is not only used, but made
into the " chief corner-stone " on which all else depends.
Let us exult together with the Psalm. The upshot of our
life is Resurrection. Even if we live a life of Calvary *and*
Resurrection, it is a life most certainly of both, and
Resurrection carries the day.

.   .   .   .   .

Compare with the above—

*Eduxit me in latitudinem : salvum me fecit quoniam
oluit me*—He brought me forth into a large place : He
saved me because He was well pleased with me—(xvii. 20).
The Latin suggests that one has been cramped to suffoca-
tion in some spiritual prison, and that the Lord has led me
out into wide spaces, because He was determined not to
lose me. People laugh at the cliché about " wide open
spaces " ; but claustrophobia is a real thing, and you
can have it spiritually too, and feel as though all formulas
and practices had gone dead, and were worse than stone
walls, which, they tell you, need make no prison. Thereupon the Lord takes you out into the great world of His
Catholic Truths : " I opened my mouth and I drew deep
breaths! " Lord, when I begin to struggle and gasp
and am all mentally tied up, do not forget that You have

decided on me. It is a settled thing with You. You are not going to allow me to die on your hands, so to speak! Probably the words mean : " because He took pleasure in me." Well, one may feel that one doesn't see how He can possibly do *that*. At such moments, when the consciousness that God loves me has gone numb, I will at least remember that He has made up His mind about me, and does not at all intend that I should be suffocated.

THE FRUITS OF THE LAND

Terra dedit fructum suum. The earth hath yielded her increase.—Psalm lxvi. 7. Tues., Lauds, 3.

1. The Psalm is a thanksgiving for a rich harvest—so precious to Palestinians. But it looks much further than the year's field-produce. When St. Aloysius discovered himself to have done wrong, he said in simplicity : " Behold, O Lord, the fruits of my garden." He was sorry, but not surprised, and certainly not " scrupulous." Left to ourselves, our life *would* produce but a very feeble crop of virtuous acts ; indeed, how can we tell if it would produce any ? For God never leaves anyone to himself ; the Protestant, the Pagan, may visibly be producing very noble, unselfish acts : but God is helping them! At anyrate, we know that apart from God we can do *nothing*. " Nihil est in homine—nihil est innoxium ! " That does not mean that human nature is so essentially corrupted by Original Sin that it *cannot* ever do anything good—that it is intrinsically vile throughout : but, that it will do little enough that is even " naturally " good, and *can* do nothing that is supernaturally so.

2. But the supreme Fruit of the Land was to be the Messias. This notion of the destined Stem, or Shoot, rising from deep-buried roots, became more and more definitely " Messianic." In Isaias iv. 2, it is used vaguely

for the saving work, produce, of The Lord (see too Isa. lxi. 11) : but in Jeremias xxiii. 5, xxxiii. 15, it refers definitely to the Messianic King ; and in Zacharias (ii. 8 ; vi. 12) the word has become one of His *titles*. The work of a priest, and in his measure of every Christian, is to implant, and to nurture, *Christ* in human hearts. " Conversion " to the Church is not changing from a small sect to a larger one : a mere exchange of allegiance. We have to be satisfied with nothing less than the development of Christ in our own hearts ; the extension of His influence through us, as of a growing, fructifying tree ; and producing the same all around us.

.　　　.　　　.　　　.　　　.

The lovely Psalm is yet more consoling because of the clearness with which it announces the salvation of the Gentiles. " That we may know Thy Way upon earth —Thy saving help among all people : Let the peoples praise Thee, O Lord! yea, let all the peoples praise Thee! . . . It is Thou that judgest the peoples in equity ; and guidest the Peoples on the earth. . . . Let all the ends of the earth fear Him! "

This almost forces us to enlarge our minds till they become truly Catholic and take in all the world. But with this enlargement of our minds must go also a practical will in regard of Catholic Missions, about which we are still very apathetic.

SAFE THROUGH THE FIELDS OF DEATH

Et si ambulavero in medio umbrae mortis, non timebo mala, quoniam tu mecum es, Yea, though I walk through the midst of the shadow of death, I will fear no ill, for Thou art with me.—Psalm xxiii. 4. Thurs., Prime, 1.

1. The Psalm must be dear to us also for Our Lord's sake, who will scarcely have failed to have it in mind when speaking of the Good Shepherd who was Himself (Lk. xv. 4–7 ; John x). Throughout Hebrew history, God is seen as shepherding His people. The rod and staff (4b) were more for keeping off thieves or wild beasts, than for rescuing the sheep : but under Christian influence the " crook " has become definitely the bishop's pastoral crosier. Even the loveliest Old Testament symbols become lovelier still under the Christian light. The " waters of refreshment " were the rare refreshing springs of Palestine, making things green around them—in the Commendation of the Soul, we ask that the dying man may be admitted to the " lawns of Thy Paradise for ever green." We can repose our thoughts in this serene idyllic spiritual landscape.

2. " He hath brought back my soul "—He hath brought *me* back, if I strayed : " Like any sheep that is lost, so have I strayed—Seek Thy servant ! " (Ps. cxviii. 176 : p. 151). He gently leads me back into the right paths ; and whether it be just the day that is ending in deep darkness, or my very life that disappears into bodily death, still is He with me, giving me rest and security—I fear no ill !

3. The second half of the Psalm uses the image of a banquet. " My Cup is Overflow," says the concrete Hebrew—My cup, that is ever full, how splendid it is ! " Accipiens et hunc praeclarum calicem." " Taking, too, this glorious chalice into His hands," says the Consecration Narrative at Mass. Towards Mass, then, let us look during these verses which may appeal to us less than the preceding ones. Our only adequate Feast is Communion.

THE TRUSTFUL SOUL

*Sicut oculi servorum in manibus dominorum suorum
. . . ita oculi nostri ad Dominum, donec misereatur
nostri. As the eyes of a slave are upon the hands of
his master . . . so are our eyes upon the Lord, our
God, until He have mercy upon us.—Psalm cxxii. 2, 3.
Tues., Vesp., 1.*

1. A Captivity Psalm ? "Too much glutted are we
with contempt ; too sated is our soul with the scorn of
them that are at ease—the disdain of the supercilious!"
But the Israelites felt that it was always God who put them
where they were. They could hardly bear their subjection
any more. Their eyes were fixed on their Lord's hand,
to catch the first glimpse of His no more thrusting them
down and away. May no living man have to feel like that
towards any human master! Great is our responsibility
towards servant or employee.

2. But there is a happier way of watching one's master
—almost a dog's way. He adores his master : he runs on
a little way—looks back for the slightest sign—wags his
tail even when asleep at the least word addressed to *him*,
though inattentive to the loudest talk in which his master's
voice may intervene but not for *him*. A dog may also
" pine " when his master dies—a master, too, who has
always *been* a master, and has never accepted " naughtiness "
from his dogs. So be my soul unto Thee!

3. God is a Master, but no tyrant, slave-driver, critic
waiting to pounce. Neither absentee, nor " interfering."
But a *dear* Master, for chances of doing whose will I shall
be always looking out—for whose signified approval I
shall hardly openly look—but how glad I shall be when
I get even a side-glance from Him implying that He is
pleased!

THE CHILDLIKE SOUL

Domine, non est exaltatum cor meum . . . neque ambulavi in magnis neque in mirabilibus super me. O Lord, my heart is not puffed up . . . I walk not among great things, not in things too marvellous for me!—Psalm cxxx. 2. Wed., Vesp., 4.

1. The Psalm should probably be translated thus—

> Indeed do I humble my mind
>   And exalt not my soul.
> Even as a weaned child is upon its mother's breast,
>   So rests my soul upon me.
> Let Israel hope in the Lord,
>   Henceforward and for ever.

2. The child is weaned from its mother, and suffers. Yet none the less does it know and love and trust its mother, leans back upon her breast, feels her arms clasping it to her—and the peace is more than the pain.

3. Once maybe the intelligence clamoured to understand all mysteries: the will was urgent to attempt and carry through many achievements. But I shall hardly begin to understand any of life's deepest things: never will hopes be caught up with: so small a fraction of what was to be done—what needed to be done—will be fulfilled. No matter. Cannot my tiny soul trust God? Cannot my feeble, fleeting, foolish soul rest back upon God, the Strong, the Lasting, the Wise, and above all, the Loving? Unfathomable peace is his who can thus turn back to His God and abdicate all save *His* will.

SLEEP IN PEACE

Ego dormivi . . . et resurrexi, quia Dominus suscepit me. I went to sleep . . . and arose again, for the Lord accepted me.—Psalm iii. 3. Sunday, Matins, Noct., i. 3. In pace in idipsum dormiam et requiescam, quoniam tu, Domine, singulariter in spe constituisti me. In peace will I forthwith lay me down and take my rest, for Thou, Lord, as none other, hast established me in trust.—Psalm iv. 9. Sunday, Compline, 1.

1. These two Psalms (clearly connected) may have been sung before and after battle. In the former, David laments that his foes are many : they say that God is powerless. But nothing will disturb his trust : already he can lie down and sleep, so sure is he of God's assistance. In the latter, he exults : he has conquered ; God has put " joy in his heart, more than was theirs when their corn and wine and oil abounded." And again he can lie down in peace and rest.

2. If David could thus sleep in peace before his fight, it did not mean he had not got *to* fight, was not in real danger, or relaxed his vigilance afterwards. Rarely does one battle win a war. One decision *may* alter the course of a whole life : one heroic choice make the difference between eternal gain and loss. But most men have to fight, and to go on doing so, and not to be astonished that they, Christians, have so hard a time.

3. But, God helping us, there is an interior calm that can be preserved throughout. " I will never leave thee nor forsake thee " (Hebrews xiii. 5). " Himself hath care for you " (1 Peter v. 7). This " sleep " is neither indolence nor presumption ; still less, that lethargy which besets those who for long have not *tried* to do

something for God. They are too numbed by prolonged inactivity to begin to try.

REST FOR MY BODY

Insuper et caro mea requiescet in spe. Yes, and my very flesh can rest in hope.—Psalm xv. 9. *Tues., Compline, 3.*

1. This Psalm is most often used by priests or by Church students because of its verses 6 and 10. But we are thinking of it here from the point of view of serenity due to trust in God. God does not *need* any of my good things ; yet how generous He is to me—hence I keep God always before my eyes, and God always remains close to me. Hence joy, confidence, and perfect peace.

2. Hence, while verse 10 is rightly applied (Acts ii ; xiii) to Our Lord and His resurrection, and again, to the immortal soul, we use it here to reflect that however deep we may be sunk in sorrow, God will not *leave* us there ; and so bright will be God's sunshine that it will seem impossible that the night ever was so black.

3. But we have to remember that our own daily " resurrection " depends wholly on two things—God's free grace, and our free co-operation. We are often told to work as if everything depended on us ; and to pray, as if everything depended on God. It certainly is God who takes the initiative in all good things—in making us want to pray, for example ; and even more, in making us pray when we do *not* want to. To be helped to will to pray, when we do not want to pray, is a very great grace. But in the midst of this double activity, work and prayer, we have to keep our trust fully upon God, so that our mind can " rest in peace," and even our body experience that rest which it never will so long as anxiety or " nerves " are harassing it.

I SLEEP, BUT MY HEART WAKES

Qui statis in domo Domini . . . in noctibus. Ye that stand in the House of the Lord in the night-watches.—Psalm cxxxiii. 2, 3. Sunday, Compline, 3.

1. This little Psalm is addressed to those who kept the night-watches in the Temple, and exhorts them to fervour in prayer. We do not as a rule rise during the night, or watch late, for the sake of Prayer ; still, it is possible to habituate our mind to turn to God if we do wake, and we may be able rapidly to praise Him ; or to pray for those who are awake in pain, or in sin, and so, to sleep again.

2. Priests may regret that they cannot as a rule, or usually, say Compline the last thing at night : but it is certainly possible to grow very familiar with the prayer : " Visit we beseech Thee, O Lord, this house ; and drive far from it all snares of the enemy ; may Thy holy Angels dwell therein, to keep us in peace, and be Thy blessing on us evermore, Through Christ our Lord." This is a very good prayer to say wherever we are, and at any time of day ; it may cause our coming into a house, or a railway-carriage, or a lecture hall, or any other place, bringing many blessings with us.

3. We shall, however, wish to make our night-prayers as well as possible which certainly implies peacefulness and trust. Catholics were often exhorted to end the day by reflecting on death, their coffin, and the grave. Yes, if the thought of death has become pacifying and restful : not if it causes us to end the day in anxiety and possibly wakefulness. When the New Testament uses the word " sleep " in connection with death, it does so tenderly and lovingly ; perhaps it is death that should be thought of in terms of sleep, rather than sleep in terms of death.

IV

REBELLION AGAINST GOD

Personal Sin

THE opposite to having " awe " for God, to reverence and service of God : to giving Praise to God and showing gratitude to Him, is Sin : nor only the definite act of grave sin, but also habitual disregard of God ; casualness in regard of Him and of what we know of Him : and there is what can be called an inclination to sin—if not a definitely sinful mood, at least an innermost seemingly ineradicable tendency to worship idols or simply to God-less-ness.

The Psalmist is conscious of every shade of meaning that can be attached to this word " sin." So, too, in Mass we present the Bread at the Offertory to God, asking Him to accept it on behalf of our innumerable " sins, offences and negligences." Sins and omissions are easily understood : but how vast a field is covered by " offences "—wilfully imperfect, jarring, un-Christianised acts and tendencies!

But " no man liveth to himself." The Hebrew Scriptures are sincerely concerned about what we now call " social sin," especially when it was committed by men whose whole reason for existing in their office meant that they should not only act justly but administer justice. Usury, but also the taking of bribes by judges, is a recurrent theme in psalm and prophecy, together with the " grinding of the faces of the poor."

But the Israelite saw still further, and understood attacks on the Nation as attacks on God himself, and that practically every nation of whom he was aware sooner or later and even simultaneously attacked his People and Jerusalem in particular. Both in peace-time and in war-time it was, moreover, the heathen who seemed to prosper, which was a terrible temptation to the " righteous " to cross over to the successful side.

Hence some of the Psalms are steeped in profound melancholy, not only because of the Psalmist's sense of personal sin or disaster, but because he seemed to see that it was useless to serve God : God broke His promises ; His hand grew weak ; He sold His People for a song. But melancholy never cured anything : it leads to distrust in God, His reality, His goodness, or His power. The Psalms then very often contain this sequence—an expression of despondency verging on despair : a marvellous recovery and proclamation of God's rescue and of absolute trust in Him justified by experience : and, a determination not to keep any of this private, but to announce it " in the great assembly," yes, so that future generations, too, might know of it.

It is impossible, as a rule, to " isolate " Psalms or even verses which deal exclusively with the personal *or* the social aspect of sin or those miseries which, the Psalmist felt, must in the long run be due to sin, because, as we said, the Hebrew felt himself to be part and parcel of the People— nothing was purely " individual " for him. Hence our arrangement of the meditations is, in a sense, arbitrary. Still, we repeat that these pages are not a commentary on the Psalms, but contain meditations, or thoughts, which can rightly arise out of verses *in* the Psalms. It remains that while every constituent element of true repentance is emphasised by the Psalmist—confession, contrition, firm resolution—he never fails to recall that he must try to spread what is good over as wide an area as possible and not merely avoid what is wrong : even that most " personal " of Psalms, the *Miserere*, insists that I, I the penitent, so terribly needing a new-created heart, " will *teach* Thy ways unto the wicked, that the sinner may be converted unto Thee."

SIN AND CONVERSION

*Beati quorum sunt remissae iniquitates, et quorum tecta
sunt peccata. Happy the man whose transgressions are
forgiven, whose sins are covered up !—Psalm xxxi. 1.
Mon., None, 1.*

1. The history of a soul " coming round " to repentance.
The Psalmist (as so often) begins with a general declaration.
Happy the man whose sins have been forgiven ! Then he
recalls the time when he would not confess : however much
he complained and " roared " all day long, that would
be but silence—not prayer—in regard of *God !* So his
very bones—certainly his soul—grew old, lost all freshness,
shrivelled up. At last (verse 5) " I began to make my
sin known to Thee, nor any more hid my sin. I said : ' I
will confess,' and Thou didst forgive me my impious trans-
gression." At once he is forgiven. St. Augustine says: "The
voice is not yet so much as upon the lips, when—the wound
is healed ! " The change of heart can occur in a flash ; " in
tempore opportuno"—at the right moment, the apt moment
when God touches the soul just so as to win His response
without forcing its will. Then the Psalmist gives thanks.

2. Then God speaks : " Now I will give you understanding, and instruct you how to walk. I will keep My
eye upon you. And don't become like horse or mule which
have no intelligence ! You have to muzzle their jaws with
bridle and bit—else they would never so much as approach
you ! " Therefore attend, dear Soul, to My Law and My
Holy Spirit !—And the Psalm ends with a free acknowledg-
ment of the discomforts of the sinner, and the mercy that
envelops him who puts his trust in God.

3. Here, surely, are contrition, confession, and a firm
resolve for the future·—which cannot but be happier than
the past!

AM I INNOCENT ?

*Si est iniquitas in manibus meis . . . decidam merito.
If there be sin on my hands . . . I shall deservedly fall
down. Psalm vii.* 4, 5 *; cf.* 9. *Mon., Compline,* 2, 3.

1. The Psalmist often disconcerts us by appealing so
strongly to his innocence, and almost challenging God
to reward him " according to it," and to punish him if he
has sinned—so sure is he that he has not. Yet we know
that David did sin ; and that we do too ; nor would we offer
our virtue to God as an argument for His being gracious
to us. Yet we do—*divina institutione formati*—dare to
say : " Forgive us our trespasses *as we* forgive them that
trespass against us."

2. Still, David did know that he worshipped God :
that others did not : that he was the Anointed of God,
and the People, the Chosen People. His personal life,
like any man's, was a mixture. He sinned, but repented
and began again and did not abdicate from his vocation.
When we observe people to be " mixed " in character or
behaviour, it is good to concentrate on the best in them
and try to develop that : God wishes it to triumph and we
thus co-operate with Him. We can also gratefully recognise
that there is *some* good in ourselves. God puts it there :
let us ask Him to make it better still. Anyhow, encourage-
ment of what is good produces better results, as a rule,
than criticism of what is bad.

3. But the Christian can do better still. Incorporate
with Christ, he can and does appropriate His Person and
His Holiness ; and he can offer these to God as an irresistible
plea, and so indeed he does at every Mass. He can therefore
ask God to see His Son, when He looks at *him.*[1]

[1] Verse 8. The Lord is asked to sit publicly as Judge ; " Return (to Thy
Throne) on high, above the assembly"--15. (The sinner) is pregnant with injustice:
he conceived disaster (for others), and brought forth sin.

THE SHEEP THAT WAS LOST, BUT FOUND

Erravi sicut ovis quae periit : quaere servum tuum !
I have strayed like a sheep that is lost : seek Thy servant !
—Psalm cxviii. 176. *Sun., None,* 3.

1. Picture the sheep caught in brambles, or fallen over a precipice. It *cannot* free itself. Someone must seek it. God does so. He always takes the initiative. If I pray, like the sheep bleating, God has already been working at my soul. St. Augustine puts this the other way round— Thou wouldst not seek Me, hadst thou not already found Me! That is, deep down, the soul was already attending to God's touch, to His call.

2. "We love Him because He first loved us" (1 John iv. 10). We are constantly told to "love God": sometimes that seems difficult if not unreal. How much easier it becomes if we remember that *He* loves *us*. What a change in our feelings, if we discover that someone we did not like, has said something kindly about us behind our backs. Our Lord, dare we say, *does* kind things "behind our backs." He is always seeking for us "until He finds us" (John v. 14). He is willing Himself to be torn by the brambles and risk life and limb over the precipice, if but He finds and saves us.

3. Help your devotion to the Sacred Heart by remembering *that*—that God and Our Lord are always loving us. Amazing that They should love such colourless, irresponsive un-loving people as we. Yet They do. "Who shall separate us from the love of Christ ?" Read 1 Corinthians xiii, about Charity, and see how all that St. Paul says about it is more than verified in the person and love of Our Lord!

THE DEATHLY SLEEP

Illumina oculos meos ne umquam obdormiam in morte.
Give light to my eyes, lest ever I go to sleep in death.
—Psalm xii. 4. Tues., Compline, 2.

1. In this Psalm, the Psalmist is almost desperate: God goes on and on "hiding His face" from him; "turning the light of His countenance away" from him. No divine light, or favour, shines upon his eyes, and his very eyes have grown dim and lustreless. Let not this go on *any* longer—"Lest mine enemy ever say: I have triumphed over him."

2. This can well be applied to any long-enduring temptation, or trial: we feel that we never shall conquer "the sin that doth so easily beset us" (Heb. xxi. 1); that the future is as black as the present, and that our faith and trust are going to give out.

3. But there is a much deeper "sleep" than this—which is theirs whose conscience has become what St. Paul calls "cauterised"; who have become insensible to the difference between right and wrong—or perhaps have ceased to "mind"—let alone to "try"—in regard of some particular sin. This is perhaps chiefly brought about by un-resisted habits of sensuality; or again, by habitual use of dishonest ways of making money. At first they say: "How can I help it?" Then they take it for granted that they cannot. Then it ceases to occur to them that "wrong" enters into the matter. Their conscience is silenced. Give even the most painful light to my eyes, lest *that* happens to me!

Nequando . . . assimilabor descendentibus in lacum.
Lest ever I be made like to them that go down into the grave.—Psalm xxvii. 1.

I am alive, but my life can shrink. I can sink from plane to plane of life until, so far as the higher planes are concerned, I am as good as dead. I can become sensual, having been spiritually perceptive : a man whose virtues have changed into their own parodies : I can try to find my satisfaction in a world of idols, where things are no more images of God : I can become practically a machine, having no choices in life. The veriest slave can preserve within him his spiritual independence : in proportion as I gravitate towards what is external, I lose that : I sink into a grave.

THE DEEPEST DEATH

Inter mortuos liber, sicut vulnerati dormientes in sepul-chris, quorum non es memor amplius. I am cast off among the dead, like slain men that sleep in their tombs, of whom Thou hast no more heed.—Psalm lxxxvii. 6. Sat., Compline, 1.

1. Undiluted melancholy. The Psalm does not—as is usual in despondent Psalms—end with the triumphant assertion of triumph, and the public recognition that God approves the Psalmist. He is already as good as dead : " My life draweth near to Sheol : I am reckoned as among those who go down into the Pit : I am like a man without any help—set loose, isolated—even among the dead . . ." What is the *good* of that, he asks ? what is the good—to *God ?* Thou wilt not, assuredly, work wonders among the Dead ? Shall physicians arouse them (so the Latin : Hebrew ; Shall the Ghosts rise up) that they may give thanks to Thee ? Shall anyone, in the Tomb, relate Thy mercy ? or, in the world of Destruction, Thy loyalty ? Shall Thy wonders be made known in the Dark ? and Thy justice, in the land of Forgetfulness ? "

2. We know much more about the next part of life, i.e. Purgatory, than the Hebrews did : in fact, of its purifying

element, they knew nothing. But it is possible to insist too one-sidedly on the pain of that Purification, and too little on its joy. *There*, no atom of suffering is wasted. Here, all of it may be. It may be embittering, hardening, stupefying. There it is sweetening, spiritualising, vivifying.

3. Is it then a " terrible " courage that we require, to pray : " Give me here my Purgatory " ? Can any prayer involve a more complete trust in God, or a more perfect throwing of oneself upon His mercy and gentleness ? After all, the more fully Christian a life is, the more joyous it is : so the more we are purified, though at painful cost, the gladder our hearts will be.

    .   .   .   .   .

Oblivioni datus sum tamquam mortuus a corde. I am given over to forgetfulness, as though dead from the heart up.—Psalm xxx. 13.

Presumably this means : " I am given over to forgetfulness from the memory (the " heart " was the seat of memory), like a dead man. But there is a meaning in the literal translation. The " heart " can become " dead," insensitive, irresponsive. What used to mean so much to me may cease to make any appeal at all. Soon enough it fades quite out of my memory. I may be astounded by reading spiritual notes I took years ago, and seeing how much this or that meant to me, which no more means anything. We have then to ask God for resurrection—renewal of life. " What value is there in my blood, should I go down to the grave—to oblivion ? " Oh God, what waste it would be, were I lost!

THE NEW-CREATED HEART

Cor mundum crea in me, Deus ; et spiritum rectum innova in visceribus meis : Create a clean heart in me, O God, and make a new right spirit within my breast. —Psalm li. 12. *Wed., Matins, Noct. iii,* 3.

1. We can pray this Psalm even with the mind of the Psalmist, in so far as it testifies at least to an unconscious need of super-natural grace. He doubtless did not allude directly to our doctrine of Original Sin : nor to that of man's absolute need of redemption and re-creation : but he does affirm that even though a man may have sinned constantly from birth onwards, God—but only God— can and will blot out his sins, not merely condone them or cover them up. When God " turns His face from " anything, it *ceases to be :* man's spirit is the in-breathing of God and he simply cannot give that to his own self.

2. Experience, too, shows us that we absolutely need such a gift. Even when we cease to commit sinful acts, we are too often conscious that our innermost self seems un-changed: we *would like* to commit sin: we stop ourselves from doing so—that is already an effect of Grace—but we need the very fountain of our appetites, instincts, tendencies, self-worship to be altered—a new self, in short : and who but God can provide that ? " *Create* a clean heart in me! "

3. But forthwith I shall want to contribute the good new thing that is mine—that is I! Save me, O God, from acts of spiritual blood-guilt—from that soul-slaying of which I shall be guilty if I do not, so far as I may, transmit Thy Grace! God, who has given me the broken heart; then, the mended heart ; then, the pure heart, gives me, too, a Spirit-indwelt heart, so that what is pure, purifies.

．　　．　　．　　．　　．　　．

In verse 10 he cries that the bones that were broken, shattered, shall rejoice. He means that the very structure of his life had been broken to pieces. We have the ex-pression : " I feel it in my bones," when we mean that we are sure of something, we don't know why, but we *are* sure, in our very innermost. In Psalm xxxiii. 21, he cries that the Lord guardeth all their bones—not one of them shall be broken. We have then the right to apply this to

the beliefs that are *structural* in our creed. We have God's
assurance that not one of these shall be proved false or
in any way unreliable. The pagan who tries to build his
life out of false dogmas—like necessary progress, goodness
without God, the self-sufficiency of this world—is certain
to find bone after bone broken. Less than 100 years ago,
all those ideas were held as ascertainedly true : yet the world
they built up has been smashed into splinters. Every
limited " cosmos "—worlds built out of money, pleasure,
convention—explode or are crushed, come down about
their inhabitants' ears or bruise them badly. But not one
bone of the Faith shall be injured. Thus I live strong and
undismayed. Dismay is for unbelievers only.

IN THE LONELY LAND

Deus, Deus meus, ad te de luce vigilo. God, my God,
towards Thee do I watch from break of day !—Psalm
lxii. 1. *Sunday, Lauds, 3.*

1. The Psalm indicates that its Psalmist was far from the
Temple and was longing to return to it. But we take it
simply as the expression of thoughts which, please God,
arise in us the moment we awake—especially if life is at
the time monotonous, disappointing, or positively difficult.
" My soul doth thirst for Thee—yea, my very flesh—ah!
in how many ways—in this lonely land, where no water
is nor way! " So the Latin. Even so he used to yearn
to " see " God in His Temple—but then he would have
before him God's Power, and Majesty, and also tender
Mercy—which was more to him than life—than any other
life ; than " lives," as the Hebrew says, as though however
many versions of " life " and experience the world might
give to him, they would never come up to what *God* gives. So
may we long for Mass or even a private visit to the church.

2. Verse 7 offers an easy interpretation to those who

hold that if we try, last thing at night, to remember what we propose to meditate on next day, we shall indeed be the better able to meditate : and that is true. Still, the verse means what is equally true, we trust—that when I wake, during the night or at the time for rising, God will come into my mind ; my heart will be richly consoled ; I shall at once praise Him with exultant lips! Many find the simple process of *waking* up—even if they *get* up—very hard. Their brain is clogged. But a good habit *can* be formed : the mind can be trained to go at once to God.

3. May it indeed be our experience that God's wings shelter us, and that we can retire under them and their warm fostering whenever anxiety distresses us : we cling to Him, and He embraces us. Nothing can injure us. Absorb the Psalm, rather than dissect it!

FROM UTTER DESOLATION TO UNIVERSAL TRIUMPH

Deus, Deus meus, quare me dereliquisti? . . . Non sprevit neque despexit deprecationem pauperis. . . . Apud te laus mea in ecclesia magna . . . annuntiabunt caeli iustitiam eius populo qui nascetur. My God, my God, why dost Thou forsake me? . . . He hath not scorned nor disdained the prayer of the poor! . . . In the great Assembly shall my prayer mount up to Thee. . . . The very heavens shall proclaim Thy righteousness to a people yet to be born.—Psalm xxi. Fri., Prime.

1. This is the greatest of the Psalms which prophesy the Passion : Our Lord used its first words upon the Cross. But we must not try to apply the words of each verse equally to the events of the Passion. Prophecy as a rule saw within some contemporary or imminent event greater and deeper things—usually disasters culminating in the triumph of God ; and so it is here. Thus it is the entire " flow " of the Psalm that we need to study.

2. It is, too, a perfect example of those Psalms which begin with a cry of bitter distress only to end with a triumphant affirmation of the goodness and justice and loyalty of God ; hence while the Psalmist begins by contemplating his own, and perhaps his people's woes, and feels, as so often, that God has totally abandoned him, in verse 25 he rises into a declaration that God has *not* deserted him and instantly he feels the need of announcing publicly that God has rescued him—telling *all* the People of God's goodness that they may share in it—the Poor shall feast and praise God and " their hearts shall live for ever and ever" (verse 27).

3. But his gaze goes further—God's triumph is to be co-extensive with the world—" All the families of the Gentiles, the pagans, shall come and worship Him " : and again, it must reach to the farthest future : " My descendants shall serve Him . . . a People yet to be born, a People fashioned by the Lord! " So the Psalm is one also of Resurrection, and of Christ's Life continued in the Church.

MY FRIENDS FAR OFF

Domine, ante te omne desiderium meum ; et gemitus meus a te non est absconditus. O Lord, all my desire is before Thee, and from Thee is my cry not hidden !—Psalm xxxvii. 10. Tues., Matins, Noct. iii. 1, 2.

1. The Psalm is so sad because the Psalmist feels himself absolutely alone—" even those who were closest—akin—to me took their stand a long way off." Compare Job and his counsellors. If the Psalm is due to sickness, recall that the Israelites tended to put sickness down directly to the act of God, an act inflicted as punishment for sin committed. Here he feels quite at a loss even what to say next : " I am like a deaf man—dumb—a man that hath no rejoinder in his mouth " (14, 15).

2. *Gemitibus inenarrabilibus* (Rom. viii. 26). Groans that have no words. Prayers that cannot be put into words. Maybe, the best prayer! Formulas seldom fully represent *me*, save those few transcendent ones which are, simply, the consecrated prayers of the Church, in which I can take refuge, meaning what the Church means, even though we cannot exhaust that meaning—but certainly it includes all that *I* mean! I may even risk listening to myself praying, and think : " That was a very fervent prayer! " In liturgical Prayers, the priest effaces his personality and leaves the words of the Prayers to express their meaning of themselves.

3. If I am " towards " God, I *am* a Prayer. I simply put myself before God, and maybe can do no more in word or even thought. But it is enough. The whole of me cries to Him. No words could correspond to that total self. *In Te proiectus sum :* I simply am cast on Him. And I leave Him to do what He wills in my soul. But the moment I see I am beginning as it were to " moon," I will have recourse to my carefully recited formula!

.   .   .   .   .

Factus sum sicut homo non audiens—Et non habens in ore suo redargutiones.

He had said that his friends stood at a distance, while those who wished to ruin him were talkative enough, but with treacherous words. " But I, like a deaf man, gave no ear : I was like a dumb man, that openeth not his mouth." And then, " I made myself like a man that heard not— who had no rebuttals in his mouth." He could not answer back. He had no retorts, or, if he had, he had no heart to make them. Job (xxiii. 4) wished that he could find where God was—if only he could find Him, he would set forth his cause before Him, and *fill* his mouth with arguments! On the other hand, when the Servant of God was brought before His judge (Isa. liii. 7) he refused so much as to open His mouth. So Christ before Herod. Lamb to the slaughter.

Sometimes I feel : " What is the good of talking ? "
Voluble earnest agnostics, reformers, up-to-dates, deluge
me with talk and miss the whole point. I don't know where
to begin. Better just hold my tongue. This may be lazy ;
cynical, uncharitable. Catch hold of *one* word of theirs !
Try, with *one* word of yours. " It shall be given you in
that hour what you shall speak ! "

I feel : " On their grounds, they have won. I don't
know what to say. They make divorce seem so reasonable ;
contraception ; untrustworthiness of the Scriptures ; in-
efficiency of the Church. Even if I could administer a whole
series of lectures to them (which I can't, in a chance meeting),
what I'd say would sound so feeble. " You haven't answered
my question—Yes, or No ! " Better not say anything !

Go home without having answered. How they will
laugh. " I met him, and of course he had nothing to say,
when it came to the point. "

" Oh Lord, all my yearning is present to Thee ! my howling is not hidden from Thee ! " You do not mind if I am
undignified and just howl. I don't so much as explain
what it is all about. *He* can't see the point : *I* can't state
the point. He has scored all along the line, so far as everything save Truth goes. But how am I going to explain
that to him ? I can't. I have no rebuttals in my mouth.
Well, Lord—what I *wanted* is all of it before Thee. Thou
seest it ; not one inarticulate outcry is hidden from Thee ! "

*Obmutui et silui a bonis . . . et in meditatione mea
exardescet ignis. I kept silence and refrained even from
good works ; but my anguish was but renewed : my heart
burned hot within me ; and the more I brooded, up blazed
the fire !—Psalm xxxviii. 3, 4.*

Confronted, before God, by his enemies, the Psalmist
refuses to speak even in his own defence. But that simply
threw him back upon himself, and he became more and

more indignant. I have to judge when it is good to accept
a situation in silence : I may easily delude myself into
thinking I *ought* to " answer back." Yet there are such
things as spiritual sulks, or moroseness, or a cynical (and
lazy) notion that it is never any good saying anything.
But that shrivels me, and hardens me, and makes me in-
accessible. Even shyness may make me keep silence when
I ought to speak. If charity habitually rules in my heart,
I had better be simple and speak, trusting to God, what
comes into my head. He will put it there. " It shall be
given you in that hour what you shall speak." It is no good
being a frozen-up man. (See next Psalm, verses 10, 11.)

HAD IT BUT BEEN MY ENEMY . . .!

*Si inimicus meus maledixisset mihi, sustinuissem
utique. Had it but been mine enemy who cursed me, I
could indeed have borne it.—Psalm liv. 13. Wed., Terce,
2, 3.*

1. This is a passionate cry for sheer solitude—deliverance from enemies, not so much by their destruction, as
by self-isolation. Had I but wings, like a dove, I would
fly far away and find rest—far would I fly away and dwell
in the desert! (The dove was regarded as a timid bird,
constantly escaping from birds of prey and cowering into
the crannies of the rocks.) So too felt Jeremias, ix : " O
that I had even a traveller's hut in the wilderness—I would
forsake my people and go forth from them. "

2. Had then the Psalmist not a soul in whose company
he wished to be ? No, for it was, precisely, his dearest
friend who had done him the cruellest wrong. " Had it
been my open enemy who slandered me, I could indeed
have borne it—had it been he that hated me who spoke
arrogantly against me, doubtless I could have hidden. But
thou, man of one mind with me! my comrade, my friend

whom I *knew*—who didst share sweet food with me—with whom I walked one-heartedly in the very House of God! " So in Psalm xl. 10. " Ah, even my friend, my ' man of peace,' in whom I trusted, who ate my bread—it was *he* that hath fiercely raised the heel against me ! "

3. In Our Lord's mouth, this will have meant Judas. But I will apply it at once to myself—I, baptised ; I, confirmed : I, fed again and again upon food sweeter than any imagined by the Psalmist—*omne delectamentum*—all deliciousness *is* in the Blessed Sacrament, whether or no I am able to appreciate it : I, maybe ordained or in other ways specially called : I who *thought* I would be for ever loyal, and that my mind was that which also was in Christ Jesus, and my heart like unto His Heart! And after all this, maybe, a cooling off : secret hostility ; open treachery. God preserve us from that.

．　　　．　　　．　　　．　　　．

Vani filii hominum in stateris ; ut decipiant ipsi de vanitate in idipsum. Psalm lxi. 10. *Men are deceitful in the scales, so that in their emptiness they utterly deceive. (They are lighter than a breath : Hebrew.)*

The more I can trust my fellow-men the happier I shall be even if they fail me at times ; nor is it true that to trust just anyone will, as it were, *make* him honest. But sometimes it is better to take a man's word even if you feel fairly sure you are being tricked. There is always a *chance* that the man is honest or may change and act honestly. It is not idle self-delusion, to hope that there is but a minimum of lying in the world. God must be pleased that we *hope* truthfulness exists, because it is like Himself, the perfect Truth. And *He* will somehow create it.

．　　　．　　　．　　　．　　　．

The dove was not much esteemed by the Hebrews : it did not in this Psalm suggest, for example, sublime and silver soaring, but mere flight. In Isaias xxxviii. 14, the Latin says that "I meditated like a dove," but this apparently meant that I moaned like one. Now on the whole, moaning is not to be recommended, though both Vergil and Tennyson say that doves do it. But the French *roucouler* is a charming word, and far more picturesque than our monosyllable *coo*. It suggests a kind of contented gurgle—and really one could be spiritually worse off than sitting in a kind of dove-cote of a soul-house, peeping out occasionally from the sill of its door, seeing God's world, being pleased with it, grateful for it, and making one's queer Deo Gratias.

Now in Psalm xxxviii. 12 the Psalmist says that God has "made his life to melt like a spider." This certainly is odd ; and as a matter of fact the Hebrew says "moth." In Osee v. 12 the idea is put the other way round—it is God who acts the part of moth to Ephraim, and wastes him away as the insects do to the stored riches in the gospels ; and Job (xiii. 28) regards himself as "moth-eaten," though no doubt in viii. 14 he says that the trust of the godless man is a mere spider's house. Anyhow, here in the Latin we have "spider," and we ought to attach *some* imaginative meaning to it ; and it is quite legitimate even in "meditation" to see if such words cannot, they too, be of assistance to us—even of a rather quaint or unusual kind.

Well, a moth, if it flies into a candle-flame, crackles and shrivels. But when a spider is ill or frightened, it may not exactly "melt"—but it pulls all its legs in and shrinks into a little lump, even in the middle of his web or when dangling at the end of his long thread. And my soul can get cold and unhappy and scared and quite unable to do anything. It huddles into itself and retracts all its filaments. I am more likely to do something like that, than roar like a lion, which David quite often says he does.

And possibly I shall find, as I read, that my thoughts

make a web of very fragile connections ; in meditating on these Psalms I may think that my fancies are but precariously joined on to the real sense of any one verse : but they *are* " connected," anyhow for me, and I need not be afraid of them.

Almost anything is legitimate in hours of " meditation," provided, of course, I do not declare that my thoughts *are* the meaning of David's words. Let David's words suggest anything to you that they can. You are making *your* meditation, not his: he helps you, and will not at all mind if he causes you to think even what he did not. No artist should be huffed if a spectator sees more than *he* did in his work.

Besides, we may trust that the Holy Spirit, whom we constantly invoke when reading His book, the Bible, will *guide* your thoughts " into the paths of peace," and not allow them to take you into dangerous places.

NOT ONE COMPANION!

Sustinui qui simul contristaretur, et non fuit : et qui consolaretur, et non inveni. I waited for one who should share my sorrow, but there was none : for one who should comfort me, but I found none.—Psalm lxviii. 21. Thurs., Matins, Noct. iii.

1. This is the secondary Great Passion Psalm, and is often quoted in the New Testament as Messianic. But we are concentrating only on the idea of loneliness. " I was a stranger, and you took Me in," said Our Lord. The " stranger " had literally no one to whom he could turn and *claim* roof or food or friendship. When we reflect on the destitute, the sick, the prisoner and so forth, we may also remember how desperately lonely numbers of people are in the midst of our crowded civilisation, especially those who are becoming unattractive and can make no

return for kindness. Our duty of being kind is therefore doubled. But we have to seek for such people. The very fact of their loneliness makes them invisible.

2. Some people love to complain that they are " not understood." These are usually selfish. But people may really be living in an environment which does *not* " understand " them—there being no fault on either side. If then I can get into spiritual touch with such people, I should be grateful to God. Even if they feel no more than that they can freely express themselves to you, you do a great kindness by listening and not showing scorn or indifference towards them.

3. Our Lord experienced loneliness. " Could you not watch one hour with Me ? " We often ask Our Lord to be " with *us* " in our daily tasks : but *He* has a work to do in His world, and needs companions, and I am right in often asking Him to allow me, His servant, to be where my Master is : I shall hear Him call me " no more ' servant '," but " friend."

.   .   .   .   .   .

We recall that no one is obliged, or even able, because this Psalm, like e.g. xxi, is a " Passion " Psalm, to apply each verse equally to Our Lord or even try to. The characteristic of Hebrew Prophecy seems to have been that it kept its eye both on the nearer plane *and* on the farther, but not always simultaneously, nor equally. Thus the fierce recriminations of verses 23 to 29 cannot without violence to their meaning be put upon Our Lord's lips. On David's, they have this to be said for them—he definitely intended them to correspond to deliberate sin on his enemies' part. In 1 Kings xxvi. 19 . . . he makes his point of view very clear. If it is *God* who has roused Saul against him, then God must certainly be right, even though angry : may He receive a propitiatory offering ! But if Saul's hostility was wholly due to human agencies, then may those wicked men

M

be accursed, for they were aiming at nothing else save driving David away from worshipping *God*. "They drive me forth to-day so that I may have no part in the inheritance of The Lord, saying: 'Begone! worship other gods!'" It has been already pointed out (and see p. 165) that the Hebrew constantly saw the future *in* the present; so, when he *foresaw* with absolute certainty that God's enemies *would* be overthrown, he *demanded* that they *should* be, and his curses were no more, in a sense, than the anticipation of God's own verdict. St. Paul at any rate (Rom. xi. 9 sqq.) does not regard these curses as spoken by Our Lord, even in type, but by David. Again, here (6) and in Psalm xxi. 2 ("Far from my rescue is the catalogue of my sins"—the Latin is anyhow misleading: the Hebrew has "lamentation": i.e., I cry, but am not rescued: the Latin presumably means that a great gulf is fixed between his sins and God's succour), the Psalmist confesses to sin. It seems exorbitant to make this mean that Our Lord—whom the Psalmist is assumed to be impersonating—had made our sins His own. In a sense He did so: but we cannot extract that from the Psalm. Only if we insist that every verse of the Psalm is to be spoken as by Our Lord, are we driven to seek a way in which He can have called Himself a sinner.

    .   .   .   .   .

Lest verses 6 and 7 be so obscure as to cause us a distraction, their meaning may be as follows—(i) "Even until now, my prayer is (opposed to) their desires—Their judges are dashed against the rocks and swallowed up, and men shall hear of my words that they are powerful!" That is, "I will have nothing to do with sinners or their courtesies ('oil' poured over a guest's head): I will pray against them; their chief men shall be hurled down rocks and made an end of—so shall it be seen that my prayer wins its response!" And (ii): "Like clods scattered about over the earth—so are our bones strewn beside the pit of Sheol." This is not like the Hebrew; but it provides a sense, especially if we regard it as an exclamation on the dying lips of those who had been thrown down a precipice. Probably it is best to allow the mind to slide quickly over these verses, retaining merely the general idea that the Psalmist will have nothing to do with the wicked, prays against them, and obtains their elimination.

LONG-DRAWN ABANDONMENT

Singulariter sum ego donec transeam. I am all alone until I cross over.—Psalm cxl. 10. Fri., Vesp., 4.

The Hebrew means: " Let the impious all together fall into their own net: but *I* pass on " (safely). We cannot here take this into account.

1. The general sense of the Psalm certainly shows that the Psalmist is lonely: the world is hostile to him, and even to us it is often aloof and alien. There is, in our land, a very strange mixture of deep hostility to and distrust and of course ignorance of Catholics, combined with a curiosity about them, and a desire to know more of them, and even, an attraction towards them. Well, it is at times inevitable and even right that we should be " out of sympathy with our surroundings." The Christian can love the world in one sense, and in another he cannot without committing himself to its ideals. And certainly the pagan world will never love the true Christian. Very well. Accept that solitude; it never need be loneliness. In it, God will always be your companion, till you cross over from your exile into your true home.

2. Verse 2 must be dear to us because it is so often used in the Liturgy; and the Apocalypse, too, has the image of " incense " to represent prayer. It seems clear that the Psalmist, as we see in other Psalms, was being kept

far from the Temple and its worship. We cannot be content if we have no appetite for public, collective worship. Even at our private prayers let us unite ourselves with the immense volume of prayer which is ascending from all over the world towards God. Why, men understand so little of their own hearts that we may trust that many are praying who are not even aware of it: God is aware of and understands the strange mingled motives and methods that are ours. Many spices go to make up the scent of incense.

THE BITTER PAST

Quantas ostendisti mihi tribulationes multas et malas, et conversus vivificasti me! How many, how great, what bitter tribulations hast Thou imposed upon me! But then—Thou didst turn, and give me life anew!—Psalm lxxx. 20; Thurs., Compline 2: read, with this Psalm, Psalm lxix, ib., 1.

1. This and the previous Psalm, and others, have many verses in common: yet Psalm lxx has its true individuality. The Psalmist looks back on Israel's long history, and sees that God has not deserted him nor yet the People: he on his side has ever made God the theme of his song: let Him not abandon him now he has grown old!

2. He does not refuse to remember harsh experiences, all of which he takes directly as from God's hand. God, at any rate, has always brought him safe through them. We have courageously to admit that it is better for us to experience times of stress, humiliation and fear. Without these, we should be a very untempered steel! The man who has not *suffered* will not understand suffering in others—not even in Christ.

3. The Psalmist, as so often, declares that far from grumbling, he will give the maximum of " publicity " to the goodness of God, experienced by himself or observed

in history. Verses 15, 16, probably mean—" My mouth shall proclaim Thy righteousness—all the day long, Thy help. I cannot reckon up the list thereof—but I will come forth with the mighty works of God—Lord, I will announce Thy righteousness—yea, Thine only! " It is quite possible to pray, while reading history: to make acts of contrition, or praise: and also, it may be a false humility, never to let others know how God, in our life, has helped us.

THE HEALING PAIN

Priusquam humiliarer ego deliqui ; propterea eloquium tuum custodivi . . . bonum est quia humiliasti me, ut discam iustificationes tuas. Before I was humbled, I *did wrong : that is why I obey Thy decrees : It is a good thing that Thou didst humble me, that I might learn Thy righteous rulings.—Psalm cxviii. 67, 71. Sunday, Terce 3.*

1. We may hope that we are reasonably modest : maybe we begin by being diffident. When we meet others who are so, let us encourage them ; pick out the best in them, and praise and develop it. Even if we find one who is self-sufficient, it is probably better not to snub him, lest we embitter him, throw him back upon himself, and destroy the early shoots by frost-bite.

2. We may be called, by our position, to check others, to correct inventiveness by experience, ardour by prudence— even to snub impertinence. But the moment we see we are doing this out of pique, irritability, or mere dislike for being disturbed, our rebuke is sure to be badly administered. Often life itself will administer the check required : sometimes God will. The Saints went through " tunnels " of complete blackness—more than any of us are likely to be called to—but they emerged stronger than ever precisely

in proportion, as they had " humbled themselves beneath the mighty hand of God " (1 Peter v. 6).

3. But God so humbles us that He may be able to exalt us in the day when He visits us. His treatment is never sterilising. Even a field must lie fallow. When I want to be " up and doing," to see results, to chafe at " marking time "—then must I remember that God is training me : nor must I say : " It is not God : it is my timid or old-fashioned or unsympathetic superiors "—God is mightier than any superior or circumstances. " For them that love him, God makes all things to co-operate for good " (Rom. viii. 28). So, far from repining, we shall say : " We are glad for the days when Thou didst humble us— the years, in which we saw ill-fortune ! " (Psalm. lxxxix. 15).

HUMILIATED INTO WISDOM

Homo, cum in honore esset, non intellexit : comparatus est iumentis insipientibus et similis factus est eis. Man, when he is held in honour, does not understand (Hebrew ; does not endure) : he must be likened to the senseless beasts—yes, he is no better than they!—Psalm xlviii. 13, 21. Wed., Matins ; Noct. ii, 2, 3.

1. The first verses show us so often, that, for the Hebrew, the prosperity of the wicked was a continual problem. The Psalmist's solution is : Such prosperity does not last. Probably the sense of verses 8 and following is : No man—no man—can buy himself off! (That is, from Death.) No man can pay his own ransom unto God, not though he should toil for ever that he may live for ever. He will not even contemplate his own death, even when he sees that even the wise *do* die! The point is : (i) Death sweeps all men equally away : and (ii) What folly not to realise this!

2. Certainly it is almost impossible for anyone—certainly for a young man—to realise that one day *he* will die. Even

the old and the sickly often cling to life obstinately.   It is true that others " let go " of everything all in a moment ; know they are dying, and are hardly interested. It is improbable that we shall be able to pray, when we are dying, in any *exceptional* way. We shall do what we have been accustomed to, and probably more apathetically even than we used to. Hence let us often recommend " the hour of our death " to God ; and attend separately to those words in the Hail Mary. We shall need all the " outside help " that we can get.

3. The Psalmist probably does not refer to the kind of insensitivity that great riches often produce. Yet that point needs to be considered. A very rich man can get all he wants without effort, and so, does not care for it when got. Nor can he understand and sympathise with the poor and powerless. Nor can he, as a rule, extricate himself from the sort of life that convention dictates to him, nor does he question it. Riches *stupefy* their possessor.

GROWN OLD AMID ENMITY

Inveteravi inter omnes inimicos meos. I have grown old among all my foes.—Psalm vi. 8. Mon., Compline, 1.

1. The Psalm is one of profound melancholy, though as so often changing into final exultation—as if in the very midst of his prayer God made Himself present to the Psalmist's soul. But meanwhile, he has felt as good as dead—and among the dead who so much as remembers God ? In Sheol who will praise Him ? He has wept so much that his eyes are dull and dimmed like an old man's.

2. The pagan notion of old age combined a sort of respect for the aged (because helpless : the same, not innocence, was usually the reason for " respect " being had for childhood, or the blind), with a pity due to the " melancholy " attached to anything that was " dying out "—

that had nothing ahead of it. We cannot permit ourselves so to think. In any case, it is difficult for the young to believe they ever will get old. At 20, 30 seems already old. At 50, men do not permit themselves to think they are old. After that, time goes so very fast that a year slips by unnoticed : at 60, they find they still have characteristics they remember from their childhood. The extreme form of this is, that few, either young or old, can admit that they will ever die.

3. But die we do. And we have to envisage the fact without fear, or repining. The Hebrew hardly could do so. Our imagination defeats even our Christian selves. How can we imagine that when the body dies, *we* shall be far more alive than before ? May we so *believe*, and advance towards our bodily death humbly, hopefully, with determination, and even with exhilaration.

A BROKEN SPIRIT

Incurvaverunt animam mean. They beat my spirit down.
—Psalm lvi. 7. Wed., Sext, 2.

1. " They bend down my soul "—there is a mood different from sharp fear, despair, or even agony. It is almost worse. It is when I have come to feel *cowed :* I am beaten : I cannot stand up to any more : I wait dumbly without knowing whether things will grow better and not venturing to count on their doing so or even to expect they will. Prolonged unsuccess ; consistent snubs and unkindness, may risk bringing the soul to this pass.

2. A strange word is used about part of Our Lord's Agony in the Garden. He began to be " sick at heart," sickened, disgusted ; to be utterly dis-heartened. This was different from the fear and grief which also were His. None the less, He went forward to what was to be still worse, His Passion itself.

3. And the Psalmist himself exclaims : " My heart is fixed, O Lord ; my heart is fixed—set—steadfast : in spite of everything, nothing shall prevent my praising Thee! " And, as ever, he looks far further than his interior recovery : he foresees himself as praising God among the heathen—he sets no limit to the glory of God nor to his share in extending it. God, when all around me is so utterly unstable, yet so overwhelming—grant me this steadfastness!

. . . . . .

Whether or no he meant : " They have spread a snare for my feet, to trip me up and made me fall over it," the Latin is very exact—I get all bent-backed, doubled up, chin on my chest, " all in a heap," when I am conscious of how many chances of mistakes life supplies me with— because I am not conscious of any really malicious persons trying to upset and injure me. So I am not much moved by the Psalmist's frequent assertion (as in verse 7 part 2) that " they digged a pit for me—and fell into themselves! " I don't want anyone to fall into pits ; and if they did, I should want to pull them out at once. But duties themselves give you as many chances of going wrong as right, and you are always wishing that you hadn't behaved or spoken just as you did. Well, one has but a Mixed Chalice to offer. God trans-substantiates it.

PENANCE IN PAIN

Cum mihi molesti essent, induebar cilicio. As for me, when they harassed me, I put on sackcloth.—Psalm xxxiv. Tues., Matins, Noct. i.

1. This is a very bitter Psalm of protest against the Psalmist's enemies. The Latin here suggests that the more his enemies tormented him, the more did he do penance. Do I do that ? Or when things go badly, do I just try

to find compensations ?   But in the Hebrew, the Psalmist appears to be contrasting his behaviour towards his foes with theirs towards him. *They* paid me back evil for good —barrenness, bereavement, for my soul! But I, when I found them sick, put on sackcloth—I fasted—I showed sympathy as if it had been my brother, my own kin : like a man that grieved and was dismayed, so did I bow myself down (Latin) ; I bowed down mourning as one that mourneth his brother. . . . Again, I can ask myself if I ever do anything like that ?   Do I show any sympathy for those who show none with me ?

2. But what was extraordinary in a Hebrew—loving compassion for a persistent enemy—must become normal for us Christians. Not least in hours of crisis, when men get " worked up," and " hate " is deliberately inspired, do I lovingly pray for my enemies ?

3. If in normal times I say I *have* none, that no one does " trespass " against me, I had better go straight to the fountain-head of dogma, and recall that many undoubtedly are persecuting *Christ ;* I identify myself then with Him, and earnestly in His Name, in His Person, through His very lips, pray that His Father, mine, and theirs, will forgive them—whether or no they are aware of what they are doing!

BUT THE CHRISTIAN SHOULD BE RESCUED!

Me expectant iusti donec retribuas mihi. The righteous take heed of me, waiting for Thee to do me justice.—Psalm cxli. 8. Fri., Vesp., 5.

1. The Psalmist has painted a deplorable picture of his isolation. He looked for help—not a man came near him. Flight was denied to him ; not a soul tried to rescue him. All the more did he turn to God, arguing that it was *expected* of God that He should rescue him. God was

righteous : David was righteous. How then should He *not* rescue him and do him what after all was but justice ?

2. Our Lord's life and death has taught the Christian that visible justice is not always done in this life either to the individual or to the group, even when they seem to be innocent. We accept this : the whole of an evil past has poured into us, and because of our " social solidarity " not only with the whole contemporary world, but with the past—and all too truly with the future—justice *is* in reality being done. We remember, however, that by prayer we can obtain from God that mercy, out of proportion to all accurate justice, shall be done to us.

3. But it is certain that others " keep their eye " on Catholics. They expect something " different " from us, even if they know not what. Since we profess something indubitably special, they expect us to *be* something special. But within this general " something special," ought they not to recognise something " specially special "—the fact that we *are* getting a reward if we are faithful, however much we may be suffering—a certain serenity ; ability to retain our interior peace, a peace which shall even shine forth to a real degree, so that it is recognised even ex- teriorly, and even envied ? Is that peace " exulting," or at least shining, in my heart ?

. . . . . .

In verse 11, the Psalmist, you would say, had been falsely accused and tried—" Lying witnesses rise up, and ask me about what I know not—they requite me evil for good—barrenness (Hebrew : childlessness) for my soul ! " Or he may have been just slandered and more vaguely " tried " before the bar of public opinion. All sorts of accusations, slanders, can be set floating around, and a man can well be unable to prove a negative. People can make no end of accusations, suggestions, about my Faith, to which I know no answer : I cannot know everything : I can be quite sure that I am right—that my Faith is impregnable—and yet I can be made to look—and even feel—a fool for believing it, and be quite unable to show to unsympathetic listeners that the Faith is *not* folly. I may feel that I have " let the Faith down " in public : I may be not so much ignorant but slow—not a good debater— I think of the right retort afterwards. All this leaves me with a sort of sick and hopeless feeling, especially if in my heart I *do* want to uphold the Faith and defend the Church and strike a blow for Christ. I am " barren," useless. I neither derive nor contribute comfort. This test is a severe one and prayer is my only refuge—" What *I* cannot do, do *Thou!* "

FLESH DIES, TO FLOWER AGAIN

Refloruit caro mea, et ex voluntate mea confitebor illi. My flesh hath flowered anew, and with all my will do I give thanks to Him.—Psalm xxvii. 7. Mon., Terce, 3.

1. Take the Latin as it stands, for it is more vivid than the Hebrew. There is a myth that sexual and emotional experience causes the flesh to " blossom " and become its true self. In so far as that is true, it lasts but a little ; meanwhile, the soul is shrivelling, and this displays its counterpart even in the flesh and the features. It does so, that is, if the mind settles down into sensuality. If there be a strong counter-effort, the sterilisation of the personality does not take place, still less, become visible. Hence courage, not least for those who find temptation " too hard " for them.

2. Dreadful are the elderly years of those who have squandered what should have been alive and life-giving, in barren acts. What belonged to the body has been transferred to the mind and the desire, and empty yet

aching years are spent by those who long for what they can no more have.

3. But if the Christian realises from the outset that chastity is not a negative virtue—merely *not* doing things for which the instinct wishes—that Christ wishes that " they might have life and have it more abundantly " (John x. 10), then he will never find his life shrivelling and shrinking. And if, after a history of mistakes or wrong-doing, he somehow corresponds to God's unceasing vocation, he will find that his life " re-flowers " and has its second spring.

THOUGH I VANISH, GOD ENDURES

Dies mei sicut umbra declinaverunt. . . . Initio Tu, Domine, fundasti terram. . . . Ipsi peribunt, tu autem permanes. My days have fallen away like a shadow (Hebrew : Are stretched out like a shadow—in the evening, when it will soon be there no more.) . . . In the beginning, Thou, Lord, didst establish the earth and the heavens. They shall perish, but Thou endurest. Psalm ci. 12, 26, 27. Sat., Terce.

1. This Psalm contains the majestic words quoted in the Epistle to the Hebrews : " In the beginning, Lord, Thou didst establish the earth ; yea, the very heavens are the work of Thy hands. Yet *they* shall perish, but Thou endurest : they shall all wax old as doth a garment ; and as raiment shalt Thou change them, and changed they indeed shall be : but Thou art the Self-Same—*Thy* years shall not fail! " (Hebrews i. 12).

2. The Psalm consists of a double, then a triple contrast : the Psalmist feels how fleeting is his own life, but draws consolation from the permanence of God's Chosen People, which shall not perish, but shall see a New Sion built upon the ruins of the old one—and there is a prophecy in this that the Psalmist hardly guessed : the Church

is the New Sion. Then again he sees himself as but fleeting
and vanishing in comparison with the created universe ; but
then—how transitory is even that, compared with GOD!

3. It is good often to realise how rapid, impotent and
futile is the life of any one man—of myself—merely *as*
such. The older you become, the less you see yourself
to have done, or have mattered. But I never need be
thus " alone " : the Christian's life is " hid with Christ
in God " (Col. iii. 3) : our Lord can " eternalise " our
work and make it for ever effective—nay, co-redeeming.
We repose upon, are rooted in, eternity. Vastly do we
" matter." Nothing that is united with God can be futile.

.   .   .   .   .

The birds of 7, 8, cannot be identified. Pelicans are
not solitary nor do they live in deserts but by water : if
the second bird be indeed the owl, the Latin can mean
" the owl in *its* house," probably a ruin, like the " moping
owl " of Gray's Elegy in its ruined tower : as for *passer*,
it means any little bird. Still, we may naïvely liken our
soul to a sick little sparrow, deserted by its companions,
wizened and tiny : or in other moods, to the old owl,
huddling itself into itself, not really wise at all and easily
flurried by anything unaccustomed, like a sudden light.
As for the " pelican "—we had better just allow a picture
to form itself of some great gaunt bird—and indeed one
sees such birds in other continents—perched or stalking
all by itself in barren places, and we need make no attempt
to give it a name! Pictorial impressions, not scientific
data, are what the Psalms may be expected to provide ;
but it is a pity to allow even one verse to slip by ineffectively.

.   .   .   .   .

" *In imagine pertransit homo* " (*xxxviii.* 7).

One's friends die ; but, much worse, they don't, but
inevitably drift away. It is impossible to see them often

or even to write to them often or ever. A man, in a hospital, the war, on a boat, flits into your life and out of it ; you have really loved him and tried to serve him, and you know you won his affection and trust in return, and you want him to be happy, and for all you know he is, and that is good ; still, you would like to know about it and share in it, and the same if he is unhappy. Well, he doesn't exist *for me ;* I am not meant to hold anyone captive ; please God I did my job by him, and must hand him on and this is where prayer comes in so gloriously, because God does not forget him : though I may hardly ever think of him, and do forget his name, yet not *him*. I can, by praying rapidly for him, put him still deeper into God and re-meet him hereafter all the more profoundly. Others come and disappear like ghosts—the person sitting opposite you in a 'bus. . . . It is almost good fun to pray for him, not having the slightest idea what will happen to him in consequence—but some *good* thing *must* happen ; nor does he know he is being prayed for or " suffering " a gift from God.

This self-rescue from melancholy is quite in keeping with this psalm. The psalmist is confronted by the " sinner," and gets so indignant that he thinks he had better hold his tongue altogether : he doesn't exactly sulk, but it was not quite a good silence, because he simply got angrier and angrier, and the more he brooded, the more his feelings became worked up, till at last he blazed out— luckily, to God, but even so, almost (at first) in the spirit of classical common-place—you pile up wealth, only for your heir to dissipate it. Everything passes like a dream. " Tell me my end ! How many days remain to me ? How fleeting am I ! Thou hast made my days " measurable "— each one is a definite tiny measurable span—one inch out of so many miles of life. Even so, my "duration" is as nothing before Thee—ah ! everything—everyone—is emptiness ! Men pass like ghosts, and all their busy-ness is for nothing !

But just because this is a Psalm, and not an ode by Horace in one of his glum spells, he flings the whole of his weight—his trust—his assurance—his self, upon God. *Substantia* should probably be much the same as "expectation," *i.e.*, hope : I can rely on nothing save on God, but it *is God* on whom I do rely. However, I like that idea of "substance." "My substance is with *Thee*." I *am* not a ghost. My life is not a mere illusion. Things, like friendships, that have vanished, haven't gone nowhere. There *is* reality, in myself, my friends, my actions : in God, they become real, solid and enduring.

THE SPIRIT SUBMITS, THAT IT MAY CONQUER

Nonne subiecta Deo erit anima mea ? Shall not my soul submit herself to God ?—Psalm lxi. 1. Thurs, Matins, Noct., 1.

1. Little though we think it, this is the very hardest part of the spiritual life—and yet, the most essential. I stiffen myself against God : and then, I discover how very weak I am ! My enemies attack me ; they just push me over, as a man might do to a wall already tottering, and a falling fence. It is only when God puts His arms under me and holds me up that I shall no more be shaken (verse 2). "Humble yourselves beneath the mighty hand of God" (St. Peter, i. 6). It is this doctrine of self-submissiveness that they so hate who wish to be "their own masters" in the world. No one can be that—even were there no Judgment to follow it.

2. In verse 10, we are told : "Should riches flow in upon you, set not your heart upon them" ; and this is just what St. Paul suggests when he writes : "The *love* of money is the root of *all sorts* of evil" (1 Tim. vi. 10) not just "money," nor just "all." We can, with God's help, get the upper hand in regard to money, position,

or anything else created which tries to dominate us: but the upper hand of God—No.

3. We can repeat again and again with St. Augustine: "Nostras etiam rebelles ad Te compelle voluntates"— "Even when our wills rebel—Lord, our wills towards Thee compel!" That sounds indeed a paradox—that our free wills can be in any sense "compelled." But we freely give God leave to do that! or at any rate so to dispose of our circumstances that we shall freely choose what He wills. Then indeed is our heart not "set upon" any created thing: and our soul is indeed "submissive" to the Almighty but most merciful God.

N

V

THE SOCIAL SIN

It is possible to confine our " acts of contrition " to sins committed in isolation, *i.e.*, without any regard to anyone else (like not fulfilling one's Easter duties), or to those which affect perhaps only one other person—someone to whom, for example, we have been " uncharitable," *i.e.*, unkind. (It would seem that the word " uncharitable " is often relatively lightly used, because it has become " technical," and does not bite so deeply as the more human word " unkind " does : nor do we often hear the word " ungrateful " used in Confession.) And perhaps we shall not be in sufficiently powerful positions (whether financial or not) to commit sin on a very wide scale. Hence the notion of " social injustice " may pass us by, nor shall we examine our conscience to see if we are guilty of any. We often read phrases like : " The days when the Church used to be in the van of civilisation—the chief force making for social righteousness," and so on. To-day, we are given to understand that the State has " taken over " much that the Church used to do ; and even, that the Church no more attempts to do it, but concentrates on personal piety. The great social Encyclicals suffice to prove that this is false ; but few save Catholics read them, and how many Catholics attend to them ? Hence Catholics are not manifest to all as preaching a " social crusade "—they appear to leave that to other groups, Communist or Fascist. We might indeed observe that these have a " social programme." The non-religious " Right Wing " has none. And we . . . ?

True, Christianity is not meant to concern itself *directly* with, for example, drains : but it is meant to affect, to " convert," the *entire man*, whether the individual or the social man : and if bad material conditions are examined deeply enough, sin, *i.e.*, offences against truth, justice, charity, and certainly the practice of the love of God and of one's neighbour for His sake, will be discovered. The Christian is forthwith concerned.

The Hebrew Law, set down in the inspired Scriptures, is full of detailed enactments destined to ensure social justice, equity and even benevolence—*i.e.*, the periodical freeing of slaves or re-distribution of property : the well-being of the widow or orphan or the " stranger within thy gates " ; but we are here meditating on the Psalms.

They suggest no *system* of charity, nor any " organisation " of charitable work ; nor do they allude to any group of persons having charitable endeavour as their life-vocation. But they certainly allude often to Judges, whose whole business it is to see that justice is administered ; and again, to the Rich, by whom something very different from the " prosperous " is intended. The Hebrew thought that men *ought* to be reasonably prosperous, and that prosperity was a sign on the whole of God's favour, and that calamities were a mark that the sufferer had sinned. Hence his continual protest—" I suffer, but I have not sinned! " " Si est iniquitas in manibus meis . . .! " But there were, he freely recognises, men who accumulated riches at the expense of others ; who took bribes : and the frequent allusions to " usury " make it clear that in the Psalms the " poor " at any rate sometimes, means, quite simply, those who have not enough of this world's goods. This, he implies, is wrong ; and means sin somewhere.

It is true that the Psalmist applies the words " egenus et pauper," " pauper et inops "—poor and needy—to

himself when he feels he is friendless, isolated, persecuted :
and regards the nation as " poor " when for any reason
it is in distress—in exile, for example. But any national
calamity always did bring impoverishment in its train. He
also applies these words in the sense which became, later on,
very nearly technical—the gentle, quiet folk, who did not
take part in politics and still less in militarist aspirations or
enterprise. All these senses can be discovered in the Psalms.

But we can usually recall yet again that no Hebrew—
and certainly no righteous king—we may in fact insist,
and say *no* Hebrew—ever thought of himself in isolation
from the People ; he was part and parcel of it : he might
and often did sin against his belief, but it *was* his belief,
and it was based on the general oriental sense of the tribe,
or clan, as coming *first*—you were what you were because
of your incorporation into *it ;* and this unity was, in
the Hebrew's case, lifted to an incalculably higher level
because that unity had been guaranteed by the Promises,
the Covenant, of a Righteous God. As Catholics, we
are bound to think similarly, though on a far higher plane
still : we are one, all of us, in Jesus Christ : and it is
our vocation to summon the whole world into that Universal
Unity. But this supreme Union has to manifest itself on
every level ; so, in using the Psalms, with their passionate
appeals for justice amongst all, we may very well examine
our conscience from, so to say, bottom upwards, and
see whether we are fulfilling our more elementary duties,
and not forgetting them when we congratulate ourselves
on being members of the Church.

Psalm ix (see verses 10, 13, 19, 30, 31, 33, 35, 38, 39)
and Psalm lxxi, verses 2, 4, 12, 13, 14, are pre-eminently
to the point : see also Psalms x. 5 ; xi. 6 ; xiv. 5 ; xvii.
28 ; xxii. 17 ; xxv. 10 ; xxxiii. 7, 11, 19 ; xxxiv. 10 ;
xxxvi. 14, 21 ; xxxix. 18 ; xl. 2 ; liv. 12 ; lxvii. 6 ; lxviii.
30, 33, 34 ; lxix. 6 ; lxxxi. 3, 4 ; cxi. 5 ; cxii. 7 ; cxxxi.
15 ; cxxxix. 13 ; cxlvi. 13–17 ; cxlv. 9.

THE GENEROUS GIVER

Dispersit, dedit pauperibus. He divides—he gives to the poor.—Psalm cxi. 9. Sunday, Vesp., 3.

1. The Hebrew had no "system" of charity; no organisation. He "scattered"; he gives largesse: when anyone arrived needing help, the true servant of God *gave*.

2. It is, however, right that we should have "order" in our charity. The members of a family are right first of all to think of their home, and be of *service* within it. A priest's family is his parish; a bishop's, his diocese. There is no one with directly universal mandate save the Pope.

3. All the same, it is easy to develop the vice proper to our virtues; to hoard rather than to administer prudently; to grudge anything to anyone not connected with our personal or even official concern. No doubt it is good for everyone, priest or not, to have something *central* on which to concentrate: but it is also good, at least from time to time, to behave generously towards what is definitely not "my" affair, like the Foreign Missions. Disperse! Scatter! Loosen the bonds of your imagination! We can all of us share in the *spirit* of the Universal Father, which is that of the Redeemer of all men, Christ our Lord.

.   .   .   .   .   .

Verse 4 probably means: *He* has risen up, a light in darkness, for the upright . . . those men of innocent life, especially, who have no other aid. He is merciful, pitying, just, kind and generous.

THE INTELLIGENT GIVER

*Beatus qui intelligit super egenum et pauperem. Happy
is he who taketh heed of the poor and needy.—Psalm
xl. 1. Tues., Sext, 1.*

1. The Psalm is proper to one lying sick : but it begins
thus with words that may have been proverbial, and
applied by the sick man to himself. Take, however, the
words in their most literal meaning : Happy is the man
who takes attentive heed of—puts his mind to—the
un-moneyed. To all who cannot for various reasons lead
the free and stable life that is their right. Who are " in
need." It is possible to be quite unaware of what is
happening at our very doors.

2. The Church is of good repute in England for her
care of the poor ; and Catholics—especially the poor
themselves, as always—are generous. But giving generously
is quite different from paying attentive heed. Priests and
people alike need to look as deeply as they can into the
causes of the misery of which there is so much ; we dare
not be content with everlasting palliatives. It is possible
for a parish to become a " comfortable unit," living a
life sufficiently varied and self-contained to exempt it
from knowing so much as the struggling parish next
door. Such a group, and the individuals that compose it,
do not try to " understand " about the " needy," and
so, miss the Blessing proper to those who do.

3. There is a " pity " for those who are in distress—
dis-comfort—which is not an " understanding " one. It
is due to the sight of discomfort making *me* uncomfortable. " Kind " actions due to this are not much more
than acts of self-indulgence. They do not show that we
are looking for the roots of the sufferer's discomfort :
they make no attempt to reach and cure *that*. All the

same, a pitying heart is good : it means insight, imagination, responsiveness—all of which soon enough exact real
self-sacrifice on the part of the pity-er. Genuine pity will
overcome shyness, condescension, inclination either to
intrude or to hold aloof. " He knew what was in man "
(John ii. 25); " He knoweth whereof we are made ;
He remembereth that we are but dust " (Ps. cii. 14).

· · · · ·

*Dum superbit impius, incenditur pauper. The godless
man luxuriates, and the poor man is set afire.—Psalm
ix. 23.*

Because of the proud insolence of the rich and godless,
the poor are in a blaze of anger or a fever of fear for their
future. Inequalities of fortune are natural, inevitable and
so, not wrong in themselves. But pride and godlessness
due to wealth are wrong : and wealth obtained unscrupulously is wrong : *vast* inequalities of possessions nearly
always mean sin somewhere and extreme inequalities of
life—all the ease on one side, all the hardship on the
other—is shocking, and engenders hate. No harm in
thinking of the violent oriental contrasts between palaces
and poor men's hovels literally the easy victim of fires in
which *all* their possessions are lost—all their " means."

THE FORGOTTEN FOLK

*Non in finem oblivio erit pauperis : patientia pauperum
non peribit in finem. The poor shall not be forgotten for
ever ; the endurance of the poor shall not come to
nothing in the end.—Psalm ix. 19. Sunday, Matins,
Noct. ii. 2, 3 ; and iii. 1, 2.*

1. This is largely an alphabetical Psalm ; so its verses
may seem disjointed : but its theme is clear—neither
foreign foes, nor oppressors within the land, shall for ever

lord it over the " poor " and helpless : but all alike, who set themselves up too high, shall learn that they are but men (21). The " poor " in the first part of the Psalm do not mean the financially-poor so definitely as in the second.

2. Again we examine ourselves, to see if in any way we are living *at the expense* of others : priests are very seldom rich ; still, the faithful support them, and they should wish to use what does come to them in the shape of alms in *as priestly a way* as possible. We have also to be careful thus—What may seem to us (and be) a very moderate way of life, or house, can seem downright luxurious to the very poor. People ought not to " take scandal," but perhaps we ought to be doubly careful not to give excuses for it.

3. *Time* is a real and very precious asset. Some priests are overworked : but others, especially in the country and alone, have much time " on their hands." They would not wish, and usually could not, spend it in amusement merely : it provides a splendid opportunity for study—for revising seminary studies ; or, studying problems which could not be tackled there—*e.g.*, this very question of the " poor," and the rectification of social injustices.

　　　·　　　·　　　·　　　·　　　·

This is not a Messianic Psalm, at least directly : but the Kingdom or Triumph of God is a triumph of Justice. " The Lord shall be *recognised* by His exercise of justice (17 ; and compare 5 ; 8b ; 9 ; 20b and 21) ; and contrast the insolence, and fraudulence, of the wicked (23 ; 26b ; and 20–31). Verse 30 gives a vivid picture : " He lies in wait to seize hold of the poor man : he seizes hold of him and drags him along." Verse 31 can hardly but mean : " With his noose—lassoo—he brings him (the poor man) down to earth : he (the poor man) collapses and falls, when the enemy masters him." No wonder the Psalmist turns to God, who helps *in opportunitatibus*—at the very right moment! " To *Thee* the Poor is left over! 'Tis

Thou must be the orphan's helper! . . . The Lord doth
grant the yearnings of the Poor—Thine ear doth hear
the strong longing of their heart—even that Thou wouldst
give verdict for the helpless child and for the lowly, so
that no mere man may any more again exalt himself upon
earth! "

THE DIVINE PROSPERITY

*Parcet pauperi et inopi et animas pauperum salvas
faciet. He shall have pity on the poor and the helpless ;
yea, he shall save the lives of the poor.—Psalm lxxi.
13. Thurs., Prime.*

1. This glorious Messianic Psalm concerns the Kingdom
of Peace and Righteousness (the two are indissolubly
connected) that shall belong to the Anointed King. His
own grandeur occupies but a few verses, and they, not
the first or last, nor is it they that contain the " guiding
words " of the Psalm. At once, God is implored to bestow
the grace of justice and giving of right judgments to
the King—yea, the Royal Son—that in Justice he may
judge Thy People, yea, with righteous judgment Thy
Poor. . . . Let the mountains bear Peace, yea, the Hills
Justice ; (then shall He give judgment for the poor of
the People and rescue the children of the Poor, and bring
low the oppressor. . . . He will rescue the Poor from
the powerful ; the Poor, who hath not a helper . . .
from usury and injustice shall He save their lives ; and
precious shall they be in His sight.

2. There is a real inversion of due order when Charity
is placed before Justice. Catholics are generous : they
willingly give alms even without knowing accurately about
that for which they are requested. But this is a palliative
on the whole : the condition of the poor is not only sad—
it must not stir only our sympathy : it is *unjust*, and
we must see *sin* in it, and beware lest by apathy we share

in another's sin—a social sin. We want to make those alms *unnecessary*.

3. Certainly the picture of the vast extension of the Messianic Realm is impressive ; also its eternity—the Anointed King shall reign as long as sun and moon endure. (*Ante lunam*, verse 5, *ante solem*, 17, mean in Hebrew that the King and the sun or moon as it were confront one another. Neither shall perish first.) But the essence of Christ's Reign is Justice and Charity ; for *us* to establish these *here* and *now*.

.   .   .   .   .

The Latin of verse 14b means : " Their name *i.e.*, the name, the persons, of the Poor shall be held in honour in his (the King's) presence. The Hebrew says : " And precious is their blood in His eyes." This word *precious*, also used in the verse *Pretiosa in conspectu Domini mors sanctorum eius* (Ps. cxv. 15), means " grievous," *i.e.*, " heavy," *i.e.*, to be taken into serious account—the Poor are *valuable*. There is to be no such thing as a mere " proletariat," in which the individual is lost in the multitude, nor is the nameless multitude to be merely at the service of the few. The Spanish word *hidalgo*— " son of *someone* "—had a sinister bearing : the mass of the people were " nobodies," as we, too, used to say. —The next verse, too, quite possibly means : " And he, *i.e.*, the poor man, shall live ; and there shall be given to him of—a share in—the gold from Arabia ; and men shall pray for Him for ever—all day long shall men bless Him."

Verse 15 is obscure. *Firmamentum* may well mean the sustenance given by corn—" There shall be crops in the land even on the summits of the mountains—its fruit shall be taller than Lebanon " : but the Hebrew more picturesquely, less exaggeratedly, says : " Its fruit shall rustle, wave, like (the forests of) Lebanon." It remains that the Messianic Kingdom was to be one of " peace and plenty " for all.

.   .   .   .   .

Cognoscetur Dominus iudicia faciens : The Lord shall be recognised in His doing of justice . . . Constitue Domine legislatorem super eos, ut sciant Gentes quoniam homines sunt. Appoint, O Lord, a Lawgiver over them, that the Heathen may know that they are but men.—Psalm ix. 17, 21.

Wherever you see Justice being done, you see the activity of God. This may take place outside the Catholic frontiers. No matter : praise God for the *infiltrations* of His Holy Spirit wherever you detect them. And grieve if injustice be done by Catholics or among them. Let us praise, praise and praise good when we meet it : and openly confess our sins when we commit them. Therefore, we must pray for statesmen and governors, as the Church keeps urging us to do in her Liturgy—for all rulers and not only Christian ones for whom we pray officially. For all Authority comes from God, and if it does not act according to God, this means that it has usurped the place of God ; man is in God's sanctuary—an " abomination that makes desolate."

THE HAPPY WORKER

Labores manuum tuarum manducabis : beatus es, et bene tibi erit.—Psalm cxxvii. 2. Wed., Vesp., 1.

1. The Hebrew felt that begging was a disgrace—" to beg I am ashamed " (Luke xvi. 3)—but also, that a man ought not to have to buy all he needed, for that could suggest that the Lord had not blessed the produce of his possessions : again, should a man be extremely affluent and yet idle, there was a presumption that he got his wealth by usury, by grinding the faces of the poor, or by laying hands on what was really his neighbour's. Hence a man was expected to work, to earn, and the sons even of well-to-do families were brought up to a trade.

2. The only gift that is absolutely free, is Grace : and

even with Grace I ought to " trade." (Recall the parable
of the Talents, and the rebuke given to him who wrapped
his talent in a napkin and left it unused.) " I will do as
little work as possible : I will do only what I must : I
wish I had no responsibilities" indicate a mood that
should be alien to us. Work is as healthy for the soul
as for the body : idleness should be shocking to us when
we reflect that many have to work too hard in order to
supply us with our superfluities. If I am wilfully idle, I
should blush at the sight of a working man. Pius XII
spoke to the Roman nobility of the " original and
universal law of work."

3. On the other hand : " I will get more and more—
all I can " is no ideal for a Christian. Once money-making
becomes the centre of gravity of my life, I develop a
" love for money "; and it is *love* for money (not just
money as such) which St. Paul calls the " root of all sorts
of evils " (1 Tim. vi. 10).

. . . . .

Verse 3a. " Thy wife is like a fruitful vine on the walls
of thy house." But the Hebrew has, not walls, but " in
the inner parts " on thy house. It means, then, " Thy
wife, in the innermost parts, etc., is like, etc." The Hebrew
woman, like the Roman one (" domum servavit : lanam
fecit "), was expected to stay quietly at home for the most
part. Proverbs ix. 13 sqq., pictures Folly as a woman who
sits at the door of her house, or even on seats in the high
places of the city, to call to the passers by. Much worse
is the woman in vii. 11, whose feet " abide not in her
house."

THE PROUDEST PRINCE WILL DIE

*Ego dixi : Dii estis . . . vos autem sicut homines
moriemini. I said : " You are gods ! . . . None
the less, like mere men shall you die ! "—Psalm lxxxi.
6, 7. Fri., Terce, 3.*

1. A stern rebuke of authority unjustly exercised. God enters the judgment-court of the powerful but unjust: He denounces them for their injustice towards the poor and helpless. But they will not attend—they cannot understand—the very foundations of the earth, the very principles of Justice, have collapsed. And God says with dreadful irony: "Yes, they feel themselves to be great as gods—sons, all of them, of the Most High. None the less, as men die, so must they: even great princes fall— so shall they!" And the Psalm ends with a passionate cry that this should indeed come to pass.

2. We may be terrified at times to see how frail are the foundations of elementary justice. Almost any trader's log will show that it does not even occur to him to make money off Natives otherwise than as trickily as he can. At home, he would be reasonably honest: but when confronted by the ignorant, the easily cheated, nothing stands between him and immediate fraud. There is an old question —"What would I do if I were *sure* no one could see me and that I would not be found out?"

3. The moment I have a little extra power—and money provides that—I am tempted to think disdainfully of those who have less. But the moment I despise anyone, I am already sinning by injustice: for, I have no right to think anyone beneath me. We are all equally small before God—or, if I use His Grace, equally great.

SHALL EVIL LAST?

Ad nihilum devenient tamquam aqua decurrens. They shall come to nothing, like water streaming down.— Psalm lvii. 7. Wed., Sext, 3.

1. It is unjust judges who stir the Psalmist to this torrential indignation. "If indeed ye be judges—pronounce verdicts—judge what is *just*, ye *men*!" Thus may we trans-

late the first verse. But then he proceeds to indict them for their utter perversity; their hands weigh out and weave injustice from one end of the land to the other. They are as venomous and as unheeding as the deaf serpent—and yet, God shall shatter their teeth like lions' teeth: they shall flee away like a mountain torrent that vanishes in the pebbles as swiftly as it bursts forth: they shall melt like so much wax in the sun before they so much as catch sight of it. (The Hebrew may well mean —and how picturesquely!—They shall melt away, as they go, like snails . . . they shall vanish like an abortive birth that the sun never sees.)

2. But what probably disconcerts *us* is, not the impermanence, but the unaltering endurance of evil. We look back over history and see that though men, at times, have been less violent, less outrageous, than at others, when have they not been sinful? when has not power corrupted them? Despite the extraordinary things that have happened in the world—the Incarnation: the daily renewal of Calvary at Mass—no *substantial* improvement seems to have been made. Profound discouragement! black disillusionment! It is when we feel thus, that our Acts of Faith and Hope have a supreme value before God.

. . . . .

This line is so picturesque that it remains in the mind throughout the puzzling verse about the thorns, and the unpleasant one about washing your hands in the blood of sinners. Not that I want my enemies to " come to nothing, like water rushing down " . . . That is just what one so fears about one's own character or work. The Palestinian torrents—spouting and roaring at the top, then spreading and fussing, and then thinning and being drunk up and disappearing in the fissures and the unproductive dusts! One's work! Amateur—erratic— flimsy—impermanent—dissipated—non-character-building

—defeated by the rocks and by the sands! *Apud Te substantia mea!* Certainly one observes fantastic but so-energetic anti-Christianities, in Russia, in Mexico, in Germany—weakening, becoming ordinary, producing nothing; that is one human reason for never losing one's head: Rome never loses her head, if only because she has seen the same thing happen a hundred times. Not that Rome is wise merely because of her immemorial experience, unshared by any secular government of to-day; she has her certainty, her promises and her faith. In consequence she sometimes looks as if she didn't really mind very much about the contemporary incident. She does; because souls are at stake. But presumably God will not allow millions of poor little souls to suffer eternally because they are at first whirled away by the waters in spate. I presume that even the noisy torrent carried down with it a number of seeds, of fertilising stuff; and even when the water vanished in the sand, it left behind it much material that worked at turning the sand into good soil. Still, the retiring waters do leave a lot of mess behind them. Recurrent ferocities like those we are witnessing destroy a great deal as they make their mad plunges: they also remove a lot of good soil from one place and even if they transport it to another, it *is* removed from *that* place, and is thinner where it comes, and sometimes remains in smears of perfectly useless mud. Well, Christ was killed, and then, " rising from the dead has re-generated us, too, into a living hope." Be content to see but a fraction of your hopes realised: trust that more is realised than you see: want your work to prosper in His way, not yours: ask pardon for your obstinate adhesion to *your* way: " do not look back at my sins, but upon the Faith of Thy Church ": " to us, too, sinners—yet servants of Thine!—out of the multitude of Thy mercy deign to give freely unto us *some* part along with Thine Apostles and even with Thy Martyrs! "

VI

MAN'S WORLD-SIN

We have seen how the Israelites never forgot their history : how they recalled and lamented with the utmost frankness their disasters : how they saw, in these, very largely the result of their own infidelities, either downright apostasies, or at least compromises with the pagan invader or environment : and how they were none the less quite sure that God was faithful; would always be merciful to the penitent, and would conquer at the last.

We have, then, placed first the Psalmist's laments, expostulations with God, and references to particular events in the People's history—not that we can indicate with certainty what these were; but the sequence of *moods* mentioned above is constantly to be found throughout Old Testament literature, and indeed is frequently found in almost any Oriental. But towards the end of this section, a few considerations are to be found expressive of the double upshot of that series—the Psalmist is conscious of his, and the nation's, intrinsic helplessness and of the utter uselessness of reliance upon force : and, of the Omnipresence, Omnipotence, and All-Goodness of his God.

THE WORLD'S HEART DESECRATE

Deus, venerunt gentes in haereditatem tuam : polluerunt templum sanctum tuum. O God, the Heathen have come into Thy possessions ; they have defiled Thy holy Temple.—Psalm lxxviii. 1. Fri., Matins, Noct., iii. 1.

1. Our Catholic ancestors knew the Psalms well; and this one, expressive of the anguish felt by the Jew when he saw Jerusalem and the Temple sacked and defiled, must have been often on their lips. We still can say it, as with their minds; and yet again, when we watch the sacrileges of our own times about which perhaps we do not pray enough.

2. We can too refer it to the desecration of millions of young souls being deliberately brought up without Catholic education, and infected by pagan philosophies.

3. But the Psalmist is always candid, and ascribes these disasters to ancient sins. His thoughts move so fast that he almost takes those sins for granted—hardly needs to confess them: the Lord is implored not to remember them: let His loving mercies actually take the lead, swiftly come in ahead—*cito anticipent*—of anything that man can think or do. And finally, he displays the serenest trust in God: " As for us, we are Thy people; yes, the sheep of Thy pasture: we will give Thee thanks for ever and ever—from one generation to another, we will proclaim Thy praise! " We have but to change one or two vengeful verses into a prayer for that " revenge " that only love and succour can provide.

.   .   .   .   .

The Psalm provides a vivid example of " mixed motives." The Psalmist was genuinely horror-struck at the sight of God's special possession, the Holy Land, being invaded; the Temple defiled; Jerusalem reduced to no more than a field-hut such as those in which watchmen spent the night. . . . He was in anguish at the sheer distress of the people; corpses unburied and the prey of beast and bird: he was bitterly sensitive to the mockery which, like all conquered peoples of old, the Jews were having to endure: He agreed that such calamities must be due to God's wrath—and that wrath could not be aroused save

by sin : he implores God to have mercy on His people—
because their humiliation involved the mockery of God
Himself—" Where is now their God ? " He longs alike
for deliverance and for revenge ; and he thanks God even
beforehand for that ultimate rescue of which he feels so
sure.

Perhaps we shall never have a perfectly " pure intention " : a genuine sense that I " ought " to do something
kind or apostolic may be shot across by a feeling of vanity
because I think I shall do it well and be applauded : or
the duty of reproof may be confused by my desire to pay
someone back for injuries received. Well, we ought not
to refrain from good, or from duties, till we are *absolutely*
clear that we have none but *absolutely* pure motives : and
after our best actions, we may still ask God to forgive
us.

STIFLE THE FEASTS OF GOD !

*Dixerunt in corde suo cognatio eorum simul : Quiescere
faciamus omnes dies festos Dei a terra. They said in
their hearts—the whole gang of them together—" Let
us cause every feast of God to be silenced off the earth ! "*
—Psalm lxxiii. 8. *Thurs., Sext.*

1. It is very likely that this Psalm was written, or
re-written, after the attempt of Antiochus Epiphanes
(168 B.C.) to subjugate the Holy Land : he pillaged and
ruined the Temple ; forbade the offering of sacrifices :
set up his own image in the shape of the Sun-god in the
Temple precincts, and tried to cause the Jews to fuse
their religion with a sort of general worship which should
be part of a homogeneous world-culture. Hence the revolt
of the Maccabees, see especially 1 Maccabees i, iv, etc.

2. The times we live in are unprecedented in this—that
we witness a *concerted* attack upon religion *as such*. Ancient
persecutions were directed for various reasons—mostly

political, as many are now—against Christianity: but a variety of cults were encouraged, and certainly the cult of the State and its Governor, which still is operative in our world. But never has the world seen in so many parts of itself an "anti-God" Front, attempting indeed the impossible, for God exists and wills to be worshipped, so that religion "comes natural" to man, but working appalling havoc especially among the young. But a veto upon public acts of religion—the driving back of religion into sacristies—is an old story. Even that re-emerges.

3. So the saddest verse of all is the ninth. "Our signs we see no more: now there is no more prophet." No symbol of religion (or miracle-sign?) was to survive,—worse, for 400 years before the appearance of the Baptist, there was no "prophet," no manifestly accredited spokesman of God. We must agree that there are few Catholics who can make their voice inescapably audible throughout even one country—or Europe—or the world. Would there were more! But there are those who *should* be inescapably audible! From Leo XIII to Pius XII, all our Popes have deserved to be. Therefore we must pray for the opening of deaf ears, and for the imparting of piercing strength to such prophetic voices. Yet after all, the greatest prophets, and even Our Lord Himself, were hardly listened to! Pray, none the less, for spokesmen, and for contact.

    .   .   .   .   .

That this Psalm may be easily prayed without distractions due to obscurities, we recall that verse 3 means: "Lift up Thy hand against their uttermost malice—ah! *what* malice have they displayed within Thy Sanctuary!" 4b and 5; "They have set up their standards and trophies (pagan standards, waving in the very Temple-precincts) —high over the gateways—they knew not what they were doing." (This must suffice to give a meaning to the Latin, and it also presents a vivid picture of desecration.) 6;

" As in a forest of trees, with axes have they utterly hewn down its gates—with hatchets and axes have they broken it down. . . . To the very ground have they defiled the Dwelling of Thy Name." 11 ; " Why turnest Thou away Thy hand—Thy right hand from Thy bosom for ever ? " God withdraws His hand with which He had been carrying Israel against His breast, and the child falls to the ground. But the Hebrew may mean that He keeps His hand *in* His bosom—the folds of His robe—instead of reaching it out to help. Yet it is *God* who worked mighty marvels of old—won victories over beasts alike of sea and land. The Dragon is no doubt the " primeval monster " that legend placed in the bottom of the sea : God flings him as food to the " jackals "—the " desert folk " (the " Ethiopians "). God makes waters to break forth, and dries up " flowing streams " (" flumina ethan ") —He is all-powerful! Let Him therefore look in mercy upon His people and remember His covenant (20), " for the people of Thy land are in darkness, and glutted by (the cruelties of) the homes of iniquity (*i.e.*, the iniquitous invader)." This is but an attempt to provide *a* sense for the Latin words as they stand. When Henry VIII began to rob the poor of their homes and lands, he created a whole race of " hidden," " dark " people, and the land lay, it was said, under " the blanket of the Dark." Russian serfs, too, are said to have been called the " dark," invisible folk.

WHERE ARE OUR SAINTS ?

Defecit sanctus : diminutae sunt veritates a filiis hominum. There is no Saint : truths have dwindled away from among men.—Psalm xi. 1. Tues., Compline, 1.

1. The Latin can mean : " The Saint has disappeared," *i.e.*, there are no Saints to-day. " Truth has lessened

among men." The modern generation, we sometimes feel, produces no heroes—perhaps because of the prevalent agnosticism, itself largely due to " undogmatic teaching." Where you are not sure of anything, you have no over-whelming motive to *be* anything, to sacrifice everything to one thing. The Psalmist was speaking rather of *telling* the truth : but in proportion as we have to acknowledge a prevalent vagueness of mind, a decay of " religion " generally, a dwindling of Faith among so many to actual vanishing-point, it is but likely that there will be a dearth of Saints, just when they are most needed.

2. But Catholic History shows that God always does raise up Saints when they are needed—and Saints of the *sort*, or sorts, that are needed—as different as St. John Bosco, St. Thérèse de Lisieux, and (not to anticipate) Charles de Foucauld and Mat Talbot.

3. All the same, we pray that God would raise up Saints also in England. We see very many very good men—but not Saints. Yet perhaps they are there all the time. If they are, God can reveal them if He chooses. How else would the Little Flower ever have been heard of? Let us pray for a great out-pouring of the Holy Spirit, into our own hearts, and into hearts better prepared than ours for receiving Him!

.   .   .   .   .

In opposition to the " disappearance of truths " (no doubt this meant, originally, " loyalty "—being " true " to your word—to your belief) are the *lies* of which the Psalm makes so much : " they speak with double hearts " —their real thought is not what they express. " We shall make proud our tongues: our lips are our own "—we will say exactly what we please. Thank God that the Truth, taught us by the Church, saves us from endless mistakes—unconscious falsehoods of thought or word.— We can admit as a meaning for the last verse : " The

wicked walk freely round about : *but Thou* dost multiply
Thy race of men—the righteousness—according to Thine
own greatness." God is independent and paramount.
He does what He does on a scale proportionate to what
He is.

SEIZE HOLD OF HIS SHRINE

*Haereditate possideamus Sanctuarium Dei. Let us
take possession of the Holy Place of God as though it
were ours by right.—Psalm lxxxii. 12. Fri., Noct.,
iii. 3.*

1. No human person must ever *possess* another. You
hear : " I can't call my soul my own." But that is just
what no other person must *dominate*. The wish for
domination can become a real disease. Even a priest may
feel injured if he finds that parishioners, or people whom
he directs, have independent ideas and choose for themselves. The soul is *God's* Sanctuary, and no mere man's
possession.

2. But more than in recent times do Governments wish
to be absolute possessors of men's minds. It is the duty of
every Catholic, in these days of renewed persecution, to
understand what are the rights of the State—the State
has *no* rights over conscience : but it is quite possible that
the very people who protest against the State for persecuting
the Church, fall short in their *duty* toward the State in
many ways, and try to avoid paying it its dues. Am I
ready to *cheat* the State ?

3. The Psalmist boldly asks God to make the Oppressor
" like a wheel," *i.e.*, like whirling dust—chaff before the
wind—food for a forest fire among the mountains. It
may be a real spiritual difficulty to desire intensely the
abolition of what we know to be wrong—involving the
destruction of him, too, who is engineering the wrong.
All the more must we sincerely pray for those whom we

believe to be in the wrong, and doing wrong. And indeed, in the Psalm, the ultimate motive is (19) " that they may realise that Thy Name is ' The Lord '; *i.e.*, that *Thou art* ' Yahweh,' and all that that Name means—that Thou alone art Most High over all the earth." It is true that the Psalmist wanted the heathen to learn this from God's relentless crushing of them : we have been taught that He wishes " all men to be saved and come to a knowledge of the truth "—He *loves* all those heathen. Still, the Psalmist's main preoccupation *was God*.

O LORD—AWAKE!

Exsurge—quare obdormis, Domine?   Awake—why sleepest Thou, O Lord?—Psalm xliii. 23. Tues., None.

1. The Psalm begins with a retrospect towards God's great work for His People in the past, and a profoundly sincere declaration that it was not the power or merits of Israel itself, or of any one man within it, which had been responsible for past victories. This idea is continuous in the Old Testament—Israel was God's People because of His free choice, sanctioned by Promises—and it draws near to the Christian doctrine of Grace—never by our own merits or work can we earn grace and we never shall. We have nothing in or of ourselves to warrant our boasting, as St. Paul often says. But the memory of our nothingness should make us lean the more trustfully upon God, our Saviour.

2. Yet the Israelites suffered dreadful calamities : their City and Temple were ruined and they were exiled. God has sold His People " for nothing "—He seemed to think them so worthless that He did not trouble even to get anything in exchange. Sin can ruin even a soul that had been highly graced. St. Aloysius had seen, he wrote, the

very pillars of heaven falling. How then could he promise
perseverance to himself?

3. The Psalm contains what sound like bitter reproaches
to God. We allow for Oriental audacities : but again
we wish that our own prayers were not so languid! Yet
even the intensest prayer should be calm : if we become
agitated and as it were shout at God as though He were
really asleep, we are trusting too much to our efforts, and
not remembering that in all circumstances He cannot be
other than perfect love.

·   ·   ·   ·   ·

*Posuisti nos in similitudinem Gentibus ; commotionem
capitis in populis* (15). *Thou hast made us into a
by-word for the heathen—a nodding of the head among
the peoples.*

Certainly, at times everything seems to go wrong, and
Catholics seem to do everything worse than anyone else.
People say : " How exactly like a Roman Catholic! "
" You are as bad as a Catholic! " And when a Catholic
provides a scandal, people nod : " There! Just what one
expected! What did I tell you ? " Smug, self-satisfied,
Pharisaic nod! Yet one does much to deserve it. Lord, I
deserve it. I am always letting your Church down!
Confiteor ! Extraordinary how reluctant we are to own
up to our bad behaviour in our " apologetic " life, whereas
we are always being made to do it in our liturgical life,
and have a whole Sacrament precisely for Sinners. If the
Reformation (the Reformers were ex-Catholics) devastated
the Church and the world, that was possible because
Catholics were bad ; and I am bad ; and I am injuring
God's cause in England and Europe and the Missions!
Confusio faciei meae co-operuit me (16) : my blush of shame
covers the whole of me—I blush from head to foot. . . .

·   ·   ·   ·   ·

*Non egredieris Deus in virtutibus nostris. Thou marchest
not out, O God, with our forces.—Psalm xliii. 10.*

We work hard, and sometimes feel that a blight, a
paralysis, is upon our efforts. It seems incredible that
" Catholic Action "—technical or not—produces so small
an effect upon the world or even the country. There is,
of course, resistance due to the world, which is almost
pagan, and the devil. It is always possible that we go
forth on our expeditions alone—without God; our
actions are not shot through with divine activity. Yet
nothing is worth doing unless it be done " by means of
Him, along with Him, and in Him." If but we came to
our committee meetings having spent long enough at
least to purge our hearts of self-will, self-seeking; to
remove all obstacles from the way of God's advice;
God's energy.

FRET NOT THYSELF!

*Noli aemulari. Fret not thyself.—Psalm xxxvi. 1.
Tues., Noct. ii. 1.*

1. As so often, the Psalmist is disturbed by the sight
of the wicked prospering. Sometimes his distress amounted
to real anguish and hot anger: here, the notion (twice
repeated: 7, 8) is rather what we mean by " fretting."
" Fret not thyself because of evil-doers: nor grow hot
against the workers of iniquity. *Fret* not thyself because of
him who prospers in his path, who works unrighteousness.
Cease to be angry . . . it can but issue into sin on thy part
too." Such, probably, is the meaning of the last words:
anyhow the assertion holds good.

2. " Fretting " is one of those " moods " which we
must conquer if we are to grow holy. In a " mood," one
loses clearness of vision and peace of soul: we cannot
attend to anything, let alone to prayer. Our Lord tells us

not to "fret," to "worry" about material things: this
does not mean that we are to be indolent, or parasites,
nor can we always help being anxious, nor yet, indignant
with, *e.g.* the persecutors of the Church. And there is a
certain placidity which is irritating. We feel: "He
ought to be more upset!" But if our calm is based on
trust in God, and not on a sort of stoical recollection that
"things have been as bad as this, or worse, before now,"
then we can not only be at peace ourselves, but spread
peace round us. Yet the Psalmist, taking this long view,
did consider he had always seen the "wicked" fading like
weak grass in scorching sun. *Did* he? Do *we*? Whether
or no we "see" it, that is not the criterion of Faith.

3. The tragedy of allowing ourselves to get hot and
angry even with wrong-doers is that the devil has got his
own way with *us too*. For being angry with sinners does
not stop them from sinning, but it puts *us* in the wrong.
Hate breeds hate: if we want to take revenge on wrong-
doers and feel that "nothing is too bad for them," we
are sinning in the way in which they are and are un-
Christ-like.

.   .   .   .   .   .

Verse 4. "Find thy pleasure in God, and He will give
thee all the petitions of thy heart." "Ama et fac quod
vis," said St. Augustine: if you but love God, you can do
as you please . . . (for you will not even want to do
what He does not wish!). As time goes on, we can do more
than just desire to do God's will, and feel unhappy if we
do not do it. We can positively "take delight in God"
—be overwhelmed, at times, with gratitude that God *is*
God, and is all that we know Him to be. Certainly we shall
then "entrust our life" to God, and hope in Him—"and
He will bring it to pass" (5). This is one of those brief
sentences that can take up its lodging in our minds, and as
it were peep out from its room at us, and whisper itself

to us when we are least expecting it. This "alphabetical" Psalm contains many such short, disconnected sentences : but in this meditation we would wish its supreme lesson to be "not fretting," and a trust so simple that it might almost be taken for a "simpleton's."

THE WORLD IN TUMULT

Quare fremuerunt gentes, et populi meditati sunt inania? Why are the heathen in a turmoil? why do the pagans plot?—Psalm ii. 1. Sunday, Matins, Noct., i. 1.

1. Christian feeling may not like so warlike a Psalm about the Messias. Yet we have to recognise the *fact* that the powers of the world are—and perhaps for long will be—in revolt against belief in God and in Christ. Not only ignorance ; but hatred. No wonder if God is angered with much in our world. We dare not eliminate the notion of the " wrath " of God. Our Lord does not ; nor do His apostles John and Paul.

2. But the Heathen, when they revolt, are doing what is " vain," futile, what cannot succeed everywhere nor in the long run. Yet there is no promise that they shall not succeed here or there—no country is immune : nor for a very long time—our life-time might see nothing but defeats. I humble myself before God, and beg for perseverance for myself ; my fellow-Catholics ; my country ; for Europe.

3. Where the New Testament insists on the Love of God, the Old emphasises His Mercy. Yet neither there nor here is God " weak," ready to condone just anything, able to be " talked round." All the same, since it is very difficult for the human mind to retain in itself, and together, *all* that is true of God—even to that extent to which the human mind can entertain any of it—we cannot do

wrong in concentrating upon the fact that God loves us. "Blessed are they who put their *trust* in Him!"

.   .   .   .   .

The "flow" of this Psalm is as follows—

"Why are the Heathen in a turmoil—making futile plots? The rulers of this world meet and conspire against God and His Christ!" "Let us throw off Their yoke!" But God mocks them: and His Anointed King in anger declares to them—" *I* have been appointed King by God: *I* announce His decree! God has said to me: ' *Thou* art My Son! Thou hast but to ask of Me, and I will give Thee the whole world that Thou mayest rule it with absolute authority!' So now, you kings, be wise. Be obedient to God—lest He be angry and ye perish utterly. How happy are they who put their trust in Him!"

" *Ego hodie genui Te* " (7)—To-day have I begotten Thee—is a Hebrew way of saying that in the hour of His triumph God's Messiah is made manifest as His Son. St. Paul applies this verse to the Resurrection (Rom. i. 3–4, cf. Acts xiii. 33; Heb. v. 5), which indeed sealed Our Lord, for the eyes of anyone who would look, as God's guaranteed Spokesman, whom not even death could kill.

.   .   .   .   .

Ego hodie genui te : To-day have I begotten Thee.
While this refers primarily to God's declaration that the Messias is indeed His Chosen King, and could be quoted in connection with Our Lord's Baptism and Resurrection, priests, who are called "Father," can apply the text to themselves. When, for instance, they baptise a child; when they give absolution to a sinner, or the Last Sacraments; when they receive a convert into the Church. God's Fatherhood is delegated to me, His instrument. May I feel it as a permanent privilege: I must try to retain a true father's love for all such persons; not forget them;

not desert them ; justify their trust in me. . . . But since they become too numerous even for memory itself, how utterly must I transfer them into God's hands " in whom all spirits live." " Of those whom Thou hast given me " *Thou* wilt lose none!

HAS GOD WEAKENED ?

Dixi : " Nunc coepi ; haec mutatio dexterae Excelsi ! "
I said : " Now I begin (to understand)—This is a
change in the right hand of the Most High."—*Psalm
lxxvi.* 11. *Fri., Compline,* 1, 2.

1. The Psalmist begins with a cry of sheer misery (in verse 3b, *et delectatus sum* cannot be right. There is no thought of God giving him any consolation : read—' and am in distress "). The very thought of all that God used to do for him, makes the present only worse. He was on the side of His People : now He abandons them. The Psalmist meditates, examines his heart, and concludes : " Now I begin to understand. God's hand is changed : either it has grown weak ; or, He uses it no more for succour. It is a hand that strikes, not saves."

2. We know that this cannot be true : yet it is consoling that the inspired Scripture does not mind a man's feeling, and saying, that God seems to have deserted him. Many a Psalm begins with a cry of all-but despair ; continues to reflect on what God has done in the past ; and concludes with an act of trust for the future. God is " faithful." We invoke Our Lady as *Virgo Fidelis.*

3. This verse, taken by itself, has very often been used as meaning : " Now—at long last—and genuinely—I begin ! I make a resolution firm as never before ! This change in me is due to the hand of God Himself ! *I* could never thus have touched, stirred, strengthened my own heart ! " We are not forbidden thus to apply it. If, how-

ever, after an hour of extreme fervour, we break our
resolution as so often before, we shall be apt to return
to the real meaning of the words. But we must not permit
this despondency in ourselves. When the soul sags, and
always to be beginning again seems intolerable, *then* is
the very time to show *our* fidelity, to trust God, to grasp
His hand and let Him pull us up.

.   .   .   .   .

Verse 5 : The Hebrew says : " Thou holdest my eyelids " : the Latin, " My eyes forestall the night-watches "
—*i.e.*, I cannot sleep. I was in agitation, and yet could
find no words in which to express myself—I could not
find any meaning in what was happening. So I reflected
on the past—I cross-examined myself—I asked if really
God will never again be merciful ? And in fact I began to
decide that God had changed. He does *not* intend to
stretch His Hand out any more to help us.—And then he
re-reflects, and is clear that God always has helped His
People, and always will. If you have insomnia, probably
you ought to make your feet, or else your head, *warmer.*
Half of insomnia is an affair of blood-circulation. The
other half is due to your mind. It is quite useless to say :
" I *will* go to sleep." That is only an additional awakening
effort. If you say, quite serenely, " It doesn't matter whether
I go to sleep or not . . .", you have won half the battle :
you are nothing like so tired afterwards. But best of all is
not to struggle to not-think about what may be keeping
you awake, and to let your mind—without argument
—turn to *facts*, not problems : and of these *facts*, the
surest are the simplest : that God is wise, powerful, loves
me, and governs the world, my circumstances, and me
This is *certain* : in this knowledge I " sleep and take my
rest " : His fingers will be firm and gentle and cool upon
your gritty " eyelids."

VISIT THY VINE!

*Respice de caelo, et vide, et visita vineam istam!
Look down from heaven, and see—and visit this Thy
Vine!—Psalm. lxxix. 15. Fri., Terce, 2.*

1. The Psalm is of unusual beauty and pathos. Jerusalem
has been captured and ruined. The Psalmist invokes God
by glorious titles expressive of His Power, and implores
His rescue from the cruelty and mockery of the conquerors.
He recalls how God marvellously transplanted His Vine
from Egypt and tended it into luxuriant magnificence.
"Ah," he cries, "why hast Thou destroyed its walls"—
all who pass by can pick its clusters—though soon enough,
there will be none left; every wild beast tramples its
way across it!

2. So can the soul be devastated—the soul that had
been baptised, confirmed, fed upon the Holy Eucharist;
pruned by Penance. It has been intended for a great and
glorious thing: but sin has ruined it. This can be seen
in those who have *entirely* abandoned any attempt to live
the Christian life.

3. But, more often, a Catholic soul can shrink and
become unlovely though it does not die. Its promise is
unfulfilled. Innocence and early fervour evaporate; the
purity of vision becomes clouded and the sweetness of
charity soured. How can this hard, conventional-minded,
fretful man or woman be the youth or girl we knew?
The grapes are still produced, but they are acid. Even
when that is so, the divine touch restores the old-time
loveliness; and it is in such cases that we feel the *necessity*
of praying to the Holy Spirit for His interior vivifying
action. No watering, manuring, outside assistance can
really do what is needed.

TRANSCEND OUR PRIDE

Accedet homo ad cor altum et exaltabitur Deus. If a man tends towards some proud plan, yet shall God be He that is exalted.—Psalm lxiii. 7, 8. Sat., Lauds, 3.

1. Such is the sense, perhaps, of the Latin; and of the Psalm itself. It deals with the plots of the wicked against the righteous man and their ultimate defeat. The words preceding those of the text can be translated: "They examined into iniquities—they searched into them till they were exhausted." That is, they used their intelligence to the very utmost in making iniquitous plans—but however much a man may aim at proud things, it will be God who triumphs.

2. We can use and mis-use our intelligence over divine things. We are encouraged by the Church to apply our intelligence as much as we can to the Truths of Faith, and St. Anselm says that it is indolence not to. But we are not able to "comprehend" any divine Mystery: even God is not seen by us, now, face to face: it would be arrogance to fancy that we can adequately solve any of the greatest revealed Mysteries—all the more grateful are we, then, to have *had* them revealed; and to possess an infallible guide.

3. Even if we are not using our intelligence for evil, or for *proudly* probing into divine Mysteries, we can get a drying-up of the heart so that our prayer is spoilt. This is a real danger to which students or professors are exposed. Hence however "bookish" I am, I ought to ask God for opportunities for understanding, sympathising with, serving and sacrificing myself for my fellow-men. Our Lord always refreshes and consoles one who seeks so to serve *Him*. Besides the "dried" heart, there is also the obstinate mind, which will not admit even the likelihood of being

mistaken, or of *acknowledging* undoubted mistakes. This has led many a man into heresy.

MAN'S PALTRY PLOTS!

Dominus scit cogitationes hominum quoniam vanae sunt. The Lord knoweth the thoughts of men, that they are as nothing (Hebrew : are but a breath).—Psalm xciii. ... Sat., Prime, 1, 2.

1. The Hebrew did not dwell much upon abstract ideas, philosophies. *Cogitationes* means, rather, plots, devisings, schemings. The wicked unscrupulously hatch methods of achieving their ends, and say : " God will not notice."

2. Those who use this book are certainly able to attend to some at least of the false ideas that are current, and ways of looking at life and managing it, of which as Catholics we cannot approve. Therefore we need not fear, even in meditation-time, to try to make sure that we deal properly with this part of our life—the study of our Faith and of those who attack it. First, if we have any inclination to read " un-orthodox " books, we must make sure that we know what is " orthodox " properly, and have no perverse taste for the startling, or subversive, nor any contempt for Catholic literature, nor any wish to show off, or to seem " broad-minded," which too often is the same as shallow-minded.

3. However, if we choose to argue with others, we must at least know their point of view, actual doctrines, and meaning. Nothing exasperates a man so much as to find himself attacked by one who does not understand what he is attacking. Then, we need as much charity in intellectual things as when a man is physically sick. Remember that often our ideas, and phrases (like *supernatural* or *revelation*) are quite meaningless to those we are speaking to. *They* are ignorant of *us*, probably not by

P

their fault. Much good can be done by a well-informed
modest, kindly Catholic in debate or argument; but to
embark on it without very serious preparation is fatal.

IN WHAT DO WE TRUST?

*Hi in curribus, et hi in equis; nos autem in nomine
Domini Dei nostri. These trust in chariots, and those
in horses—but we, in the Name of the Lord, our God.
—Psalm xix. 8. Mon., Matins, Noct., iii, 1.*

1. This is the renunciation of the *belief* in force, even
when it is used. Too often we think of the Israelites as
blood-thirsty, or at least "militarist." They were so,
but always was there also in them the strain indicated by
verses like these. If the Psalm was sung liturgically before
battle, that makes its renunciation the more impressive.

2. Certainly, as a rule we profess to disbelieve in
coercion, and have but few chances of applying any. But
in what *do* we trust, as though, if we possessed it, it would
do anything for us? Let us *dis*trust and not use sentences
beginning with "if"—"If only I had so and so—were
here, or there—were talented thus or thus." This leads
to day-dreaming; and it is never any good speculating
on what would have happened if something else had
or had not.

3. To say one trusts in God *may* be the easier way out.
We may imagine that we need not therefore take all the
trouble possible over some task. The Israelites after all
prepared their chariots and drove them. But they did
not put their ultimate reliance upon them. It is not
material strength, nor money, that are bad; but *reliance*
on strength, and *love* of money. If, when I cannot
help someone materially, I say that I will "pray for
him," let me make very sure of doing so.—Compare
Psalm cxlvi. 10.

ON WHAT CAN I LEAN?

Fallax equus ad salutem. The horse is a cheat, as to safety!—Psalm xxxii. 17. Mon., None, 2, 3.

1. Does not the Psalmist treat the poor horse rather superciliously? After all, in Palestine (unlike Egypt or Mesopotamia) there were but few plains where a horse could be of much use in battle or even in flight. Of course he occurs here only in a list of " material " helps in which men idly put their trust—the king is not saved because of his numerous army; nor the " strong man " because of his great muscles : and however powerful be the horse, " he is a lie " if we trust in him for rescue.

2. Sometimes we may feel that " Trust God " is a platitude, or even as though God took care of mankind in the rough—" Providence " is invoked at crises or on solemn occasions—and it is not always easy for the soul to realise that the " whole " of God, so to speak, is concentrated upon *it*.

3. But the Psalmist insists. God looks out of heaven and sees every one of the sons of men. From His immutable dwelling-place He looks down upon each of the fleeting myriads that drift over the earth. He fashioned their hearts—each one of them (*sigillatim* is a strange word and ought to mean " seal-wise "—God sets a separate seal and stamp upon each. The idea, anyway, would hold good. But may it have been an accidental mis-writing for *singilatim*, one by one, each as well as all, which is certainly nearer to what the Hebrew means). God understands each act and thought of theirs. When no one else understands me, when I am a riddle to myself, what a relief to realise that God *does* understand. If I do wrong, He will punish me; but punish me *properly*, and in none of the unfair ways which are almost sure to be mixed up with any

purely human decision about me, or view of me. Yes—
what a relief to know that *God* understands ; *God* judges!

BOASTING OF SIN!

Quid gloriaris in malitia, qui potens es in iniquitate ?
Why boastest thou of evil, thou man mighty—in sins ?
—Psalm li. 1. *Wed., Prime, 2.*

1. Men exist who are proud of their mis-doings ; and
there is even a fashion of praising them—envying them—to
speak of " splendid sins." At times they seem to have
the right to boast. Everyone does seem so much stronger
than the Christian ! Constantly men boast that they have
destroyed the " orthodox " belief, or very soon will have
done so. The " lying tongue " loves every word that
" ruins " : every theory, catchword, formula, that brow-
beats the loyal Christian finds free entry into press and
on to platform—and the believer cannot get a hearing.

2. None the less, it is the Church that lasts. The Hebrew
of verse 1 is : " Why boastest thou of sin, thou mighty
man ? It is the loving-kindness of God that lasts for
ever ! " That has been seen again and again in history.
But, meanwhile, terrible destruction is worked.

3. It is true that flattery is worse. The Anti-Christian
would give anything to win the Catholic into some
compromise. Still, are we not at all to be blamed ? We
speak—but safe within our churches : we criticise and
confute, but in the columns of our own press. We talk
in short, to one another. How to make contact is our
great problem ; and often, we fear, we are cowards and
do not seek to make it. We must pray for many more
laymen able to set forth the Catholic Faith in public—
adequately, clearly, charitably. And also that we priests
may not shirk that " contact," but seize every opportunity
to make it, and, having made it, to speak courteously,

calmly, and in the language of our fellow-men. What qualities of spirit and mind this supposes! May God fit us for that! " Ut digne et competenter annuntiem evangelium! " Announce it we *must*, else we leave our vocation to apostolate to go by default.

DO WE LIVE IN VAIN?

Memorare quae mea substantia : numquid vane con-
stituisti omnes filios hominum ? Remember whereof I
am made ! surely thou hast not created all the race
of men—all for nothing ?—Psalm lxxxviii. 48. Fri.,
None, 3.

1. A Psalm that should be read continuously, and single verses ought to be selected less readily than elsewhere. Pray first that we may receive that Spirit which brought it into being, and re-act duly as its meaning reveals itself.

2. The Psalm begins with a majestic acclaim of God's greatness, and this is at all times suited to our use as a great Song of Praise. Already it mentions God's promise made to David ; but only after verse 19 is this primarily dwelt upon. Into what is said of David and his royal successors, we naturally read what is true about Our Lord and His Church. God's great Oath, sworn by Himself, holds good on yet a higher plane for those. Even should the Chosen People play false to God's Law, He will indeed chastise them; but not desert them. Then, from verse 39, the Psalmist utters the most heart-broken reproach to God. He sees the Holy City, the Temple, destroyed : the People shamed before all their neighbours —every promise seems hopelessly broken. Surely the whole of this divine history cannot have been meant to come to nothing—as it infallibly will, should God withdraw His presence and His power. At the very end, in a

doxology, *in spite of all*, God is praised, " for ever and
for ever—Amen! Amen! "

3. If we seriously apply this to the history of the Church,
and to her sufferings in many lands to-day, and to the
inevitable blackness of the future (in view, for example,
of the deliberately pagan education being forced on myriads
of children), how shall we not be brought to elicit acts of
Faith, Hope, Charity and Contrition such as we seldom
can ?

DO I WHOLLY DISAPPEAR ?

*Substantia mea apud te est : My firm foothold is with
Thee.—Psalm xxxviii. 8. Tues., Matins, Noct. iii, 3.*

1. The Psalmist finds the sight of the prosperity of the
wicked too much for him. Not only he will not comment
on it, but he will not say *anything*, partly because he feels
that nothing is any good, and, lest he break out into
murmurs against God. But that only made things worse :
his heart grew hot within him; he brooded and brooded till
the fires of wrath blazed up and he boiled over into words.

2. He was overwhelmed by the transitoriness of man.
Elsewhere, this consoled him when he saw the wicked
prospering (e.g. Ps. lxxii) ; but here he feels that even
if the wicked soon disappear, so must *he*. " Tell me
the number of my days, that I may know what still is
left to me. (The Hebrew is very different from the Latin :
but the Latin is true to the emotion of the Psalmist and
interprets him well). . . . Thou hast made my days so
few that they may be counted (in the original : " a mere
hand's-breath : four-fingers'-width ") : my very being
is as nothing before Thee. . . . Only as phantoms do men
walk to and fro : only for nothingness do they make
their turmoil. . . . Well, Lord, what then can I expect ?
All my being, my firm foot-hold, stability, is in *Thee*.
. . . Keep, then, not *Thou* silence—what else am I but

a stranger before Thee ? a pilgrim, as all my fathers were.
Relax, that I may smile again, before I depart hence, and
shall be no more."

3. Read, after this, the *Dies Irae*, which is the pro-
foundest Christian expression of what *would* be intimidation,
and dejection were it not for the stanzas that no Hebrew
could have sung. Along with the Old Testament we
renew the recognition of our nothingness before God ;
together with that of our incalculable value in His sight,
because He loves us as His children, and twice over because
of our redemption by His Son.

THOU KNOWEST ME AND DOST " WILL " ME

*Semitam meam investigasti. Thou hast searched out
(Hebrew : Thou winnowest) my path.—Psalm cxxxviii.*
3. *Fri., Vesp.,* 1, 2.

This Psalm is best meditated by reading it slowly, on
one's knees, and not by singling out verses at the expense
of the general sense. This is, God's Omnipresence, and
His incomparable understanding of all that I am. Thou
probest me—Thou knowest me : whether I sit, or stand,
Thou knowest it! Even from afar off, Thou knowest my
thoughts . . . and my road. . . . Thou fore-knowest
all my ways—there is no word upon my tongue but Thou
knowest it. . . . Thou knowest all things, the old and
the new. . . . 'Tis Thou that didst fashion me, and
clasped within Thy hand Thou holdest me. Too marvellous
is Thy knowledge for me! too sublime—I have no power
for it!—He asks how he can *fly* from God's presence ?
He cannot. High as heaven—deep as Sheol—*there* is
God. Were he to fly with the speed of light beyond the
seas—there still would God have hold of him : as for
darkness, for Him it is but as light.—Why, in my mother's
womb, where Thou wast fashioning me in secret—when

I was not even yet truly a man—Thine eyes beheld my substance : in Thy book was all my being written : day by day I was being fashioned, while as yet there was no one there.

The Psalm is an expression of overwhelming, almost paralysing awe, rather than gratitude and love. Job, too (xiii. 21 ; 27), found God's presence and intimate knowledge to be terrifying, anyway too intrusive. May that not be our " reaction " to a truth that we can realise even more deeply than the Hebrew could.

EARTHQUAKE AND AFTERWARDS

Terra tremuit et quievit cum exurgeret in iudicium Deus. The earth shook, and then was still, when God arose to judgment.—Psalm lxxv. 9, 10. Thurs., None, 2, 3.

1. This vivid verse is used in the Liturgy at Easter : in the Psalm it suggests the shock the whole world experiences when God does intervene decisively in the battle between right and wrong. It had looked as though that would never happen : then it does : and the world, after a shuddering gasp of amazement, relapses into a sort of paralysed silence, waiting for the upshot.

2. There have been heresies or perverse devotions among Catholics which induced a sort of stunned apathy in the presence of God and His majesty. Yet this is almost better than frivolity, which, together with a lack of reverence for anything great, good or beautiful, is a tendency of our age. Progressive agnosticism and material-ism reduce everything *to our own level :* the mechanical robs the world of *life.* Scientific explanations of immediate phenomena still tempt men to disregard the action of God altogether, let alone His direct action. Hence awe dis-appears from religion.

3. And yet, God's dwelling is in Salem, in the City of

Peace (verse 3). And peace must not be translated into apathy or inertia. True humility sees everything in its place, self included, and therefore gives the first place to God in everything. Forthwith I can live in peace, and profit by my chance of orderly action. The more I stand in loving awe of God, the less I shall risk *not* working for Him, with Him and through Him.

GOD MAKES MY BED

Universum stratum eius versasti in infirmitate eius.
Thou utterly changest his bed in the hour of his sickness.
—Psalm xl. 4. Tues., Sext, 1.

1. This means that God changes the sick man's bed into a bed of health. But we can "adapt" this—God "turns" the sick man's bed; "makes" it, as a careful nurse might. God wants us to think of Him in terms of tenderness.

2. Trust to this, even when friends fail you—pretence-friends may fail us and we are not surprised—yet it is better to expect sincerity and loyalty rather than treachery. The false friends in the Psalm actually *want* the Psalmist to die (6): if they visit him, their sympathy is fictitious —their heart hugs, accumulates malice; they go out; and tell their accomplices; they plot; they mutter— " *Surely* the sleeper will not rise again ? "

3. But what is that, when those of whom you *might* have expected it, thus act ? What is that, compared with treachery on the part of " the man of my peace "—the man with whom I always was at peace, intimate; in whom I *trusted*—who visited me and ate with me ? What if *he* acts treacherously towards me ?—Oh my God— grant that I, vowed maybe to your intimacy, not only to your service—" Behold, I no more call you servants— I call you friends " (John xv. 15)—I, who at all events, profess to be your Christian, your Catholic—may never

betray you! Never have to say to me: "Friend—to *what* art thou come?"

. . . . . .

We may like to think of this verse quite literally. God turns the whole of my bed upside down when I am ill. Mattress included. One has had quite enough experience of hospital nurses making beds in the most miraculous way, without hurting or even worrying you; and of how delicious it is to be in a clean, cool bed, with no wrinkles to irk you. Oh my God! the night has been so tedious! Impossible to get into a position that doesn't make one ache, that allows one to be even remotely comfortable. Then *You* come, and change everything. What is my "bed"? My state of life. "You have made your bed, and you must lie on it." No doubt I did make it—when I took my vows; when I was ordained. Or when I, as a layman, seriously undertook to serve God and not to adore the world. As a matter of fact, I would rather not think of myself as lying upon beds, comfortable or not; but, as standing up and trying to work. But I suppose my "state of life" is a sort of bed. Ecclesiastical "beds" are often extremely comfortable compared with laymen's. At least one is sure of them. . . . But it is hypocrisy to deny that from time to time any bed becomes extremely uncomfortable. O Lord, all my forgivable groaning, and my despicable whining, are before Thee. My midnight growls are by no means hidden from Thee. And all of a sudden, dear Lord, who dost not disdain to act the part of a very hospital nurse (how *should* You, when you actually used an "unjust judge" as a hint of what You were—and were *not* . . .?), a kind of Orderly in the frightful dis-comfort of a war-hospital—You come and "make my bed" so beautifully—it was worth while to have the damp, hot, knobbly "till when? till when?" discomfort, if *You* came and changed the whole of my bed in my infirmity!

VII

SACRIFICE: OUR GIFT TO GOD
ACCEPTED

To express his absolute dependence on God, Man has ever followed an instinct to give Him "gifts." Such gifts were different from all others, precisely because to *God* they were given. To express further to himself that such gifts were absolute, total and irrevocable—as no other gifts can be, for to no one save God is anything wholly and absolutely and for ever due—the custom of destroying such gifts developed. And when man was conscious of Sin, he symbolised by that destruction the fact that he himself had merited annihilation, and trusted that God would be pleased to accept partly in his stead, but also as representative of his own contrition and humiliation, the grain or the animal or the fruit that he felt to be so precious. The great law-giver, Moses, put order into the immemorial Hebrew practice of making such oblations. They were *not* wrongful in themselves. The Israelites were *not* doing wrong in offering them.

Yet it was certain that the practice of material sacrifices could and did lead to abuses. It could engender a false idea of God—as though God Himself could be pleased by blood or the destruction of anything. Also it could create a mechanical, arithmetical view of sacrifice—as though two oxen were twice as good as one. And again, it could divert attention from the essential—the sacrifice of the heart: the sense of guilt against *God*, a guilt that no human effort or gift can ever obliterate. This sacrifice of the heart, the self, is to be found, no doubt, in the Psalms: but on the whole our minds went towards that in the meditations upon sin and contrition. Here we are confining our thoughts almost wholly to the idea of the Worship of God, which at times and in special circumstances expresses itself in Sacrifice. And within this, we catch fleeting gleams of the self-offering of Christ. But, centring no doubt around the Altar, there was much else in Hebrew worship which was carried exultantly through by the People. To start with, the Israelite *liked* worshipping in active union with his fellows. He positively desired to pay his homage to God in the sight of *all* the people. He enjoyed the (to us, maybe, tempestuous) processions up to the Temple, through its courts, and round and round the Altar. We cannot expect and do not desire all nations or periods of history to behave in exactly the same way: but we are bound to declare that it is disastrous—even inhuman—when the instinct for Sacrifice to God dies out of a man or a community: that it is good if all wish to take an active and vocal *share* in the Liturgy: and that, historically, it is High Mass rather than Low which is the normal Mass. We pray then that "active participation by the People in the Liturgy" may resume its due place in our public, social religious life.

If, however, we should *wish* to think of sacrifice more especially as a Sin-Offering, we can re-read the meditations upon Sin, and work into them these thoughts on Sacrifice, and more particularly the memories of Calvary and Mass.

MY FREE-WILL SACRIFICE

Voluntarie sacrificabo tibi. With right good will will I sacrifice to Thee!—Psalm liii. 6. Sunday, Prime, 1.

1. "Sacrifice" means a gift that God accepts—a gift different from any other, because of its Recipient; and also, because it implies total worship, absolute homage, irrevocable offering, which are due to no created thing. But we take it here as the giving up of something that

we would like to keep, for the sake of something we want still more. But it is significant that the *instinct* to offer Sacrifice to God—the very linking of the idea of *God* with the word " sacrifice," has almost died out. This suggests a dying out of the very idea of God. Oh God—never die out of my mind, my desire, my *instinct* for *self*-offering.

2. The Christian life, like Christ's, is compact of " sacrifices." " He emptied Himself, taking the form of a slave " (Phil. ii. 7). We have to make a " sacrifice " to pray, when we are tired. The Christian has to sacrifice a hundred ways of making money half-dishonestly. And all self-flattery, issuing into lies. Self-worship, sure to end in cruelty—sacrificing others to Self. Grasp the nettle! All Christian life, though especially the priest's, is a self-sacrificial vocation.

3. But there is here no melancholy! God loves a " cheerful " giver (2 Cor. ix. 7). Men often display this " cheerfulness " out of sheer natural courage, even in the blackest hours. How do we respect them! May we, who have the supreme motive, never whine; never shirk; not choose the softer option. " With all my heart! " *Amen*—" So be it." *Alleluia!* " Praise be to God! "

ALONG WITH THE OTHERS . . .

Vota mea reddam Domino coram omni populo eius :
I will pay my homage to the Lord in the presence of all His people.—*Psalm cxv.* 5, 9. *Mon., Vesp.,* 2.

1. The Psalmist constantly says that he will *publicly* give praise and thanks to God. " My praise shall be given to Thee in the great assembly ; I will pay my vows in the sight of all them that fear Him " (Psalm xxi. 26). He did this because Orientals are more communicative (though also more secretive!) than we are ; because he felt himself of one flesh and blood with his fellow-Jews ;

because, were he the king, he owed it to his people to lead and give example to them : because God never does give us our graces for ourselves alone.

2. The Priest is by vocation a " public man," however small his parish. He represents his flock before God—and to a great extent also before men. He says Mass publicly : on Sundays he *has* to say it not only for the people but in their presence. Scrupulous punctuality : neither hustle nor dragging : no personal eccentricities. It is his sacrifice, but also theirs.

3. If I am not a priest, still I go to Mass along with others, not to look at them—least of all to make myself looked at. That would be deliberately to distract attention from God to myself, and be sinful. If non-Catholics are present, they will watch the people even more than the Sacrifice : if they see them convinced, reverent, *worshipping*, they will be moved to think well of the Faith : if irreverent, they will assume that they care in reality nothing about it ; that Catholic worship is " mere form." The Commandment about the Sabbath was tenderly careful that the " stranger " too " within thy gates " should profit by the Sabbath—even, presumably, the Gentile visitor. Hence for his sake, too, I should be careful—but mainly for *God's ;* and if I am indeed to offer Him a " sacrifice of Praise " (8), I shall *want* to have as many people helping me as I can.

　　　　．　　　．　　　．　　　．

Verse 1. Cf. 2 Corinthians iv. 13. The sense of the Latin is : " I *believe*, and that is why I (dare to) say : I am utterly humbled. In my desperation did I say : ' Every man is a liar.' " But even so—all the same—" How can I make an adequate return to *God?* " God does not fail me, nor cheat! I have been rescued—I lift up the thanksgiving-cup of rescue! I will acknowledge this publicly! Not a light thing in God's eyes is the slaying of His Saints—so He has rescued me! Me, His servant born actually within His household! Before all men, then, in His very Temple, will I acknowledge this!— Priests will have no difficulty in applying this psalm to their own conditions.

NOT FOR EVER OUT OF TOUCH

Quare tristis es, anima mea, et quare conturbas me?
Why be sad, my soul? and why shouldst thou disquiet
me?—Psalm xli. 5. Tues., Sext., 2, 3.

1. The song of every exiled yet trusting soul. The Psalmist is far from his home, and from the Temple— he yearns for them. When shall he again stand within God's Sanctuary? Where he is, he can join in no worship: his pagan associates mock him and ask what has become of his God? He goes over and over again in memory the happy days when he joined in the True Worship: his heart is bruised: his spirit aches. Still, he pacifies himself: "Trust thou in God; for I shall yet give Him thanks— the salvation of my countenance, my GOD!"

2. Have we any of that appetite for Mass? for the very church? Are Sundays irksome to us? Are we relieved when legitimately dispensed? Am I almost annoyed when a holiday of obligation comes round? Do I arrange my holidays quite regardless of whether Mass will be accessible?

3. My exile may indeed be physical. I may have to live in the country where no church *is* accessible. Do I do anything on a Sunday which shows that I would go to Mass if I could? Or I may be ill. How do I compensate for being deprived of Mass? But my exile may be of a different sort. My soul seems isolated: God seems "far off." Nothing can please Him better than my going on trusting Him even when He seems to have withdrawn Himself; yes, even when *I* have withdrawn myself by sin.

.   .   .   .

Verse 5, in the Hebrew, means : "I brood on this, and
pour out my soul within me—how I used to pilgrimage
with the throng, moving slowly towards the House of
God, among exultation and praise—a festival multitude!"
And now he is kept far from all that! How should he *not*
be grieved ? Yet, in spite of all, he must not be! (Verses
9, 10). (For) in the daytime doth God send forth to me
His Mercy—Yea, in the night the song of His praise is with
me! (So—). A prayer to the God of my *life !* To God
will I say : "Thou art my Protector . . ." and the rest.
—We know of no method of adequately explaining the
reference to Hermon, near where the Jordan rises and
proceeds in cataracts. Possibly the Psalmist was there, and
could not leave the district for Jerusalem.

IN TO GOD'S ALTAR!

Introibo ad altare Dei ; ad Deum qui laetificat iuventutem
meam. I will go in to the Altar of God—to God, who
gave joy to my youth.—Psalm xlii. 4. Tues., Lauds, 2.

1. This Psalm doubtless formed part of one song with
Psalm xli ; certainly its mood is similar, and so is its
refrain. It should anyhow be studied carefully, if only
because it always occurs at Mass save in Masses for the
Dead. To love it will certainly ensure my arriving in
good time for Mass, if I am a layman : and will help my
concentration if I am a priest. Servers should learn to recite
their part carefully, and not to overlap the priest; else so
much of the continuity of the Psalm is lost! It becomes
hard for the priest to attend to more than his own half of it.

2. Many feel anxious—perhaps too anxious—because
of the thought that in their youth they were nearer to
God than they have become under the pressure of business
and the disillusionments of life. No doubt a youthful
effervescence of piety may have simmered down : this

need not mean that the reality or substance of my religion has deteriorated. The astonishments, excitements, discoveries of youth disappear because of experience. Often the Saints undergo their more thrilling ecstasies at the beginning of their career. A series of flashes becomes a steady glow : thunderclaps change into a solemn continuous music. The soul becomes able to see in some single truth and all the while, what it learnt by fragments, or only now and then, when it could bear it. May such be our development.

3. Yet it is possible for us to become deadened. The impermanence of created things may indeed have disillusioned us. The inferiority of our own character and its seeming incurableness may tire us out and leave us too discouraged to try. But God is the selfsame : He *is :* we never have cause *in Him* for disillusionment.

. . . . .

Verse 3 probably means : " Send forth Thy Light and Thy Truth (Loyalty ; fidelity to His Promise), and they shall lead me—or, that they may lead me—back to Thy Holy Hill and to Thy Dwelling "—escort me back to where once I was so happy. This is more according to the trend of this and the previous Psalms. But also we can use the Latin : " It was ever they that led me, on my long-ago pilgrimage, to Sion and to its Temple. Send them forth yet again, and once more shall I go in to the Altar of God—to God who will give joy to my older years, even as He did to my youth."

I HAUNT GOD'S ALTAR

Circumdabo altare tuum Domine : I will go round Thine Altar, Lord !—Psalm xxv. 6. Wed., Prime, 1.

1. The Priest recites part 2 of this Psalm while he washes his fingers after the Offertory. The Choir originally

sang it at this point, because his fingers had genuinely been soiled by handling the gifts that the People brought up. The reason has now disappeared, but the washing remains, and there is a risk of the Psalm's becoming a sort of " interim occupation." Perhaps the verses *Circumdabo . . . Domine, dilexi . . .* can " come to life," light themselves up, and illuminate the rest.

2. I have loved—I love—the beauty of Thy House— the place where Thy Glory dwelleth! And yet, many of our churches—so small, poor, even shoddy! But " art " is not what really gives them their glory. Westminster or Canterbury are just as architecturally beautiful as ever, but the life has gone out of them : any tin-roofed, wooden- or mud-walled chapel in Australia or Africa, that contains the Blessed Sacrament, is now more " magnetic" than they.

3. " I will go round and round Thine Altar." In great Basilicas I can do this, or in churches where the High Altar has an " ambulatory " behind it. Perhaps the Psalmist saw himself moving in procession round and round the altar in the great Temple Court. Perhaps he meant that he was " magnetised " by the Altar, and that from every angle he came back to it. Those responsible for churches might reflect whether really it is fitting to hide *e.g.*, Benediction candlesticks behind the altar or even to store odds and ends within it as within a cupboard, or to decorate only the front of it. Decoration is a Sacrifice to God not a bait for the people. Compare verses 1, 4, 5, 12 with Psalm i.

And note (verse 7) that the Psalmist wishes both to listen *and* to be " vocal," to chant of God's marvels.

I FAINT FOR GOD'S ALTAR

Concupiscit et deficit anima mea in atria tua, Domine.
My spirit yearns, yea, faints for Thy halls, O Lord.—
Psalm lxxxiii. 1. Fri., Sext., 1.

1. The thought is simple—may it be sincere! The sparrow finds its home—the dove, a nest: even so, my homing spirit makes for Thine altars, Lord; Thy tent! O happy they whose lot it is to *dwell* within Thy House! Even one day there is worth a thousand outside of it: to be the simplest servant in that House is better than to be master in any sinful palace.

2. The Priest especially is encouraged to love, to haunt, ever to revert to that Altar where he performs incomparably the most tremendous action of his day: where Christ is "always at home." Anyone who is responsible for Jesus Christ being "at home" in yet another Tabernacle has achieved a wonderful, a heavenly work in the world and in his life. May all the laity feel that they *need* to hark back to the material church itself, as to their home, for the sake of the Tabernacle in it.

3. But then every human heart is at least the potential Dwelling-Place of God. Either He *is* there, by Grace; or He is trying to be. And we are right to go further, and remember that so long as men and women, and their children, have not got decent houses in which to live, it is harder for them—humanwise and short of special graces—to keep their souls fit for their divine inhabitant.

·　　·　　·　　·　　·

Verse 6: *Ascensiones*, means directly the pilgrimages up to Mount Sion on which the Psalmist had set his heart: but we can also see that thus to make the Altar the sublime centre of our life draws us ever higher out of the sorrowful lowlands of mere materialism or tepidity. And far from wearying, we shall go (8) "from strength to strength," till we contemplate our very God in Heaven.—In verse 7 the Hebrew beautifully says: "Going through the Valley of Tears, they make it a place of springs!" Tears are salt and bitter and sterile: love changes them into "waters of refreshment," cool, sweet, fertilising.

GUARD THOU MY SOUL!

*Custodi animam meam. Guard Thou my soul !—Psalm
xxiv. 20. Tues., Prime.*

1. This is an " alphabetic " Psalm, so that its sentences are separately significant rather than forming a
close-woven texture. Yet how many lovable lines it
contains! " The sins of my youth and my ignorant
acts—remember them not!—O Lord, be good to my
sin, for it is great!—My eyes strain ever towards the
Lord . . . look back towards me, and have pity on me
—for I am all alone and poor. . . . Guard Thou my
life! *Guard* me! "

2. " May the Body of Our Lord, Jesus Christ, guard
thy soul—unto eternal life. . . ." So speaks the Priest
when giving Holy Communion. Perhaps he can protect
the act from becoming mechanical by concentrating now
on one word of the formula, now on another : " thy *soul*
—His *Body*—*eternal* life—"why, even upon " unto," or
" into " : the act is not a final one : what a process, a
fleeting series of changes, must yet be this Communicant's!
May it not be out of place, even here, to remind the laity
that they must not make it difficult for the Priest thus to
concentrate on what is spiritual, nor force him to think
of the physical element of his act only. Head not drooped
far forward : mouth properly open : lips not exorbitantly
painted with risk of sullying his fingers or even the Sacred
Species : tongue not snapped suddenly back : no hat
or veil that can *interfere*.

3. The thought of God's guardianship is sweet. Even
the officer, before battle, said : " I shall forget Thee this
day : forget not Thou me! " Legitimate pleasure ;
business ; sleep itself : " He slumbers not, nor sleeps—
the Guardian of Israel! " (Psalm. cxx. 4). The humble

Humanity of our Lord stands sentinel over the susceptible, easily beset, very foolish soul. May He be a Soul within our soul!

O GUARD MY SOUL!

Custodi animam meam quoniam sanctus sum. Guard my soul, for I am Thine Elect.—Psalm lxxxv. 2. Fri., Compline, 3.

1. How can we possibly say: "for I am holy"? We know we are not: if we were, we would not think we were: if we said we were, we would not be. But "sanctus" really means "selected," segregated; put aside for some special purpose by God. David was still the "holy" king even when he sinned: the Land and Jerusalem were always "holy" despite their crimes. Not even now are they finally rejected.

2. In how many ways has God chosen me! I need not even have been born. I still live. I am a Christian; I pray—I put myself into vital touch with God. Anyone has his special "purpose" in life, simply because God cannot act *without* a purpose: but why should I have these special privileges unless He has some special purpose for me? O God, let me fulfil the whole of that special purpose! I cannot see what it is, or was, until I can look back upon it from "afterwards": but I know by faith than I *am* His true adopted son, brother of Jesus Christ, and "son of His handmaiden" (verse 16).

3. If I am a priest, or religious, or called to become one, that is a further selection. People talk of a "holy" priest—they *can* do so, in the sense of "selected"; they ought to be able to do so in the sense of "morally" holy. Yet if I am not selected for that, I cannot but be selected for something: "non in vanum"—not for nothing does God create us human men and women. No wonder we ask Him to "safeguard" our souls. At Communion

the Priest always prays that Our Lord may " guard " our souls unto eternal life.

.   .   .   .   .

The Psalm is, however, not only a prayer for personal protection, but full of " missionary " hope. " All the Peoples that Thou hast made shall come, and shall do homage before Thee, O Lord, and give glory to Thy Name " (9) : but as though realising that this was indeed a distant hope, a tremendous assertion, the Psalmist recalls that " Thou alone art great, and marvel-working —Thou alone art God! " The prayer and the hope are all the more courageous, because at the moment the Psalmist feels himself overwhelmed by " the hordes of the mighty " (14) ; he requires to be rescued from the nethermost abyss. There is, however, a profound difference between the Old and the New Testament " hope "—again and again, in the Old, we are told that the Gentiles shall " come " to God, shall flow together towards Jerusalem. Christ tells us to " go! " His apostles must not stay merely waiting. Such was the Good Shepherd who sought for the lost sheep until He found it. Contrast the " Elder Son " in the parable of the Prodigal. He stayed at home, and actually grudged his brother's return. *Our* Elder Brother travelled into our far country, and *brought* us back, at His own very heavy cost.

LIFT HIGH YOUR GATES, MY SOUL

Attollite portas, principes, vestras . . . et introibut rex gloriae. Lift up your gates, ye princes . . . and the King of Glory shall come in !—Psalm xxiii. 9. Mon., Prime, 1.

1. The Hebrew is : " Lift up your heads, ye Gates ; and lift yourself up high, ye everlasting doors! " The Ark, or the King, is approaching the rock-citadel of Sion.

The very gates are invoked to lift their lintels higher still, to admit the towering Majesty of the Lord. The Choir begins by proclaiming the Paramountcy of God: the crowds, maybe, therefore ask who then can be allowed to accompany Him into His Sanctuary? " The pure of hand! the clean of heart! " The righteous, as in act, so in will. The Procession then demands admittance for the King of Glory. From within, it is asked: " Who *is* this ' King of Glory ' ? " None but God Himself. Such is this magnificent brief drama.

2. Yet contrast it with Christ's coming to the soul as described in Apocalypse iii. 20. " Behold—I am standing at the door and am knocking. If any man hear My voice and open to Me, I will come in to him, and eat with him, and he with Me." How quiet; not trumpetings, but the gentle though urgent knocking of a hand that has been wounded. No command or even demand : " *if* any man hears . . . is kind enough to admit Me . . ." Not a flamboyant festal banquet, but the intimate association of one with One.

3. All the same, my Communions are triumphant feasts with the Lord—infinitely beyond any royal " command " banquet in an earthly palace. Nor must I ever forget that to enter into Communion with the One, *involves* me in Communion with all who are in Communion with Him. Intimate though my Communions be, they are not meant to be a private prerogative : I am *intended* to consolidate thereby my communion with all who are " in Christ," or are called to be. And all are thus called.

SING, MY SOUL!

Ascendit Deus in iubilo : God has gone up amid triumph-shouts.—*Psalm xlvi.* 5. *Mon., Lauds,* 1.

1. The expression was first used of triumphal processions of the Ark, but afterwards on any triumphal occasion that

seemed suitable. We shall be out of tune with many Psalms if there is no triumph in our lives. Liturgically, the Corpus Christi *Pange Lingua* expresses this spirit supremely well, and uses Psalm cxlvi. 1 (Thursday, Lauds). *Sit laus plena, sit sonora, sit iucunda, sit decora,* etc. We have to remember that triumph-less as the Christ-less world certainly is, Our Lord *is* triumphing in Himself, and carrying off triumphs in souls.

2. But we have other triumph-hymns—the *Vexilla Regis;* the Passion-Tide *Pange Lingua*. We have the triumphant feast of the Exaltation of the Cross. A Kempis rightly speaks of the " Royal " Way of the Holy Cross. We wish therefore to be spiritually triumphant in material defeats. We must never plaintively ask why we should *suffer*—why *we* should suffer!

3. The Imitation with real rapture cries : " I have taken —up have I taken—from *Thy* hand the Cross : I have carried it, and carry it I will—right to the very end! " That is no stunned pagan acquiescence! That is the enthusiastic Christian acceptance. Not " any cross but this one! "

BE AT REST, MY SOUL!

Haec requies mea in saeculum saeculi—hic habitabo quoniam elegi eam. This is My resting-place for ever and ever : here will I dwell, for here is where I have chosen.—Psalm cxxxi. 14. Wed., Vesp., 5.

1. The direct theme of the Psalm is the pilgrimage of the Ark throughout its history, and the determination of David to build a proper home for it, and the establishment there of the Messianic King. But it is a superb Psalm for all priests, and indeed for all who want to help in building churches or even caring for the Tabernacle. " I will give no sleep to my eyes—no slumber to my eyelids—no rest to my aching head—Till I shall have

found an abiding place for the Lord—a dwelling for the
God of Jacob " (4, 5).

2. " Let Thy priests be clothed with righteousness "
(9). Priests long to be prayed for! A priest's task,
adequately done, is beyond all human strength, even
allowing for his ordination-graces. God does not do
everything through the Sacraments, but expects co-operation
of every sort, and one sort is, the prayer of the laity for
priests. May the laity respond more and more consciously :
" Et cum spiritu tuo," when the Priest prays : " Dominus
vobiscum! "—May the Lord be with you! Oh, to have
all the laity praying throughout Mass that the Lord may
be with the spirit of the Priest!

3. " I will clothe her priests with salvation " (16).
The clothes become as it were part of the personality.
The Priest becomes wrapped up in, compenetrated with,
Salvation. God's Saving Power soaks into him : and he
exhales it in his turn. A priest can never be un-priested
any more than one can be un-baptised. But how may
our baptismal robe, our priestly vestment, become stained
and tattered!

.   .   .   .   .

The last two lines are to be regarded as spoken by
God—" Here is My resting-place for ever—Here will I
dwell, because I have desired it—chosen it." David had
sworn an oath (2) that he would bring the Ark to that
resting-place—" We heard of that oath in Ephratha; we
learned of it in the ' forest-fields,' or wild wooded
country " (6). Now Ephratha means " fruit-lands," so
the Psalm may mean that people in the fertile south, and
again in the wilder less cultivated north, *i.e.*, throughout
the land, had been apprised of David's determination. But
David's own town, Bethlehem, is thrice called " Ephratha "
(Mic. v. 2 ; Gen. xxxv. 19 ; Ruth iv. 11) ; and indeed
it is natural that Bethlehem should know the will of Him
who had given it such glory owing to His birth there. So

parallelism suggests that "wilds of the woods" is also a proper name; it would then be the "Town of the Forest" where the Ark remained neglected till it was taken to Sion (1 Kings vii. 2). But the words may very well be taken up by priests, who have resolved for ever to serve the Ark, the Tabernacle, in God's churches; and, more widely still, they can be spoken by every loyal Catholic, who prays for God's grace that he may remain for ever in His Church, and serve Him there.

ETERNAL PRIESTHOOD

Sacerdos in aeternum, secundum ordinem Melchisedech: A priest forever, after the manner of Melchisedech.—Psalm cix. 4. Sunday, Vesp., 1.

1. The Divine King, the Messias, is proclaimed also Priest—even as the ancient king of Sion, Melchisedech, was also priest (Gen. xiv. 18). The Psalm, therefore, sees in God's Anointed at once the everlasting King and Priest and Judge. Though this fierce chant is not what would have been written about Our Lord since we have known Him as man, we must not let our response to His " meekness and gentleness " eclipse our true sense of awe in His regard. St. John in his Apocalypse does not allow that to happen.

2. St. Paul (Hebrews) traces Christ's priestly " descent " from that ancient king rather than from Aaron, partly because His own sacrifice, ever-enduring, now involves no more blood-shedding, and our own probably will not do so, though how many martyrdoms has our own generation seen! But in any case, Sacrifice must be the centre-point of every Christian: nor only of ordained priests. We all must offer all that we are, together with all that Our Lord is, to His Father.

3. Mass is certainly the central *act* of our spiritual life;

but by uniting ourselves, through a sincere act of the will, to Our Lord, we can be "priests" not only for ever but all the time. We can incorporate our lives with that Mass which is going on all the while somewhere within the world; and with that eternal offering which is exhibited before God "on Thine Altar on high" (Canon of the Mass).

ACCEPTABLE SACRIFICE (I)

Si esuriero, non dicam tibi. If I am hungry, I will not tell thee.—Psalm xlix. 12. Wed., Matins, Noct., iii. 1.

1. Austere Psalm, that must humble but not discourage us. God does not need us nor any of our material services. Verses 1–8 describe the majestic Advent of the Lord, and the collecting of His People before Him. He says: "It is not in the matter of your sacrifices that I will rebuke you—why! your whole-burnt-offerings are ever before Me. But I will not accept calves from your farms, nor kids from among your flocks! For Mine (already) are all the wild beasts of the woods, yes, and the herds and oxen on the hills. I know every bird that flies; the beauty of the fields lies open to Me. If I am hungry, I will not tell thee—appeal to thee . . . for Mine is the round world and all that is in it. Am *I* to eat the flesh of bulls? or drink the blood of kids? Ah! Offer *praise* to God, as sacrifice! To Him that is high above all, pay thou thy homage. *Then* shalt thou call on Me in thy day of trouble, and I will rescue thee."

2. We no more offer blood-sacrifices to God: but we work for Him; we may wear ourselves out with work that seems—and humanwise is—necessary, and very likely with work that seems just desirable; or even, done purely for God's sake. But I can become "attached" to work begun purely for God. I get ill. My work is interfered

with; not supported; stopped by authority. Do I think
that something fatal has happened? Even disastrous,
though no worse? or even, just galling? God had no
need of *any* of that work. The whole question is, whether
He wanted me to do it. So long as I honestly think He
does so want it, let me do it: but let me not force it on
Him, nor on my fellow-men.

3. Do I pray about my work? I must not cheat myself,
nor bluff God with " laborare est orare "—Work is
Prayer. That is true—thus: When I ought to work, I
should not " say my prayers "; when I ought to pray,
I must not *substitute* exterior work. For which have I a
taste? On my guard, about *that!* Re-read Psalm cxxvi.
1, 2.

ACCEPTABLE SACRIFICE (II)

*Peccatori autem dixit Deus : Quare tu enarras iustitias
meas. . . . Existimasti, inique, quod ero tui similis?
But to the sinner did God say : " Why dost thou set
forth My righteous law . . .? Didst thou suppose,
wicked man, that I was like to thee? "—Psalm xlix.
16. Wed., Matins, Noct., iii. 2.*

1. This part of Psalm xlix is even more alarming, and
seems to silence the sinner altogether. At first, God had
been upbraiding the righteous for too exterior a service.
Here He bitterly upbraids the sinner for claiming in any
way to be His spokesman. True, He sets the " scale " of
sins very high—adultery, theft, identifying oneself with
the wicked (" off you ran with him! "). We trust that
God preserves us from these greater sins. But sinner or
not, every professing Catholic to some extent claims to
speak for God: and the priest, how guilty so-ever he
feels himself, must do so.

2. But alas if we even feel just self-satisfied! God is
not so. If He does not rebuke us, He is keeping silence,

and that is still worse. " Did you really think, sinner, that I was like you? " Cared no more than you did? No! The time will come when I shall challenge you, and confront you to your face. Realise that—you that forget God! Lest God lay hold of you, and there be none to rescue you!

3. May I pray that there be in me no so deep-seated a clash between my words and works, so profound a dis-harmony, that I do not even realise it! Onlookers may see that there *is* : even, that my salient fault is just what I would deny had any place in me. Oh God—send into me Thy Holy Spirit, to burn, rinse, re-create my innermost!

SELF'S SACRIFICE

Eduxit me de lacu miseriae et de luto faecis, et statuit super petram pedes meos. He drew me out forth from the dreadful pit, out of the mire and slime, and set my feet upon a rock.—Psalm xxxix. 2, 3. Tues., Terce.

1. The Psalmist begins by acknowledging God's rescue, and how a new song was once more upon his lips—a psalm of gratitude. Then he proceeds to ask what return he can make.

2. Sacrifice and burnt-offerings were not Thy will—but ears hast Thou opened for me: burnt-offering and sin-offering hast Thou not demanded of me—so then I said : ' Lo, I myself am here! " In the scroll of a book it is written of me that I should do Thy Will—My God! that *will* I—and (to do) Thy Law is in the midst of my heart! " (This translation corresponds exactly neither to Hebrew nor to Latin : it tries to give the sense without altering the Breviary words too much.) " Ears hast Thou digged —pierced—for me " may mean no more than " opened," that I should hear, but much more probably refers to the piercing of a slave's ear (Ex. xxi. 6 ; Deut. xv. 17)

and the fastening of the pointed instrument to the door-
post: thus the slave was admitted to the " family." The
point throughout is that God does not require material
sacrifices, but service—even though this may mean—and
should—the gift of our whole self.

3. In Hebrews x. 5–7 the verses are quoted according
to the Septuagint " but a body hast Thou prepared for
me," and the whole passage is referred to Our Lord,
whose one sacrifice of Himself for ever annulled the
ancient sacrifices of animals. Any book upon the Psalms
ought easily to show how the change occurred: but,
during meditation, we reflect again on Christ's total
self-sacrifice, which, since He took up our human nature,
is indeed a human one, and owing to our incorporation
with Him, becomes ours. Mass must last all day.

VIII

COURAGEOUS APOSTOLATE

It is difficult to be sure that the Jew felt he had any personal mission actively to work for the conversion of the world. He often felt that the world *would* be converted: that all men would worship the Lord and flow towards Jerusalem: but that is more clearly announced by the Prophets than by the Psalmist. The Psalm included in the book of Tobit (xiii. 4, 5) contains, however, the strong assertion: "For this hath He scattered you among the Heathen, who know Him not—that you should narrate His wondrous works, and make them understand that there is no other God Almighty save Himself. So regard what He hath done with us, and with fear and trembling give praise to Him. So turn ye, O sinners, and work righteousness before God!" But on the whole, what was to impress the Gentiles consisted in the *sight* of the redemption of the Jews from captivity, and the Victories of God. We cannot find here much sense of an "apostolate." The Gentiles, if converted, would be so by sheer force of events. However, there is much in the Psalms about the *character* needed by Apostles—above all, firmness of soul and reliability, and enthusiasm and the desire to do *great* things for God. In the first of the following group of meditations, we do not profess to be doing more than attaching a meaning to the Latin words that they *can* bear; and, more often than elsewhere, perhaps, it is the "applied" sense that we may be using in this section. But this group of meditations seems rightly placed here, if only because the Psalmist always perceived his "conversion" from sin as issuing forthwith into the proclamation of God's goodness both to his immediate environment and to the world at large.

THE WORD AT WORK

*Dominus dabit verbum evangelizantibus, virtute multa.
The Lord shall entrust His Word to His Evangelists
with great power.—Psalm lxvii. 12.   Thurs., Matins,
Noct., ii.*

1. It is well-known that this Psalm (which contains fragments from very ancient hymns) is, in many parts, unintelligible, save that it must be a chant of triumph over enemies. Still, it contains many single verses which, taken at the face-value of the Latin, can inspire us ; *e.g.* verses 1, 7 (*unius moris* does not really mean "men of one mind," "like-minded men"—a very good idea of a Community—but "men of solitary disposition," or rather, just "lonely men": God gives them a home); 19, 20, 29 (confirma hoc, etc.). As for verse 20, its direct meaning is that God will entrust the victory-song to messengers, or proclaimers, in great force—by which we may mean that they are very numerous (and may our preachers be so!) or that they sing powerfully. But we accept it as translated above.

2. God powerfully entrusts His Word to all whose office it is to preach, and indirectly to all Catholics, whose duty it is in some way or other to herald forth their faith. But it is *His* word, entrusted by *Him*. Meditate the little Prayer before the Gospel. "Cleanse my heart and my lips . . . by Thy free mercy deign Thou me to cleanse, that I may fittingly proclaim *Thy* Gospel. May the Lord be in my heart and on my lips, that fittingly and competently " I may declare *His* good tidings.

3. Once more, then, we have to work as though all depended on us—prepare our material ; practise our voice if need be, strive to understand our audience—

and yet, to abdicate all that " our," and trust as though all depended upon God, as though all were " His," as indeed it is. Effect produced by me as *me* would be exactly co-extensive with *my* talents—I may impress; but I cannot *save*.

.   .   .   .   .

Bonorum meorum non indiges. Thou hast no need of my good things.—Psalm xv. 2.

This thought can humble us, when we are prevented from doing a good work—God does not *need* that I should do it. Others perhaps will do it (does that make me jealous ?); or it may not be done at all (then at least I am not responsible : if I grumble, and kick at what prevented me, I am embittering a situation which might have been embalmed with the myrrh of self-sacrifice); or God may—He certainly *can*—do it in His own way. Thus I can entrust the matter to Him, with far greater peace of mind and security than if I had to do it myself. For it is at least probable that I shall do even a good thing *partly* awry.

THE ESCALADE

In Deo meo transgrediar murum. In the power of my God will I escalade the wall !—Psalm xvii. 30. Mon., Matins, Noct., ii.

1. The Psalmist has been in great distress. But he cries to God, and God appears in all the stormy splendours of Sinai. Then He accomplishes the full rescue of His suppliant —sets his feet " in a wide space " : He saves him, because He *wills* him : He takes delight in him : He has chosen him and never will desert him.

2. Thereupon the chosen King starts upon his career, unafraid of the future, and able to do much more than he

thought he could. No obstacle should defeat him : walls are built across his path—he joyously escalades them. We are obviously not to attempt what seems impossible if there is no *point* in doing so ; but the moment I see that a thing is *right*, then however impossible the matter seems, let me attempt it! God *does* often ask for the humanwise " impossible."

3. On the whole, we are too timorous. The expression " inferiority complex " has become significantly popular. We can easily understand a man's shrinking from decisions, actions which imply " far hopes," and trust in the future, if he has no sense of divine backing. But we, who do trust in *God*, are right to be on the optimistic side : to be audacious : to plan largely. Especially the priest, whose vocation is a creative one, is right to be hopeful, enterprising, undefeatable by any " lion in his path! "

.   .   .   .   .

Verses 26, 27, are strange. " Towards the pious, Thou wilt show Thyself gracious : towards the righteous, Thou wilt act with righteousness : with the forthright (straight-forward, honourable) Thou dealest with directness : with the crafty, craftily." So far as we can see, the Psalmist intended to declare that God treated men according as they treated Him—if they were honest, there would be no ambiguity in His methods of disposing of their lives : if they tried to " cheat " Him, He would be found to have been at " cross-purposes " with them, however much they had seemed, at first, to prosper. It is quite true that God's justice is perfect : He *cannot* give a false verdict ; and if a man has consistently defied Him, that man will with accurate righteousness be punished. But *we* are well aware that God is in all things taking the initiative : He does not wait to see what a man will do, and then decide on His course of action accordingly : He is always " first in the field " with His grace ; always *first* with His inspirations and solicitations to contrition: "while we were yet sinners, Christ died for us"; it was not *we* who caused God to send His Son into our world: there is not and cannot be any accurate "equivalence" between man and God—and at times the Psalmist too knows that full well.

.   .   . .   .   .

Cogitaverunt consilia quae non potuerunt stabilire. They devised schemes that they could not bring to fulfilment. —*Psalm xx. 12.*

We make plans, and are right in doing so. We *ought* to have high hopes. We ought not too much to distrust ourselves—nor our fellowmen who, we fear, will not co-operate—and certainly not God. Yet it is indeed rare to see our hopes fulfilled! Even a small part of them! This is partly because the further we get, the wider the horizons that open out before us. But also, because, do what we will, we trust to some extent to ourselves *as* ourselves. Then God shows us our weakness. We did not "count the cost" (Luke xiv. 28). And the cost is, detachment from our dearest plans. Perhaps God does not want them at all! But persevere till that is made certain! He will certainly want more from us than we guess! only perhaps not what we had proposed to do. But He will get it, from the detached heart, without one's even knowing that He is doing so. We shall see, at least in heaven, that He has done so.

AT FULL SPEED

Exultavit ut gigas ad currendam viam. Like some hero, so exulted he to run his course.—*Psalm xviii. 6. Mon., Prime, 2.*

1. The skies proclaim God's glory—especially the Sun does so, exulting to run his daily course—"from one

end of the heavens is his forth-going, and to the other end his path—not one may hide himself from his heat." I, whatever my station, have the vocation to manifest God to the world, and I wish to do so exultantly, with exhilaration, not in any shamefaced way.

2. Perhaps I feel my spirits dashed if they exhort me to be " prudent " ; not to " force religion, let alone myself, on anyone." This may be good advice ; but I shall not need it if I am modest ; that is, if in my energetic performances I do not seek or even want to thrust myself forward, but am ready to work hard quite without recognition—" Himself shall do it! "

3. But the responsibility of the elderly, or the timid, or the victims of human respect, is very great if they damp the ardour of young men or enthusiastic persons, like young curates fresh from the fervent ideals of their seminary. They may be quixotic, impulsive, even exasperating, and are clearly inexperienced. Yet I may turn to see what has happened to my own hopes and fervour. . . . May I always look, first, not for difficulties, weak points, flaws ; but begin by welcoming, and go on by fostering and guiding, even if I foresee that the scheme cannot wholly succeed. Perhaps the young enthusiast may make more of it than I ever could! Then I have not to be jealous.

.   .   .   .   .

It became traditional to regard the " heavens " as the Apostles, and the allegorical language of the Middle Ages loved so to use the word. The Psalm however definitely means us to read God's message in the skies—day proclaims it to day—night to night whispers it—yet " Neither speech, nor words—No voice of theirs is heard " (Hebrew) ; still, into all the world goes forth their declaration. In verse 6, the Hebrew says that God gives its dwelling-place to the sun, which is better than the Latin, which says that God sets up His own tent in the sun. The picture is that of the sun issuing forth from his bridal chamber, and exulting to run his daily course—"Not one can hide himself from his heat!" And, even as the Sun illuminates the material earth, so does God's Law give light to the spiritual world.

WEAKNESS STRONG IN GOD

In Deo faciemus virtutem. In God shall we do strong things !—Psalm lix. 12. Wed., None, 3.

1. We need not trouble over the details of this obscure war-psalm. But we will ask God to give us a *holy ambition*. "Who will lead me into the fortified city ? Who will lead me forth even into Edom ? Surely *Thou*, O God—who dost drive us *back !* who marchest forth no more with our armies!" (verse 11, 12. Edom was immemorially hostile to the Hebrew). There are times when everything seems to go wrong—personal things ; parochial things ; Catholic life itself. God seems to desert His People. They try to do what they should, but nothing succeeds. Even if they are not actively persecuted, a sort of paralysis seems to affect Catholic endeavour. Everyone else seems more enthusiastic than we! This is the very time for reviving hopes higher than ever.

2. There is no virtue in hoping for small things only. The Psalm wishes to march into the heart of the hostile country. Certainly the " city " would be fortified. Resistance would be intense. But what of it ? Great things! great prowess! God's Will is the sole limit of my hope, and though I do not want to outstrip His Will, it is certainly not for me to dictate limits to *that !*

3. But it will always be *in God* that I must do what I do! It is a probing practice to renounce deliberately, before God, one's personal hopes and plans. To renounce them, not in the sense of no more trying, but of no longer

clinging to them should they not be according to God's intention. Then only am I free to adhere wholly to what *is* God's intention; and in Him I shall do *great* things.

THE STEADY HEART

Paratum cor meum, Deus ! My heart is fixed, O God !
—Psalm cvii. 1. Sat., Prime, 3.

1. *Paratum*, in Hebrew, meant fixed, determined, unshakable, rather than " ready," *i.e.,* " prompt." The pagan poet (Lucretius) spoke of his " infirma voluntas "; that his will should be weak was a grief to him. The Missal more than once speaks of " nutantia corda," our vacillating hearts; and of man's " fragility "—brittleness. Which of us has not suffered from the fact that he sees, no doubt, quite clearly, what he ought to do, but hesitates *about* doing it ? The two meanings alluded to above really follow on one another. If my will is fixed and determined, I readily do what I ought.

2. St. Francis Borgia said that in his day those who were ready to act, had not the needed knowledge : those who had the knowledge, would not act. Impetuous, unguided zeal is often harmful, and is not proper to a " firm " will : yet to be *too* clever, to see too many sides of a problem, is often paralysing. Often pray to the Holy Spirit that we may have both strength and light; also ardour.

3. It does not follow that we shall *feel inclined* to do what we see we ought to, and even, what we are resolved, God helping us, to do. But the " fixed heart " will do its work despite all shyness, reluctance, or indolence. The bravest man is often he who feels most frightened. It remains that however deep be my awe of God; however appalled I be at the thought that I have rebelled against Him, and that the world rebels and that much of it is a continual affront to Him, yet I know that I can repent, nay, in Christ I can atone even for sins that are not mine :

that my life can be one of gratitude for the past—trust for the future—and joy in God even here and now. And indeed the Psalm ends thus. Despite the apparent indifference of God—even, desertion by God—yet " in God shall we work mightily—do great things! " " I can do all things in Him who strengtheneth me! "

EARTH TURNED TO WATER

Liquefacta est terra et omnes qui habitant in ea : ego confirmavi columnas eius. The earth is turned to water, and all they that dwell therein : but I *do establish the columns thereof.*—Psalm lxxiv. 3. *Thurs., None,* 1.

1. The Hebrews pictured the earth as flat, and upheld by columns over an abyss of water. Other columns upheld the solid firmament—the vault in which sun and moon and stars were fixed. Above this were the " upper waters." If the " windows of heaven " were opened, those waters would rush down: should " the fountains of the great Deep be broken up," the nether waters would gush forth and flood the earth. We do not picture our world like that any more ; but we certainly are watching the break-up of all conventions, established forms, all that had been taken for granted ; and indeed the melting away of principles which hitherto had held good both for mind and morals. Also at times we feel as if we had no solidity, reliability within ourselves—as if our character were molten.

2. There are those who say that this is *right*—that nothing remains the same or can : that there is no such thing as a universal law of right or an eternal truth. This is as false as to say that the child, the boy, the grown man are not the same person. Each remains his own " I " for ever—" And thou *thyself* for all eternity."

3. But there is no permanence in anything that is not rooted in God and does not proceed from Him. Thus

we ought to try to get back to God and to Our Lord, who revealed Him, in anything that we plan or do. And we have not only to possess these columnar principles, that shall never be shaken, but to *be* " columns in the House of God " (Apoc. iii. 12), and to uphold others, and in fact the whole of society. Never flinch ; never compromise; never " hush up " the truth—yet maintaining utmost humility, and charity : for our substance, " foothold," is not in our own nature, but in God : and if others are washed away into uncertainties, is that their fault ?

．　　　．　　　．　　　．　　　．

Verse 7. Help shall not come from East, or West, " or from the desert hills." If these represent the southward rocky wilderness, the North is not mentioned. Possibly we should read : " nor from the desert, nor from the mountains," which would mean south and north respectively. The warning is in reality against alliances with pagan powers : not from *these* was help to be expected. The true rescue comes from God alone.

Verse 9. The Cup of the Lord's wrath is said to be full of unmixed wine, yet fully mixed. How is that ? It is full of wine unmixed with water, but heavily and intoxicatingly spiced. The Latin can proceed to mean that God tilts it from this side to that, and makes all the enemies drink from it, and *yet* is it not exhausted, nor will be, till all the sinners of the world have drunk from it. The appalling imagery is to be seen in *e.g.* Psalm lix. 5, and Apoc., xviii. 6, etc.

THE FUTILE FEAR

Illic trepidaverunt timore ubi non erat timor. There shuddered they with fear, where no fear was.—Psalm lii. 6. Wed., Prime, 3.

1. The impious man says that God " is not." For the Hebrew this did not mean that no God existed ; but that

Yahweh, the God of the Hebrews, was unheeding, as good as non-existent for *him*, and that he had better turn elsewhere. The pagans turned from one god, when he did not help them, to another; and the Hebrews were constantly prone to relapse into such idolatrous experimentalism and approach some other claimant for divine honours. Still, the Psalmist suggests that there were both men who trembled with awe before those false gods who were but nothingness, and others, who had no awe for anything at all.

2. To-day we are much more likely to belong to the second class—to omit God altogether. Yet we also make false gods of whom we stand in desperate awe, such as, public opinion, a political theory, money, my own will. I " bow down " if not to wood and stone, at least to impalpable and more dangerous things like those.

3. But " fear " can mean downright terror. There are those much of whose life is spent in fear—for their or their family's future—because of the precariousness of modern life and employment. Would that we guessed how much " fear " there is among our fellow-men, if not in our own safe life! Again, we can be " frightened " of God : yet His Majesty is not meant to frighten us, nor yet is our Judgment. In Him, Majesty and Mercy are one. I can fear trusting myself, my spiritual life, to Him, lest He ask too much. Or, I can be simply very shy, and terrified by calling on someone, entering a hospital ward —a military hut; of " speaking up " for my Faith in public. " Lions in the path! " God chains them, tames them, or transforms them!—Finally, the guilty man may with reason, be frightened of discovery; disgrace; blackmail. But if I "*fear*" God—of whom else shall I be afraid ?

I ALL BUT SLIPPED!

Mei autem paene moti sunt pedes—paene effusi sunt gressus mei! But my feet almost slipped—my footsteps all but stumbled.—Psalm lxxii. 2. Thurs., Terce, 1.

1. The Psalmist *begins* with the sentiment to which his meditation had *finally* led him. " How good is God to Israel—to the right in heart! " Then he looks back to see how nearly he never had reached that happy conclusion of gratitude and trust. His experience had brought him, first, almost to despair. (This is worth remembering in hours of blackness. It seems as if it would never clear! But it does! and then we feel as if we never *could* have been so depressed!)

2. The Psalmist's distress began by seeing the successes of the wicked. It was no good looking for their death . . . if they did get into trouble, they did not remain in it—their wounds did not last! In fact they did not seem to share at all in the ordinary woes of mankind : no—they grew proud ; they wrapped themselves in sin like in a cloak : their words were as insolent as their thoughts ; they put no limit to their insolence : they stare heaven itself out of face : their evil doctrines reach everywhere in the world. But worse! " My own people is turning towards them, for (say they) ' Full days are to be found among them! ' And anyway—Does God *care* ? . . . Look at the wicked! It is they who have made the money! " So the poor Psalmist feels that he had kept himself innocent—had put up with hardships—had positively been scourged all the day long— *all for nothing!* He might as well give up.

3. But he was appalled by *that* thought. " If I speak like that, I shall be renouncing, discarding, the whole Nation that are Thy Sons " and all their history. This denial of the Hebrews and all God's work for them was

more than he could endure. But the problem remained. " I
put my mind to it, to understand it . . . but it was hard
work—insoluble—in my eyes. . . . Until, until I went into
God's House, and thought about the *upshot*—the *end* of the
wicked! " He retired " into the church "—God's presence
—and reflected—not upon time and its passing pageant, but
what it mounts up to and issues into. " What doth it profit
a man ? "

BUT I CLUNG CLOSE TO GOD

*Mihi autem adhaerere Deo bonum est. For me, to cling
close to God is good!*—Psalm *lxxii.* 27. *Thurs., Terce,* 3.

1. The Psalmist places the " end " of the wicked within
this life. Snares are put close to them by God ; in a flash
they are ruined : their schemes and political plots vanish
like a dream at waking. (The Latin could mean : The very
image of them vanishes—they are simply no more seen.)
We, as Christians, " translate " the Psalms, and their
desire for visible vengeance or prosperity, for the this-world
vindication of the righteous, into what belongs to the true
upshot—our eternal life. Things are never put absolutely
right here and now.

2. And the Psalmist acknowledges that when his mind
was enraged, embittered, " worked up " about the thriving
of wrong and wrongdoers, it was *he* who (without realising
it) was being reduced to nothing : he was " all wrong " ; he
was becoming as stupid as any brute-beast before God—and
yet, and yet, God never had deserted him : " All the while,
I was with Thee—my hand wast Thou holding!"—God was
leading him home by His own ways, and was preparing to
acknowledge him in his turn, and to give him honour.

3. *Then* the Psalmist breaks into his impassioned cry :
" Ah, what have I in heaven, but Thee ? and on earth,
what, save Thee, do I desire ? " His flesh and his spirit
faint away ; but God remains his portion for ever. What

is allotted to him, is *God*. It is they who retreat from
God, who perish—who wanton away from Him, go
after false loves and miss the eternal union. And forthwith,
the Psalmist feels the need of communicating his joy to so
many as possible. The Psalmist reviews the whole of life :
suffers agonies from the problems it sets him : recovers : is
ecstasied with God—and at once becomes an apostle. Is
that like me ?

MY HOLY INDIGNATION

In matutino interficiebam omnes peccatores terrae.
In the morning would I slay all the sinners of the land.
Psalm c. 8. Wed., Lauds, 3.

1. Does this phrase really justify " righteous indignation ? " Presumably it alludes to the court of justice
which " sat " in the mornings ; and the Psalmist says
he will give verdict against all the wrong-doers brought
before him, so as to make Jerusalem and the whole Land
worthy of their name—The City, the People of the Lord.
The royal Judge declares that he will not associate with
wrong-doers nor give verdict in their favour : such
verdicts in the East too often depended upon bribes, and
went therefore unjustly in favour of the rich.

2. The world is constantly revealing itself as con-
structing and *re*-constructing its miseries because of sin
and corruption. Even for our own poor human sakes we
ought to vow ourselves to the extermination of sin—first,
from our own hearts ; then, from those of our fellow-men
in so far as we can influence them.

3. But Our Lord showed that He did not want us to
hate any sinner, however vile be his sin ; and we can
test the purity of any " holy indignation " we may feel,
by seeing whether we feel more of it when the offence
has been committed against ourselves. The only way in
which the Saints have defeated sin has been by means of

an intense love for the sinning soul—that soul which Our Lord loves with a love infinitely more intense than any that our own poor hearts can provide. Well may we often pray : " Make my heart like unto Thy Heart."

MY ABDICATION

Obliviscere populum tuum et domum patris tui. . . . Pro patribus tuis nati sunt tibi filii. Forget thy people and thy father's house : in lieu of thy forefathers, sons shall be born to thee.—Psalm xliv. 1. 17. *Wed., Matins, Noct.*, i. 1, 2.

1. The psalm is directly concerned with the marriage of a prince. " My heart is brimming with a noble theme— I will chant my Royal Ode ! " The praises of the prince continue to verse 7 ; 8 is transitional. Then follow the approach and praises of the Bride and her retinue. The Psalm is " Messianic " : the Jews would not have admitted it to their Canon had they not discerned a sublimer sense in its words. But we are not meditating on that just now.

2. Whenever the soul is called to anything great, it is also asked to abandon much. Probably the life of any priest, nun or brother is but a series of uprootings. No personal homes ; no families or kindred save spiritual. At times, the loneliness of this life may seem intolerable. It may be, better so. Their sacrifice must not only be technical. The sacrifice of parents saying good-bye to children is usually far the deeper. We need then to make an interior sacrifice. We can apply the Latin of " All the glory of the king's daughter comes from within " (*i.e.*, the palace : this makes sense, whatever the Hebrew ought to be) to the fact that the splendour of a priest's or nun's vocation are and must be spiritual, else the exterior respect shown to them is of no worth. A priest acquires a sort of social position and is more freely admitted

than others : but God forgive him if he rests his con-
tentment upon that.

3. Yet we have the duty to hope great things from our
vocation—yes, the very vocation to be a Christian in whatever status. The last verses of the Psalm indicate a great
future and posterity! Our work must last for generations!
But every such ambition must repose upon detachment.

.   .   .   .   .

" *Audi, filia, et vide, et inclina aurem tuam : et obliviscere populum tuum et domum patris tui* " (*xliv.* 11).

Verse that must have been responsible for myriads
upon myriads of sacrifices, renunciations, carryings out
of the grim command to let the dead bury " their dead."
Yet how tender—God's secret being so whispered to
His beloved soul. " Listen, daughter! Look! Bend your
ear . . .! Forget them—forget your people ; let Me
disentangle the roots and tendrils. Forget your thronging
memories, yes, and the warm narrower intimacy of your
home! " Even so, it will sound terribly bleak and harsh
to those who have no idea of what Vocation is : and even
the poor little princess, selected to marry the grand king,
wouldn't have felt much consolation just then, on being
assured that she should have a number of sons to make
up for everything she had been accustomed to—that
she should see them established up and down the world
on thrones, and that posterity would praise her. But
suppose she was in love with the prince ? Shy and nervous
in her wedding-dress ; perhaps distressed by everyone's
looking at her and half-conscious that all the bridesmaids
were—very flattering, no doubt, but also, critical and
perhaps rather or even bitterly envious ; and feeling that
ivory palaces were possibly chill and that so many scents
were suffocating—well, in and over it all was the certainty
that she was going to *him* ; and it was not his glamour

or his title that fascinated her, but himself. And happily, we haven't got to sigh (as people do at weddings) "I hope he'll treat her well—be faithful—understand her and make her feel at *home*." Because when God wills to call the soul, and marry her closely to Himself, and whispers His call, first, there is no question of His worth; or of His loyalty: or of the Home I am coming to. Nor of the fruitful work to which He is calling me. Nor even, that He will fail, somehow, somewhen, to make it up to the human hearts that Vocation may be lacerating—yes; one has again and again to say to young men or girls that it is those whom they are leaving who suffer far the most. Young and enthusiastic hearts may hardly suffer at all. When the doors of seminary or of convent shut, they may feel exultant, breathe free, experience enormous relief, and are, in fact, at *home;* and it is the sensitive knowledge that son or daughter is now feeling " at home " outside " home," that may be anguish to father or mother, even when they are proud and grateful thus to have given their dearest to God when He called. But what, when they feel no such thing as pride or gratitude ? they may not be Catholics; or, Catholics who do not "understand " " that sort of thing." Ah, Lord; if I am to leave father and mother and the rest, at the outset, do not let me come, after all, only halfway to You! Don't let me make a whole new set of selfish attachments within my religious life; after a while, You ought to be able to uproot me far more violently than you did at first! Yes— go on! uproot me. Disentangle me. My sons are to be *Thine—Thine* and mine; but no one else's. And what about forgetting these young princes themselves ? not asking to see even the results of any work done ? Certainly it will not be praise now or afterwards that we shall ask for—save indeed God's Well Done, which will be as secret as His first vocation.

MY FATHER AND MY MOTHER

*Pater meus et mater mea dereliquerunt me ; Dominus
autem assumpsit me. My father and my mother abandoned me, but the Lord took me up.—Psalm xxvi. 10.
Mon., Terce, 2.*

1. When a young man or a girl enters upon the ecclesiastical or " religious " life, it is sometimes said : " How
much they have given up," and sometimes they think it
themselves. If such has been my choice, I will begin by
remembering that the sacrifice on my parents' part may have
been very much greater than on mine : very likely a proud
and grateful sacrifice, but a very costly one, inasmuch as
youth has seldom had time to learn how to suffer deeply.
This is especially true if a child be an only one, or one in
whom the love of parents and their hopes were closely bound
up. Parents can spiritualise their sacrifice and indeed a
whole outlook on life, by often recalling in the hours when
their child is intimately missed, that at least they have provided one who is wholly working for God, great as the cost
has been. They will want their child to do the maximum for
God, and will almost instinctively do the same themselves.

2. I have to learn, when I make such a sacrifice, to love
more, not less : to keep though letting go : to be in closer
spiritual union even when separated physically. No
" vocation " can un-do the fact that my parents *are* my
parents, and, in proportion as they co-operate with my
vocation, earn also the blessing proper to those who
" hear the Word of the Lord and keep it."

3. In the course of a priestly life I shall, please God, make
many friends. Too many to see much of, to write to often,
to hear from. Often I shall give my love to those whom
business, travel, marriage, growing older and winning experience of many more men, will cause to see me as " one

of many " and even forget me, or almost. I must not chafe.
I shall find myself, too, if not forgetting them, seeing them
as paler, more remote, also as " one among many." I must
not chafe. I shall have done my work and now must serve
in another way. And I have not wished to keep them for
myself. I have handed them over to God from the outset,
and still do so.

GOD WITH ME IN MY APOSTOLATE

*Voluntatem timentium se faciet. God will do the will
of them that fear him.*—Psalm cxliv. 19. Sat., Vesp., 5.

1. The meaning is not more than that God will fulfil
the desire of them that stand in awe of Him : but we can
take " voluntas " in its stronger sense. First, God will
not coerce our free will. He did not force the Incarnation,
even, upon Our Lady. But that was an offer made by
God to man. He wishes men on their side to make requests
to Him. True, the man who habitually subordinates himself to God—" stands in awe of " Him—is unlikely to will
anything that God does not. St. Augustine Christianises
this—" Ama, et fac quod vis! " Do but love God—and
then, do as you please! For the true lover of God cannot
be " pleased " by anything contrary to that love.

2. In fact, we are encouraged to a certain audacity in
prayer. If we are at least trying to reverence and love
God, He *invites* us to trust Him a very great deal. Why,
He has done so much for us already, that no petition of
ours can *exceed* what He wants to give. He outpasses not
only our deserts (as is obvious) but our desires—*merita
excedit et vota*. How timidly we pray! How do we fear
that we are asking for more than we, poor sinners, are
worthy of! But as if any proportion could be struck
between ourselves—sinners or saints—and God!

3. Ask God to expand our hearts and intensify our
desires. Better an in some ways unsatisfactory son, who

s

yet whole-heartedly trusted his father and expected him to be anxious and able to help him *greatly*, than the well-behaved boy who expected nothing great from anyone, his father included. Our Heavenly Father cannot disappoint us, as earthly fathers may. *Quantum potes, tantum aude !*

MY RISK IS IN MY APOSTOLATE

Funes extenderunt in laqueum : iuxta iter scandalum posuerunt mihi. They have stretched out cords to make a snare for me : they have set traps by my path to trip me up.—Psalm. cxxxix. 6. Fri., Vesp., 3.

1. We expect to be tempted, and open temptations may not humiliate us. Men say half proudly : "I have a terrible temper! I am very ambitious—sensitive!" But it may not occur to us that we can be deceived. It *is* humiliating to find that one has been tricked. The Psalmist constantly alludes to the trickeries of his enemies, and is indignant about them.

2. I must be all the more on my guard about self-deception, because if I am tempted to steal or murder, I am obviously tempted to what is wrong, whereas, while I am deceived, I think I am right! My opinion seems sound ; my plan a good one. Directors or friends may see better, but it appears to me positively wrong, or absurd, to follow their advice. It is worth looking to see if we are ready, on the whole, to take advice, or whether it goes against the grain to take it or ask for it.

3. In important matters, it is well in any case to ask God's advice, of course, but also our fellow-man's, and if we go against what we have been advised, to redouble our prayers. For interior insincerity is just what we cannot be conscious of—or perhaps we are semi-conscious of it and will not let ourselves become fully so. It is certainly a good training in humility to realise that we have been fooled—have fallen into clumsy mistakes.

IX

OUR EXILE, PILGRIMAGE AND HOME

Ever since Abraham, the Chosen People were " in pilgrimage." From Mesopotamia to Palestine ; to Egypt ; back to Palestine ; back to Egypt, and again to the Promised Land. But even after that, the People were taken into exile ; and even when a " remnant " returned, it was chiefly in various ways " dispersed " throughout the world. At least Jerusalem and the Temple remained its spiritual Home ; and towards these the faithful Jew would turn and pray, each day, and even several times daily. Some of the loveliest Psalms are due to this exile, laborious return, yearning for home, and joy in reaching the Holy City. The Christian, too, knows himself in exile. He is not yet in his true country nor home. Not for that should he be melancholy ; nor should he despise nor hate this world, which is God's creation, though so much marred by sin. It remains that the Christian cannot fully feel at home in it. We need, then, a true detachment from the things of earth. But it is not upon them that our attention should be concentrated. We need to work to make this world more " heaven-like," even though we are sure it can never be fully so. And we are right to yearn for, fix our eyes upon, tend towards, that Heaven which alone will be our true, firm-founded Home. The following Psalms, many of them exquisite and pathetic in themselves—as a transcript of what was felt by the God-fearing Jew in exile or returning, or again at home —can without any difficulty at all be " Christianised " and nourish our love and longing for God.

THE EXILED HEART

Multum incola fuit anima mea! Too long hath my soul been in exile!—Psalm cxix. 6. Mon., Vesp., 3.

1. The Psalmist is held afar in exile (he may have been a trader)—he feels, unendurably long. Verse 5 originally was: " Alas for me, that I must dwell in Meshekh, and sojourn in the homes of Kedar!" *i.e.*, in (probably) the Crimea, and in Arabia—for the Jew, the far north and south. Everyone slandered or ridiculed the poor traveller : "Too long have I had to dwell—With men that hate peace!—I am a man of peace : but when I speak to them, they attack me without cause."

2. We are right to feel "in exile." We long for a world of peace, justice, charity, truthfulness, beauty. But the world does not give us these : only Our Lord can promise them. "Iesum . . . post hoc exilium ostende!" The world is full of wars, and threatens others. But even in times of technical peace, a business-life is too often a cut-throat affair. Well, it is right to feel, at times, how true it is that we have here no "lasting habitation" but look for the City "that hath the foundations, whose builder and maker is God" (Heb. xi. 10).

3. Yet we have to be careful, lest we slander our pagan neighbours or contemporaries. Who knows that the Jewish traveller was impeccable ? The Crimeans and Arabians might have had justifiable retorts! Non-Christians, non-Catholics, the laity, do not always see in the Christian, the Catholic, the Priest, what they have the right to expect. Recall the parable of the "beam in thine own eye."

HOMESICK FOR HEAVEN

Quomodo cantabimus canticum Domini in terra aliena ?
How shall we sing one of the Lord's songs in an alien
land ?—Psalm cxxxvi. 4. Thurs., Vesp., 4.

1. Israel is in exile. Its sons sit sorrowful by the water-
ways of Babylonia (perhaps they met there to pray:
cf. Acts xvi. 13) and have no heart to sing their traditional
hymns. And when the pagans invite them to sing some
national song, they feel that still less can they desecrate any
such thing by yielding to what was but curiosity and maybe
mockery. They could do nothing till they were home again
—till their enemies (Edom had shared in the destruction
of Jerusalem ; see Abdias 10–16 etc.) were overthrown.
This accounts for the ferocity of the last verses.

2. There is often a tendency to keep what is sacred,
secret. Yet it is our duty to communicate our good things to
others. We Catholics must be Catholicisers : a priest must
always somehow be acting in a priestly way. But it is no
good just bewildering non-Catholics by assertions, or by
exhibiting ceremonies, that they cannot possibly understand
without sympathetic help. Thus we must know our Faith,
and our Liturgy, as well as possible. Otherwise what we
say or do may actually become a stumbling-block.

3. Nor will the Christian or Catholic want the *destruction*
of his opponents. He will not repay hate with hate, persecution with recrimination even. That is one of the great
" reversals " preached by Our Lord. Love them that
hate you ; pray for them that persecute you! Meanwhile,
I will remember how many people are lonely ; perhaps
literally alone ; perhaps just out of harmony with their
environment ; perhaps desolate because old, poor,
unattractive. I will try to seek such people out—and
foreigners may feel quite lost in England ; or even,

converts, at first, within the Church. Visit Christ in these
" strangers! "

FROM THE WORLD'S END

*A finibus terrae ad te clamavi. From the ends of the
earth do I call unto Thee.—Psalm lx. 2. Wed.,
Compl., 3.*

1. A " missionary " Psalm. Souls are crying out from
the ends of the earth. The Psalm may have been written
by a Hebrew in exile (David himself, possibly) ; but all
souls are in exile who do not dwell " in the protection
of God's wings "—within His over-shadowing Tabernacle.
St. Paul says (Rom. viii. 22) that the whole of the universe
is groaning and straining together—a world-travail. It
has not borne its true fruits yet : it has not come to its
true self. Listen to the innumerable souls which, without
knowing it, and without being able to formulate any
explicit prayer, are none the less wanting the God who
summons them all to Himself.

2. Pray, explicitly, in their name! It is possible to
place one's soul, as it were, within that of the Indian, the
African, even of the " after-Christian," the " neo-pagan,"
and in their name, in their very person, to cry aloud to
God for help. " From the ends of the earth, I, here in
England, or wherever be my ' world-centre '—none the
less from the extreme circumference, from all over the
world, am I calling to Thee! "

3. " Missionary Sunday " is now established for the
whole world. Alas, it is known to be " observed " better
among the convert ex-pagans than among ourselves!
It comes just before the Feast of Christ the King : so the
last verses of the Psalm are appropriate. How the Heart
of Christ must be touched, when He hears the cry : " We
will have this Man to reign over us! " Pray not only
for the Missioner ; but *in* the souls for whom he labours,

or, still harder, cannot even reach! May Christ be "multiplied" to the furthest horizon and for ever!

.   .   .   .   .

Verse 5 : compare *Sub umbra alarum tuarum protege me.* Beneath the shadow of Thy wings protect me (Psalm. xvi. 8).

The Eastern liked the idea of shade because he needed a refuge from his scorching sun. This is not what easily appeals to us, whose days are so grey. But we may pray to God to deliver us from publicity that might harm us, and also from the desire for publicity. How much Catholic work is spoilt by men or women who want prominence, to have their names printed and to receive votes of thanks. They are huffed if they do not receive them : they give up the work. I must learn to appreciate especially such work as is substantial and not lime-lit. But I *must* work—and then turn over all my work to Him who alone gives the increase.

.   .   .   .   .

We can use the Psalm as above ; but its direct meaning seems certainly to be that Israel is in exile, and is praying for its return to Palestine, the re-establishment of the Kingdom with its glorious King. The second half of verse 3, in Latin (joining " when my heart was troubled " with the preceding words), is : " Thou dost set me high upon a rock—Thou guidest me." But the Hebrew means : " Thou dost lead me—or, O that Thou wouldst lead me—to the rock that is too high for me." That is, either, simply, " to a very high rock," or, " to the Rock that is higher than I," and it is this phrase which has established itself in the English language, and which is hardly less beautiful than that other phrase : " The shadow of a great Rock in a weary land " (Is. xxxii. 2). The oriental traveller comes with intense delight to some great crag jutting high above the illimitable blazing desert : he lies under its shade : he climbs it and is safe from marauders or roving beasts. Such, for the soul, is God. Recall, too, the frequent thought that God shelters us " beneath the shadow of His wings," and again, that He is a " strong tower "—a " tower of strength "—against the enemy.

HIMSELF SHALL REDEEM ISRAEL

Apud Dominum misericordia et copiosa apud eum redemptio : With the Lord there is mercy, and with Him plentiful redemption.—Psalm cxxix. 7. Wed., Vesp., 3.

1. We are accustomed to apply this Psalm to the Souls in Purgatory ; dramatically to put it on their very lips. Also, anyone who feels himself in great misery—whether spiritual, moral or even material, will need no help to savour it. But judging from its place in the Psalter, we may think that it probably expresses the utter despondency of Israel in exile, combined with unconquerable trust in God.

2. In the Hebrew the last lines go thus : " My soul is unto the Lord—strains, aches for God—more than the sleepless for the morning." This alludes rather to the Temple Levites, waiting for the morning sacrifice, than to sentinels : it can be used by anyone who suffers from sheer insomnia ; or by anyone under a long-drawn stress, *e.g.* unemployment ; but also, by those who have tried and tried to get rid of sin, or of some definite sin, and feel as if they never could succeed. " Hope deferred maketh the heart sick." We may notice, in others, the fact that they suffer in some positive way, but not notice the separate pain, the sickness of heart, due to seeing hope after hope come to nothing.

3. What special patience is needed in regard to *recidivi*, those who fall back and back into the same sin—probably one of the flesh! May we never, by harshness, or by

assuming that they deliberately act thus, quench the last glimmer of their hope; give them just that added push which makes them give up trying. Let us " wait patiently " for the Grace that will cure them, just as God waits patiently till He can give that grace without its being rejected. God often does not ask *everything at once*.

THE BROKEN NET

Laqueus contritus est, et nos liberati sumus. The snare is snapped; and we—we are set free!—Psalm cxxiii. 6. Tues., Vesp., 2.

1. The Psalmist, delivered along with his People from Captivity, is almost delirious with joy. Had not God— had not *God*—been with them, their enemies might well have swallowed them alive : the cataract might well have engulfed them ; they might have had to pass through a torrent that no man could withstand. Blessed, then, be God, who had delivered them from the fierce fangs of the wild attacking beasts : their life had been rescued, as a small bird is, from the fowler's snare.

2. There are very many—as a priest, never subjected to so dreadful a stress, may well from time to time remember with humiliation—who feel caught by terrible pincers : " Either I must be dishonest, or agree to immorality, or starve, and maybe make my whole family to starve." There are modern versions of the old arena-martyrdoms : refusal to cheat, for money's sake, is certainly one of them.

3. Others are prisoners within themselves. A habit. An inhibition. Something *in me*, seemingly forcing me to do wrong or preventing me from doing right. My will-power is captive : I have *no* will. I am at the mercy of memories, ingrained tendencies, fears, conventions. *Expecta Dominum!* Try, fail, wait, pray. *Suddenly* the fetters are broken—and I, I am set free!

HOMEWARDS

Levavi oculos meos ad montes—unde veniet auxilium mihi. I lift up mine eyes unto the mountains—Whence help shall come to me.—Psalm cxx. 1. Mon., Vesp., 4.

1. A caravan-psalm, and presumably sung " in dialogue " or, the soul communes with itself. The exile is on his way homewards : but the road is long. He strains his eyes towards the hills between him and Palestine. Who will help him over the rest of the weary path ? All help is from God—a Guardian who slumbers not nor sleeps. God protects him just where he needs Him most. (" On thy right hand." The shield was carried on the left, so that the right was the more exposed.) Neither day nor night should injure him—neither sunstroke nor the moon-rays that were so much feared. (Why ? Possibly the violent blanching due to oriental moonlight caused the Arabs to believe—they are said still to do so—that the moon caused leprosy. And we have the words : " lunatic," and " moon-struck.") But the Lord would protect his home-coming even as He had his forth-faring.

2. The mountains to which the traveller's eyes strained seemed to him, from a distance, the sign of the end of his journey. When he saw *those*, he felt as though he were practically at home. Meanwhile, the leagues of monotonous trudging. We shall need all the " perseverance " we can get, especially through the middle part of our life, when the " midday devil " attacks us and we are apt to become less spiritual—less idealist, more " fagged."

3. But not only the path may " wind upwards to the end," but the last part may be the steepest of all. God may continue to ask more and more of an effort from us. May we be ready to give it. A Psalm that indeed reminds us to ask for the special grace of final Perseverance!

GOD'S OUTER COURTS

*Laetatus sum in his quae dicta sunt mihi—" In domum
Domini ibimus ! " I rejoiced when they said to me :
" We are going into the House of the Lord ! "—Psalm
cxxi. 1. Mon., Vesp., 5.*

1. The pilgrimage is all-but at its end. The exile finds
himself standing in the very fore-court of the Temple.
He had almost fallen into ecstasy when at last he caught
sight of the city-walls—" Jerusalem, that art builded—
such a city!—each stone interknit with stone! " (Some of
these stones were 60 feet long. The simple Galilean
apostles, too, were rapt in amazement at the sight of
those colossal walls : our Lord wept that " not one stone
should be left upon another.") Then the Psalmist forgets
himself and remembers only the immemorial history of
the place ; how it was Centre and Homing-Place of his
People ; and he prays that there may be " Peace in thy
strong walls—abundance within thy towers." For the
sake of all his kin, he prays Peace for her whose very
name, Salem, meant Peace.

2. We would wish to have something of this reverence
and joy when we enter so much as the porch or the sacristy
of a church ; and we will remember how many Saints
have had these words upon their lips when it was " broken "
to them that they were dying. " Jerusalem, my happy home
—Ah God! that I were there! " Study the glorious hymn :
Caelestis Urbs.

3. Meanwhile, may we on earth " seek peace and
pursue it." It is tragic that fellow-members of the City
of God on earth, the Church, should dislike, be jealous
of, and even fight one another. The thought that all
Catholics are members of one Country, one City, one
Body—of the Bride of Christ herself—ought to over-ride

all lesser causes of variance. We must also remember that we have to play our part in the continual enlarging of the City's circuit-walls—until, in fact, she becomes co-extensive with humanity (see Psalm lxxxvi. p. 274).

NO DISILLUSIONMENT

Sicut audivimus, sic vidimus in civitate . . . Dei nostri.
As we had heard, so do we see, in the City of our God!—
Psalm xlvii. 9. Wed., Matins, Noct., ii. 1.

1. The song of pilgrims visiting Jerusalem, and finding it " up to their expectations." No disillusionment! God reveals Himself in its dwellings, for *He* guardeth it! Encircle Sion! Walk around her! Tell the tale of her towers! Mark well her strong walls, and reckon up her palaces! Thus shall you be able to assure posterity that *here* is where God is!

2. Converts enter the Church hoping so much! expecting so much! Let not one of us disappoint them. The normal inhabitant of Jerusalem no doubt took much for granted that was thrilling to the pilgrim. It is possible to take Catholic ways for granted—we are used to them—and so we dash the enthusiasm of new-comers. We ought to do all that we can to make a convert " feel at home," and indeed maybe he will make us feel ashamed of our lack of fervour. Even if he strikes us as " over-fervent," do not let us damp him down, half-snub him, " disillusionise " him.

3. Yet Jerusalem was ruined. The Church cannot fall to pieces, because of God's promises. But the individual Catholic may crumble: God grant me perseverance! And within the Church can be found much that is wrong —only Heaven can fully and for ever come up to my hopes, will never disappoint me, and of it we shall say, not: " It is as good as I had been told," but, " The half was not told me! " (1 Kings x. 7).

HEAVEN-HAVEN

Deduxit eos in portum voluntatis suae. He brought
them home into the harbour of their desire.—Psalm
cvi. 30. Sat., Matins, Noct., iii.

1. The Psalm concerns in general the history of the
Israelites driven from place to place, seeking a " civitas
habitationis," a City where they might *dwell* [" a Tower of
strength : *i.e.* a strong tower. "A city of dwelling," *i.e.*
" a permanent home "] ; and in particular their return from
Exile in Babylon ; and even, the pilgrimage of Jews from
over-seas to Jerusalem, centre of their spiritual and national
life—for till quite late the Sea played no noticeable part in the
Israelite's experience. The typical Rescue from Egypt glints
through the other parts of the long story ; and so does our
own rescue from sin, loneliness, sickness, and the impermanence of this world itself. At the end of each part the
Psalm breaks out into a refrain of gratitude, and so should we.

2. The " works of the Lord," seen by mariners, are
His raising of storms, followed by His stilling them. "Up
they go, high as heaven! Down they go, to the bottom-
most! Their spirit fainted in their distress. They reeled,
they staggered like a drunken man : all their knowledge—
their sea-craft—was swallowed up. But they cried to
the Lord in their distress, and from their grievous plight
He brought them forth. He stilled the storm to a whisper,
and the billows of the sea were still. And they rejoiced
that they should be stilled : and He led them to the harbour
where they would be." The description is unique in the
Psalms or even the Old Testament.

3. We can apply this as spiritually as we will : but
is it not a real *duty* for landsmen-Catholics to recall the
Seaman (on whom in so many ways they depend even
physically)—the Seaman, without diocese or parish ;

half his time, without home : without the possibility of Mass or the Sacraments : *with* temptations specially engineered for him : *unique among Catholics* because of his conditions, and *invisible* even to would-be helpers almost always—unlike the normal clients of *e.g.* the SVP ? May every priest and layman know of and appreciate the apostleship of the Sea ! " The Harbours of his desire " —the eternal harbour, for which, maybe without knowing it, he longs.

GOD'S GLORIOUS CITY

Gloriosa dicta sunt de te, Civitas Dei ! Glorious things must be said of thee, City of God !—Psalm lxxxvi. 2. Fri., Sex., 3.

This Psalm is so transcendent and sublime a vision and prophecy, that no " points " are here offered for meditation : we need to absorb it as a whole. It displays Jerusalem in its most universal, mystical aspect. Holy-Land becomes co-extensive with the world. For details of the paraphrase, commentaries must be consulted, and the exact sense of the last verse remains obscure. But after preliminary study, the Psalm becomes a supreme material for meditation, prayer and praise.

God's firm-founded dwelling is on the holy hills—The Lord loves the gates of Sion beyond all the homes of Israel. Glorious things must be said of thee, thou City of God ! —(Now God speaks.) " I will make mention of Egypt and of Babylon [the immemorial pagan enemies of the Holy land] as among them that know Me ! See, the Philistines, Tyre, and the Ethiopian folk—all these came into being *there !* [All were born—or to be born—within the mystical Sion, and so, had rights of citizenship there.]" (The Psalmist resumes.) So, of Sion must men say—Every, every man was born there ! Who, save the Most High, established her ? The Lord, in His registers of peoples and of princes, proclaimeth the record of them that were born within her. All, all happy people have within thee their dwelling!

Such is the general thought of the Psalm. It would be well to read Isaias xix. 23–25, where Israel is a " third " along with Egypt "My People," and Assyria, " the work of My hands "—all three shall worship together: and Zachariah viii. 23 : " in that day . . . ten men, out of all the languages of the nations, shall take hold of the skirt of him that is a Jew, saying: We will go with you, for we have heard that God is with you! " It is quite true that the Hebrews started from a nationalist vision : but they did not end there. Surely this Psalm cannot fail to fill us with a most ardent desire to extend the Kingdom of God throughout the world! Surely it must make us send forth our call, in prayer, to all parts of the world, excluding no race, no colour ; no religion, even, that has seemed impervious to the gospel ?

HARVEST-HOME

Qui seminant in lacrimis in exsultatione metent. They who sow in tears, shall reap in joy.—Psalm cxxv. 5. Tues., Vesp., 4.

1. The first verse doubtless should be : " When the Lord turned Israel home from her captivity (in Babylon), we were like men who dreamed! " We could not believe that it was true. The very pagans recognised that our God had done great things for us—and indeed He had!

2. But disillusionment awaited the home-returning Jew. He found that his enthusiasm evaporated. Confronted by the ruins of Jerusalem, he had no heart to begin rebuilding them. Even the poor little Second Temple took long to build ; and fifty years after that the City still lay half

demolished. Oh Lord, change our Captivity indeed, as the autumn rains change the mountain-gullies from aridity into rushing streams! Oh Lord, let the long-drawn periods of our sowing at last, at last, become harvest-home!

3. Most of us, and surely most priests, must have to look back on periods during which they were trying to do something from which they saw no results. Perhaps they never will see them—perhaps " one man reaps where another man has sown . . . that he who sowed and he who reaps together may rejoice " (St. John iv. 36). Such was Our Lord's generosity. He did not grudge the weary sowing—nay, not even of that Grain that must " fall into the earth and die " : but neither did He demand to have all the glory of the harvest for Himself. In any case, during this life it hardly can be but that each part is a preparation for the next, even as all life is a preparation for heaven. We are always at school; in noviciates or seminaries. Always half-way : never quite at perfection. Patience : trust : peace in the Lord's " good time."

IMPERFECT PEACE

Saepe expugnaverunt me a iuventute mea ! Oft should they have defeated me from my youth up !—Psalm cxxviii. 1. Wed., Vesp., 2.

1. Israel is at home after exile : but still surrounded by enemies. The Psalmist looks back over that long history. Enemies had attacked and re-attacked the People from its infancy ; but never had they destroyed it. Even, they took possession of the Holy Land, ploughed deep furrows on its back : but God " cut the ropes " (so the Hebrew) of the sinners—the ropes that harnessed the ox to the plough—and freed the land.

2. Yet its enemies survived. May they become like the grass that sprouts upon flat roofs from seeds let fall

by birds or blown by winds into the cracks of the plaster! Up springs the delicate shoot; but in a moment it shrivels. Not with *that* would the reaper fill his hand, not the gleaner his cloak: not because of sheaves such as those would the passer-by call "God bless you!" to the harvestess! *Grüss Gott!* (Compare the seed fallen into shallow ground, in the parable).

3. We apply this Psalm to the history of the Church and also to our own. Again and again it looks as if the forces of evil *must* defeat the Church, but they never finally do. Again and again, I feel as though temptation would be too much for me: that I cannot persevere: that I shall sink to lower aspirations: that hope can no more be helped. Well, it could not, were not *God* my hope. He is my "substantia"—my firm foothold: "In Thee, O Lord, have I placed my hope! I shall never, never be dismayed!"

COMPROMISE

Benefac, Domine, rectis corde : declinantes autem in obligationes adducet Dominus cum operantibus iniquitatem. Show goodness, Lord, to them that are good and right of heart : but them that go aside into crooked paths shall the Lord bring whither the wicked are going.—Psalm cxxiv. 4, 5. *Tues., Vesp.,* 3.

1. When the Israelites returned to Palestine, they found many pagans still there. Life was no total and immediate triumph. Even the Jew was tempted to compromise with the pagan and make the best of a confused situation. Ah, cries the Psalmist, if you would but trust in the Lord! He who does so is as immovable as Mount Sion! The dweller in Jerusalem has mountains all round him: even so, God is all round His people and will not suffer the measuring-rod (or sceptre) of the pagan to lie for ever across the land allotted to the Chosen People. If He did,

T

the Jews themselves would try to "come to terms"—to meet them half-way.

2. Half-measures imply dishonesty with God. We are not "straight" with Him. That word has won right of citizenship in our language, and so has its correlative, "twister." The "non-straight" man deserts the only right path : he "slopes off." Then he gets involved in "entanglements" (*obligationes*) : he is in situations from which he cannot extricate himself. He and the sinner will take the same way home.

3. Yet so difficult is life, and the adjustment of what is charitable, or tolerant, with what is rigidly right, that we shall constantly have to ask God to protect us lest we do not forgive, but condone ; lest we play fast and loose with principle ; and again, lest we break the bruised reed and quench the smouldering flax by our aloofness or lack of understanding. May He indeed help us to live aright in this mixed world of ours which *should* be Holy Land.

WHAT HAS GOD NOT DONE FOR ME ?

Non fecit taliter omni nationi ! Not thus hath He done for every nation !—Psalm cxlviii. 9. Fri., Lauds, 5.

1. An ecstatic congratulation to Jerusalem. Not for every city or nation has God worked such marvels! The paramount power of His Word is illustrated by the phenomenon of the snow, the hoar-frost (*nebula*) ; and the ice tumbling down the precipitous Jordan in large lumps— "Who can stand up against His cold ? " (To the Jew, such phenomena would have been especially impressive and at times alarming.) But then, God's Word, caused all this to occur, speaks yet again, and they melt : He breathes, and the waters run free once more.

2. For us, God's New Israel, the New People, is His Church. Happy am I if I "realise" her so well, that I

fall into a kind of ecstasy and love for her : do not think of her as an institution merely, governed in a special way—but in her long history, and her ever-expanding extension, and her *life* in which I share. Yet at times she may be "frozen out" by exterior enemies who allow her no part in human affairs : or, worse, the "charity of many may grow cold," and she is half-paralysed from within. "Come, Holy Ghost!" *Fove quod est frigidum*—chafe what is chilled, starting with my own unfervent heart.

3. Seldom do the Psalms offer us the chance of thinking about Our Lady; but from of old she has been called "City of God," House of God; and certainly to her God has "done great things." Congratulate her. "We give Thee *thanks* for Thy great glory!" says the *Gloria in Excelsis*—to congratulate God for what He is, and also for what He does—for the incomparable things He has done in Our Lady's soul—is an unselfish and very good sort of prayer.

WHAT GOD DOES NOT DO FOR US

*Ne occidas eos, ne quando obliviscantur populi mei.
Slay them not, lest perchance my People forget !—Psalm
lviii.* 12. *Wed., None, 1, 2.*

1. The prayer seems startling, in view of the Psalmist's desperate cry for rescue from cruel and persistent enemies —enemies that come back and back, prowling round the city like scavenger dogs, howling if they cannot find enough to batten on—since it asks that these enemies should *not* be killed, but only dispersed. But the Psalmist is brave enough to remember that when the Israelites *were* completely rescued, they "quickly forgot" (see Psalm lxxvii. 11 ; 42 ; cv. 13, 21, etc.). The story of the servant who forthwith forgot Joseph, once he had been set free from goal (Gen. xl. 23) repeated itself in the history of Israel and God. Therefore the Psalmist asks for a perpetual reminder.

2. St. Paul, too, begged to be delivered from whatever was that " stake for his flesh " with which God had provided him (2 Cor. xii. 7), and which tormented him. But God replied that His Grace sufficed. Possibly we may have to have the courage to ask God *not* to " lead us out of temptation " altogether! *Ne nos educas e tentatione.* . . . But the prayer may be too daring. Best leave our life to Him, and ask Him to " test " us as *He* sees fit, ever delivering us from the Evil One who is our constant enemy.

3. In verse 10, the Latin says : " I will preserve my strength for Thee! " and that is a fine aspiration for young men and indeed for any who do not want to squander their lives. (The Hebrew means : " My Strength! to Thee will I cling! ") And *reaction after effort* is a special temptation : we have had heavy work—it is over—we risk slacking off ; and in rushes the enemy. Deliver us in the hour of *that* temptation!

THE RIVER OF GOD

Fluminis impetus laetificat civitatem Dei. The rush of the River makes glad the City of God. Psalm xlv. 4. Wed., Matins, Noct., ii, 1.

1. The translation of the Hebrew should probably be : " A river—its divisions make glad . . . etc." There would seem to be a contrast between the stream that strongly yet sweetly sweeps round God's City, and the tumultuous barren upheaval of the sea. We recall the River which is the Holy Spirit, pouring down throughout the Holy City, New Jerusalem, causing the Grove of Life to spring up all around it (Apoc., xxii. 1).

2. It has been traditional to apply these words to Our Blessed Lady who is often called the City of God, in the midst of whom God forever dwells, and through whose soul the Holy Spirit incessantly pours. We often meditate on her Sorrows : but sympathy is deeper when it can exist with

another's joys—in sorrow, we feel that people need us : we can *give :* in joy, we are not necessary : our delight cannot but be utterly unselfish. Can we show that same sympathy with Our Lady ? " The fruit of the Spirit is Joy."

3. It is but recently that the title Regina Pacis was added to the Litany. " Salem " is derived from the word meaning Peace. " Caelestis Urbs, Jerusalem—Beata pacis visio! " The fruit of the Spirit is . . . Peace. Reflect on those characteristics of Our Lady that do not come first to our thoughts. Her peacefulness. . . . She earned all the Beatitudes. " Blessed are the peace-makers "—the peace-givers. It was through her that the enduring Peace between God and man was ratified. Pray, through her, for peace social and national to-day.

．　　．　　．　　．　　．

Perhaps the refrain : " The Lord of Armies is with us : our Protector is the God of Israel," should be inserted also after verse 4.—Verse 11 is probably addressed to the tumultuous world : " Hush! Cease your tumult and realise that *I am God!* " But how applicable to our hustled distracted life! " Come apart, and rest awhile."

．　　．　　．　　．　　．

Vacate et videte quoniam ego sum Deus (ib. 11).

Keep quiet! The psalm tells the Nations to give up their restless attacks on the Holy People. But holy people themselves often require to be told to keep quiet a bit. One is abashed when nuns write that they are " storming heaven " for so and so. Well, storming heaven is usually beyond most of us. It is difficult to get further than "including so and so " in one's memento or intention. I could not possibly describe myself as habitually storming heaven for anything whatsoever. Rather, if I began, I could imagine God saying to me : " Oh, be *quiet* for a minute or two! Am I God, or am I not ? Yes ? Very well, then! " How fussy one's prayers can become!

" Lord—Jack. Lord—Germany! " That is enough, if
only one sees it *is* the Lord. I know that the widow was
importunate ; and the judge yielded to her intolerable
pertinacity. I daren't criticise many or long prayers. But
if only I could keep spiritually quiet enough to see that
God is God—would I ever want to talk ? One look
would suffice.

ISRAEL FORTH FROM EGYPT

In exitu Israel de Aegypto . . . Non nobis, Domine, non
nobis ! When Israel came out of Egypt—not unto us, O
Lord, not unto us.—Psalm cxiii. 1, 9. *Sunday, Vesp.,* 5.

1. The Psalm is so magnificent, so Hebrew, and so
interwoven with Christian history,[1] that we may well try
so to know it as to enter fully into its jubilant yet humble
spirit when it is to be said. Every soul has its "Egypt"—
those "Egypts" in which it *might* have been enslaved
even though God has kept it clear of them : every soul
has its idols *waiting for it*, even if God has guarded it
from worshipping them.

2. We want no affected humility. We want to do great
things, and that God should do great things in us and
through us. Our Lady did not shrink from recognising that
He *had*, nor that " all generations should call her blessed."
But we do want that basic humility which will in any hour
of success *know* that God's Grace is not only what works
through us, but actually is saving us. In all things, in all
things, we need the *Gift* of God.

3. "Idols," and they who worship them—*i.e.*, put
anything or anyone *before* God—are what the Hebrew
loves to call " vanity," " nothingness." The whole fabric
disappears. Work as I may with purely human materials,
my work (together with the entire world as we know it)

[1]Dante's purgatorial souls chanted it. Milton, as a boy, translated it. Francis
Borgia said goodbye, in its words, to grandee-hood : Huguenots used it in
thanks for an escape.

comes to nothing. Work commensurate with myself *is* no more than "I" am; and since I without God, am literally nothing, so will my work be, without Him. I, and it, would "go down into Sheol" whence no praise comes: but if I *live*—if "Christ is living in me"—then both I and my work become everlasting.

LIFE IN COMMON

Quam bonum et quam iucundum, habitare fratres in unum! How good, how pleasant it is, for brothers to live united!—Psalm cxxxii. 1. Thurs., Vesp., 1.

1. Do not be disconcerted by the imagery of this Psalm. In the Hebrew, the consecrating oil is indeed poured on Aaron's head; but it is the beard, not the oil, that touches the neck-opening of the robe. We can get accustomed to the symbolism of "oil," and apply it in this case to the softening power of "charity" within a community, and "dew" again is refreshing and fertilising, which, once more, charity always is.

2. Alas that sometimes life in a community can be intolerable: everyone gets on everyone else's nerves—or even one cantankerous person—critical; seeing the mean side of things; sulking—can make life uncomfortable for everyone else. I will think this over, not fitting the cap to other heads but seeing if *I* am a disturbing element.

3. But I shall want to be, positively, a peace-making, unifying, element. May I act *dilectione non ficta* towards my brethren: this holds good as within presbytery, seminary, school, or home or parish. Not a "false," affected charity.

GOD'S WORK IN OUR WORK

Nisi Dominus aedificaverit . . . Nisi Dominus custodierit! Unless it be the Lord who buildeth . . . unless

it be the Lord who guardeth.—Psalm cxxvi. 1. *Tues.,
Vesp.,* 5.

1. This grave Psalm reminded the Israelites, on their
return from Captivity, that all their efforts to rebuild
and preserve Jerusalem would be futile, unless *God* was
the origin of their efforts. Verse 2 means : " Vain is it
for you to rise so early, and so late take rest—yet that
eat the bread of weariness—" (the Latin absolutely needs
correction here : " bread of sorrow " means the bread that
is earned at the expense of heavy toil) : for *He* giveth bread
to His beloved even while they sleep." God has no *need*
of human effort : He can give sustenance, and even
results of what would normally have needed heavy labour,
even while men sleep—and to His beloved will do so.

2. This does not mean that we can freely relax our
efforts. We *are* His " beloved " all the more, if we toil
to do His will. But results proportionate to any labour
of ours would be (i) very small, and (ii) of the same
sort as ourselves and our work—*i.e.*, only human : the
results that we long for are super-natural, grace-results.
" Paul planted : Apollo watered : but it was God who
gave the increase " (1 Cor. iii. 6). This is emphasised in
St. Matthew, vi. 25–32 ; and recall the exquisite little
parable in Mark iv. 26–28. The sower sows his seed :
" And he sleeps, and he wakes, night and day : and the
seed sprouts and lengthens—how, he himself knows not !
Of herself the earth bears her increase ; first the blade,
then the ear ; then the full corn in the ear." Work, then,
with all your strength : but have real horror at the thought
that the upshot may be *commensurate* with your strength !

3. God *wants* rich increase ! Such is the sense of the
last two verses. (*Filii excussorum* should be " sons of
youth "—sons begotten in youth, and so, adult by the
time their father would need their help. If we demand
some meaning for the Latin, say : " The sons of them
had been shaken off, or out " ; *i.e.*, exiled.)

X

TOWARDS THE MORE ABUNDANT LIFE

The Hebrew, clear that everything depends on God, and comes from Him—so clear about that, that he hardly troubled to think about what we should call secondary or intermediary causes : it was God who sent rain and spoke in the thunder ; who made darkness as well as light, and formed peace alike and war (Is. xlv. 7)—knew, too, that life itself depended entirely upon Him. " Life is in His Will " (Ps. xxix. 5) can be accepted as meaning, first, that physical life was His gift : God breathed it into the very first man ; and, since then, all living creatures do so live because of His gift freely given or withdrawn (Ps. ciii. 29). But further, there was no true life to be lived apart from God and His *righteous* Will. This Will might make itself known simply in what we might call man's conscience : all men feel that there is *a* difference between good and evil—they have a " moral instinct," so to say. This issues into the ordinary moral virtues, those proper to the " average well-living man." But the Hebrew was privileged to possess God's *Law* as no other people of the world possessed it : it had been " given " to him ; revealed to him, through Moses, on Mount Sinai. Therefore, within the Hebrew people distinctions had to be made between those who defied the Law ; those who bore it, if not reluctantly, at least without enthusiasm and with but intermittent success ; and those who loved it even passionately—and it is this passionate devotion to God and to His Law which characterises the Psalmists as well as the Prophets.

We add here a parenthesis. All sorts of literature are to be found in the Old Testament. Some of it seems purely legalistic and ceremonial; some is " ethical," common-sense, directly dealing with behaviour : some is aspiring and ecstatic. Many critics, on the strength of this, wish to assign these different sorts of literature to different authors, if not ages. So far as that particular argument goes, it seems to us worthless. You do not expect to find either moral rules or soaring contemplation in, say, the directions about saying Mass at the beginning of the Missal. You do not look for idealism or mysticism in Canon Law or a book of casuistry. Nor again do you seek for financial rulings or tables of affinity in a book on the " higher prayer." Yet all such *sorts* of things not only co-exist, as we see, in the Church, but grew up together from the outset. St. Paul, for all the sublimity of his visions, could give authoritative, practical and extremely commonsense directions about buying food in the market and how to behave at dinner-parties ; indeed he did so in the very same letter (1 Cor.) which contains his glorious panegyric of Charity ; and that very panegyric embraces not only some of the noble consequences of " charity," *i.e.*, love of your fellow-men for God's sake, but also its ultimate and wholly supernatural upshot, that is, the Beatific Vision. And St. John, who could be a very careful historian, could also spread his wings and soar to con-template the invisible ; and his Apocalypse not only makes accurate use of the most concrete contemporary facts, but also of an elaborate, traditional and technical symbolism (though he uses it powerfully, as a true creative artist should), and yet it reaches a towering mysticism surpassed by no writer that we know of—neither St. Teresa, St. John of the Cross, nor any other. Hence the mood of the Psalmist changes : his spiritual level rises, so to say, and sinks : within a single Psalm, he can begin from black despondency and end with thrilling exultation.

And with a man's mood, his style and his very vocabulary will change.

Does this mean that the Psalmist announces mysteries directly concerned with what theologians mean by Grace and the Supernatural ? In a sense, the whole of the Hebrew's religion was " supernatural," because he regarded it, as we said, as " given," revealed. He had not worked it out simply by means of his own intelligence : his faith was no human produce merely. We know with what difficulty he envisaged personal survival after bodily death, or rather, a survival which would contain any relationship with God. But (see p. 46 Sq.) we feel sure that so strong was his conviction that he was bound up with the Eternal Ever-Living God (who did not cease to be, when man appeared to do so), that with very little help he would have been led on to the perception that bodily death itself could not snap the bonds that bound him to his Lord. And of course in the later centuries of Jewish history, that perception was clear ; that conviction, vigorous. But there is little if anything of this in the Psalms, though the Resurrection, *we* can see, is prophesied there. But how deeply the Psalmist probed into the meaning of his own words, we cannot tell.

But it was not part of his genius to construct theories —even when he faced up to a problem, it was a practical one, such as, How could the pagans flourish so ? was it worth serving God ? and he solved these in terms of practical experience. There are, however, certain sentences which contain the germ of truly supernatural doctrine and which, moreover, have become part and parcel of Catholic phraseology, such as : " In Thy Light shall we see light " ; " Thou dost grant him his heart's desire." It is not too much to say that what the Christian knows, what God has given and will give, was latent in the inarticulate yearnings of the Hebrew soul.

MAN'S HAPPINESS

*Beatus vir . . . Happy the Man !—Non sic impii,
non sic !—Psalm i. 1, 4. Sunday, Matins, Noct. i. 1.*

1. The Psalms are Songs of Righteousness. This
" covering Psalm " is placed as head to the whole Psalter.
It is simple, yet full of material to be elaborated in further
Psalms. It declares only that *he* is happy, enduring,
creative, who does not throw in his lot with the wicked.
It is *they* who are sterile and come to nothing.

2. He does not accompany the wicked to carry out their
plans : nor halt to talk things over—*their* things—with
them when he meets them : still less, sit down along with
evil, whisper and nod, join in their schemes. No : his
will is " set " in accordance with God's Law : day and
night he muses upon that, and on it models his life. Hence,
when the trial comes, the wicked shall not be able to
stand up to confront their judge, nor to face the assembled
righteous. They cower, droop and fade away, and reach
nowhere.

3. The middle of the Psalm has another picture : a
palm-tree standing sturdily by a water-spring or channel.
The blank, dusty desert lies all round the oasis : clumps
of palms stand round it : their leaves help to make soil
and their roots hold it together : their fruit suffices for
life. As for what is God-less, it builds nothing. It lies
in shifting heaps : it makes dirty films over things : it
can blow high into clouds and obscure the sky, and rise
in eddying columns. But finally it vanishes : the tree
and the water remain.—In this world, the only solid
fact is the Catholic Church and the Catholic in so far
as he is vitally incorporate with her. But reflect how
widely the Church throws her beneficent shade, and
how much that is good in life is due to a forgotten Christian

heredity; and how the Catholic fruit can be, as it were, exported! May I share in giving to others, what by my Catholic privileges I possess.

THE GUEST OF GOD

Domine, quis habitabit in tabernaculo tuo? . . . Qui facit haec, non movebitur in aeternum. O Lord, who shall dwell within Thy tent? . . . The man who acts thus shall not be disturbed for ever.—Psalm xiv. 1, 7. Mon., Matins, Noct., i. 2.

1. The Psalm may surprise us. Who is he who shall never be dislodged from the Lord's dwelling into which he has been received? He who acts justly; tells the truth; does not injure his neighbour nor believe anything against him (1 Cor. xiii : Charity believeth all things . . .); disregards slanderers; keeps his word; does not lend money as usury nor take bribes.—Well! We might expect any decent man to behave almost like that: does not the Beatific Vision require more from us?

2. Yes. But the Hebrew, who knew nothing explicitly about faith, hope and charity, and supernatural grace, none the less did link up his " natural virtues " with God and His Law. He undoubtedly wished to believe in all that God had made known about Himself; and it was because of Him that he was sorry if he sinned.

3. But also, we hold that it is impossible to observe the natural virtues consistently, without Grace. And again, the habit of natural virtues makes it much easier for Grace to raise them supernaturally, so that they act quickly and decisively according to God's call, and so as to turn each ordinary act into real and meritorious service. Thus the habitually despondent man will not so easily hope : the semi-malicious gossip will with difficulty maintain true " charity " : the self-indulgent in

small things slips easily to worse faults. God forbid that we should disesteem " natural " virtues like honesty or truthfulness or kindness! Yet even people vowed to God and to perfection all too often do so.

LIFE FIRM-BUILDED

Filiae eorum compositae, circumornatae ut similitudo templi : Their daughters are placed together—set round about like a temple.—Psalm cxliii. 12. Sat., Vesp., 1, 2.

1. The Psalmist is praying for, and describing, the prosperity of Messianic days. (The Latin, as from verse 12, seems to describe the prosperity of the *wicked*. But the Psalmist is praying that *our* sons may be strong, and so forth.) May our sons be like strong young saplings ; our daughters, like corner-pillars, decked (carved) as for a temple (or palace). We can, then, pray with the Psalmist that our young men may be strong, energetic, creative of much good in God's Church ; our young women, reliable ; comely, yet, they, too, strong—like the tall, quiet colonnades of a temple.

2. We deplore the element of " flightiness," irresponsibility, whether in ourselves or others. You cannot possibly rely on *that* : nor can you make anything of it. Such persons will no doubt describe the reliable character as " heavy," hide-bound and so forth. No matter. Solidity is to be preferred to flimsiness.

3. Any life, but especially a priest's or an ecclesiastical student's, has to begin with a rigid adherence to duty. No matter if this involves routine or monotony : a firm framework is needed for such a life, and indeed for any layman's life, especially if it includes not a little leisure. Duty-works ought to be done first, at once, and gladly— not just as a bore to be got rid of. Such works should be

dear, because they are certainly right: impulsive, self-chosen works are very likely not so.

. . . . .

Verse 13. He prays that the prosperous people's "garners may be full, brimming with every kind of grain"—that their sheep may "throng their pastures," or be abundant in their young: "that there be no breach in our walls, nor goings out (into exile), nor outcry in our streets."

DISCIPLINE AND UNDERSTANDING

Bonitatem, et disciplinam, et scientiam doce me. Teach me kindness, and discipline, and understanding.—Psalm cxviii. 66. Sunday, Terce, 2.

1. Within any organised group—school—parish—there should be "discipline," using the word in the modern sense. This means that the officially inferior obey the officially superior. I dare take no balm to my soul, if I am "in office," as though I were *worth* any more than my subordinates, lay or clerical. (The Psalmist is no doubt alluding to interior discipline—self-discipline—in which what is essentially higher (mind and choice) must control the lower (senses), and exterior penances are found, to a greater or less extent in individuals, to help towards this. Hence the small scourges sometimes used are called 'disciplines'. Neither I, nor any community, can thrive if there be rebels present, active, and unmanageable.

2. One must be "patient" even with one's self. We cannot change the ingredients of which we are constructed; nor can we *give* ourselves Grace or even, strictly speaking, earn it. As for others, even the firmest-treated must know that there is true goodness, kindness, in a Superior; neither favouritism, nor affectation, nor what depends on how he is feeling at the time. Often an apparent "rebel"

may be suffering: he may have been jarred, galled; be temperamentally shy, obstinate, over-sensitive, "artistic," dull: he cannot help being it at the moment: he may really be in pain because he is "like that," but would certainly accept the firmness if he felt inwardly sure about the kindness. The French say: "Le bon Dieu": the Germans, "Der lieber Gott." The English used to say: "Our most courteous Lord Jesus Christ."

3. In this way, I shall gain "understanding," and in proportion as I gain it, I shall grow kind. Constantly pray for those gifts of the Holy Spirit which are "know-ledge, and wisdom and insight" (Col. i. 9). We need to know our men—not only know about them.

POSTERITY FOR THE PEACEFUL

Sunt reliquiae homini pacifico. There is a future for the peaceable man.—Psalm xxxvi. 37. Tues., Noct., ii, 3.

1. Probably this means there is a "posterity" for the man of peace. But take it as meaning that there is a "future," and "after," for the quiet, uncontentious man. People say: "You must fight for your rights. Anticipate attack *by* attack. If you don't *thrust*, shoulder your way to the front, you will be thrust *out*." This Psalm is full of the opposite doctrine. It is like the Sermon on the Mount. "Blessed are the meek—the quiet and gentle—for they shall inherit the land."

2. A purely self-regarding doctrine? I behave quietly because I shall get more in the long run by doing so? No. For we assume that we are thinking of the best method of acting in view of *God's* triumph, not our own. And the best way of serving God and the Church is not the method of force or retaliation.

3. It is unlikely that I shall even be able to use physical force. But perhaps I can use financial coercion, which i

a very vile thing to do. You still see wills: "If you become a Catholic, or marry again, you shall be cut off penniless." Or our retaliation may be vocal. Sarcasm is a weapon which some can wield; but if we do so at the expense of others who may be slower-witted than we though quite as sensitive, we leave scars that never can be healed, and produce no good of any lasting sort.

GOD'S WILL IS LIFE-WARD

Vita in voluntate eius. In His will is life.—Psalm xxix. 5. *Mon., Matins, Noct., iii, 3.*

1. Probably the original meaning was: " (In His anger, for a moment, is adversity); life is in His favour (or, good will)." And it continues: " Weeping may make its home, or, lodging, in the evening: in the morning, there is singing." The Psalmist may be thanking God for recovery from bodily sickness: he had but a vague conception of the future life compared with ours, so that his appeal not to die is understandable, but would be inadequate on Christian lips. " What profit would there be (to Thee) in my blood, should I (die and) go down into the Under-World? Shall the dust praise Thee, or proclaim Thy loyalty and truth? " (See also v. 3.)

2. But it is a cry that well takes its place on the lips of men who know they cannot save themselves from sin: they feel already doomed to hell—they *are* not; but they feel—" If I cannot conquer my habits of sin, I *must* be," and often give up trying. No man is necessary to God: but the Psalm allows us to expostulate with God, and ask what *use* it would be, were I lost?

3. My whole life really amounts to my doing His will. " In His will is our peace." " My food is to do the will of Him that sent Me." But more than that—What He wills me to be, *is*, simply, my only real life and self.

U

LIGHT IN GOD'S LIGHT

*In lumine tuo videbimus lumen. In Thy Light shall we
see light.—Psalm xxxv. 10. Thurs., Lauds, 3.*

1. Verses 6–10 of this Psalm can hardly be meditated
too often. The Latin transcends the beauty of the Hebrew :
all the more readily may we adhere to it. " O Lord, Thy
mercy is as high as heaven—Thy faithfulness, even to the
clouds. . . . Thy righteousness is as high as the heaven-
high hills—Thy verdicts deep as the deepest depths.
Both man and brute, O Lord, dost Thou preserve—O how
hast Thou multiplied Thy mercy, Lord ! " The pity of
God also for dumb animals is seen at the end of the prophecy
of Jonas ; and in Ps. ciii ; p. 18. Not only God's Power
and Wisdom move thrilling through all creation ; but
His mercy, His love, dominate both its beginning and
its end. Impossible to treat an animal or even a flower
irreverently : it is God who " invented " them, and is
preserving each. Touch the humblest living creature—
living with the lowliest form of life—and you may say
that it is God that you touch, in this sense, that life is the
direct manifestation of Himself.

2. " But as for the human race—under the shadow of
Thy wings it takes its refuge. " They shall be intoxicated
with the abundance of Thy House," says the Latin : " with
the torrent of Thy delight wilt Thou give them to drink ! "
We have intelligence : but God wants to flood our minds
with the knowledge of Himself : and He wants us to
delight in what we know. If we would but believe how
happy God wants us to be !

3. " In Thy Light shall we see light." The Psalmist
may indeed have meant merely : " If Thou art favourable,
we shall prosper." That is true : but how far deeper
does the Christian see ! And why ? Because, the True

Light being poured over us (re-read the Christmas Preface) we do indeed " see light " amid the obscurities of creation un-interpreted by Christ. " With Thee is the Fountain of Life! " If I am in the dark, I can hardly live. I feel stifled and I dare not move. But if world and self be illuminated, interpreted, vivified by Christ, I am all-but in heaven while still upon the earth : Heaven certainly comes into *me*.

.   .   .   .   .

Oculi mei semper ad Dominum—My eyes are ever towards the Lord (*xxiv.* 15).

Are they ? I like looking at all sorts of things, and it is often my duty to do so. Also I constantly catch myself squinting *at* myself. I know I make my " general intention " or " morning offering," which is supposed to cover all I do during the day, and supernaturalise it ; but that somehow seems *in the concrete* the quick way out, and I cannot *really* say that a God-ward intention is *really* at the back of my mind even. But can't I ? Yes ; I believe that I keep one eye, at least, on God much more than I am aware of. The Christian is always a baptised creature. The Holy Ghost, unless he expel Him by deliberate sin, is in him and at work and whispering and infusing Himself into life ; and even when I sin, I cannot prevent grace tackling me and twisting me back by little tugs and pluckings. Then after all, one *is* habitually trying, and trusting, and expecting. Lord, you know perfectly well that I *don't* expect or even wish anything to succeed independently of you. My eyes *are* always towards you. I look to You! If at any given moment You suddenly said : " Do *I* come into this at all ? " I should answer, horrified, " But of *course* You do! Apud Te substantia mea. Tibi oculi! "

.   .   .   .   .

Tibi dixit cor meum : ' Exquisivit Te facies mea' : faciem Tuam, Domine, requiram. ' Ne avertas faciem Tuam a me ! ' To Thee saith my heart : My face doth seek Thee. . . . Turn not away Thy face from me (xxvi. 8, 9).

The same thing. I keep glancing up and wanting to catch God's glance. His eyes and my eyes catching one another. My *heart* says—Lord, my face is always hunting for Thine. Oh yes! I shall always be on the look-out for Thy face! Do not turn it away. O Lord, never look away! Extraordinary, how sometimes you feel as if you had to hunt for God and could not see Him anywhere, and then suddenly realise that God is simply staring at you—but with a very loving stare—through all these things, in them all. Things simply *are* God's features : but even when you catch a friend's face and could reckon up his features if you wanted to, the thing is the mind that looks at you through the eyes ; the " he " behind his face. So present a God, and so dear a one! My eyes are always towards Thee, and Thine towards me. But grant that at least sometimes we may look right *into* one another's eyes!

. . . . . .

The verse *corresponds* to us—we are conscious that our heart's gaze peers after God : it is natural that we should pray that God on His side should look in our direction, so that our eyes should encounter each other. Yet the Hebrew is very impressive : " Thy command, says my heart, is ' Seek ye my Face! ' Therefore indeed, O Lord, do I seek it! Turn it not from me! " God *wants* us to seek Him : the very fact that we wish to—begin to —is proof that God has " made contact " with us to some extent at any rate—" Thou wouldst not seek Me," says St. Augustine, " hadst thou not already found Me." If we tend to say : We would not have sought Him, had He not already found *us*—we recall that He never loses us. Even if we sin, He is close at hand, trying to turn our faces round *towards* Him.

THE LORD OF LIFE

Placebo Domino in regione vivorum.—Ut placeam coram Domino in lumine viventium. I shall be pleasing to the Lord in the Land of the living.—That I may be pleasing to the Lord in the Light of the Living.—Psalm cxiv. 9. Mon., Vesp., 1. Psalm lv. 13, Wed., Sext, 1.

1. God has " set my soul towards life " (p. 299). I shall not die, but live. It is an evil jest of the devil's to have made religion seem a " dead-and-live " affair : to suggest that the " religious " do not " see life " ; whereas it is sin, God-less-ness, that are death—almost physical death, at times. " I am come that they might have life, and have it more abundantly " (John x. 10).

2. But it is in the *land* of the living that I am to please God. Not only in a secret and hidden solitude. True, our proper " land " is the promised land of heaven : but already here we are meant to make a version of it such as befits our state. The Christian Community ought to be happy—even, noticeably so. Not by a forced or affected happiness or heartiness, but owing to an interior fount of happiness that communicates itself all around us.

3. And again, we are to please God in the *light* of the living. Our minds ought to be clearer because of our sure knowledge of the truth and of *how* to please God. True, once more, we live now in a twilight at best ; but twilight can be exquisitely transparent—it is not a fog. And this is what pleases God. He has no delight in the death of a sinner, but wishes him to live (Ezek. xviii. 23, etc.). Would that we might understand how God Himself is the absolute Joy, and it is because He will

fully communicate Himself to us that we shall "enjoy"
the Beatific—Blissful-making—Vision. And God, on
His side, will be "well-pleased" with us. We shall be
a pleasant sight in the divine Eyes. St. Augustine vividly
said that the simplest souls could be "God's honey."
Even though the Hebrew word here may mean "walk,"
well, to walk freely to and fro, at home in our Father's
House, watched lovingly, delightedly, by Him, means
that we *shall* be "pleasing" to Him, and pleasing Him.

THE VISION OF GOD SUFFICES

*Satiabor cum apparuerit gloria tua. I shall be satisfied
when Thy glory hath appeared.—Psalm xvi. 15. Mon.,
Matins, Noct, i, 3.*

1. The right translation may well be: "I shall be
satisfied, when I awake, with Thy likeness"—*i.e.*, the
Vision of Thee. In either case, what the Psalmist says
is superlatively true for the Christian: when I "awake"
in heaven—when God shows Himself to me—I shall
be *satisfied*. "Thou hast made us for Thyself, and restless
is our heart till it finds rest with Thee": St. Augustine.
The word "satisfied," which we usually apply in rather
an enfeebled sense—"Well, I'm satisfied" means less
than "I am *delighted!*": in fact, we say: "I'm *quite*
satisfied—I'm more than satisfied!" to express *great*
pleasure—here, then, this word means its absolute
maximum: I could not wish for more—I never even
wished or hoped for so much.

2. In this part of my life I am always half alseep. I
am like a drugged man. Even when I believe a truth of
Religion, I do not "see" it; half the time it may "mean"
but little to me; at times God makes its light shine through
more vividly: but most of the time we "see" not only
"as by means of a mirror" (1 Cor. xiii. 12), but "dimly";

ancient mirrors, such as St. Paul alludes to, were seldom very perfect: shadowy reflections: even, distorted images. "Lord, that I may see!"

3. But meantime, I must be forming God's "likeness" in me: one old translation of our text was: "according to Thy likeness." And we *are* to be "like" God. Nor does this mean preoccupation with self, for God is active, creative, radiating; He sends forth His Holy Spirit of Love. To be "in His likeness," so too must I! "In His image, in His likeness." So were Adam and Eve created. But now there is a New Adam—Christ—the *adequate* "forth-shining" of God. It is to *Him* that I must be like. We must be "satisfied" with one another!

MY URGE TOWARDS LIFE

Posuit animam meam ad vitam. He hath set my soul life-wards.—Psalm lxv. 8. Thurs., Matins, Noct., i, 3.

1. The literal meaning is simply that God has rescued the Psalmist: but we will use the sense offered by the Latin—God has implanted in our soul a *tendency* towards "life," and all that God means by "life"—the "more abundant life" that Christ came to give (St. John x. 10). Human Nature, by itself, has no tendency towards the super-natural: but then, it has never been left to itself. In Paradise, it was already "graced": it fell from Grace, but was forthwith summoned back to it. Even the un-graced, dis-graced, soul has to resist God's call to "life" if it stays where it is. Yet everyone really wants life rather than death: if they deny that, they mean that they prefer "death rather than these my bones" (Job vii. 15); rather than the *sort* of life they are having to live at the moment. But it is not merely a better version of this *sort* of life towards which God has "set" me.

2. Once I realise that all "religion" is a response to

the Living God ; that it makes me more, not less : expands, enriches ; I shall experience within me that " setting " of my soul towards Life.

3. " Thou hast made us ' towards ' Thyself; and restless is our soul till it finds rest in Thee! " The Psalmist, as ever unable to keep his joy to himself, cries : " Come! listen! I will tell you what great things He has done for my soul! " In Hebrew, this means just " for me " : but link it up with Our Lady's " He . . . hath done great things for me, to and in me." Perhaps she was thinking of this very verse. It is no true humility always to speak in a depreciatory way of ourselves. Please God, we are " graced " souls, and nothing can be greater than that.

THE HEART'S DESIRE

Desiderium cordis eius tribuisti ei. Thou hast given him his heart's desire.—Psalm xx. 2. Mon., Matins, Noct., iii, 2.

1. This Psalm should probably be read together with the previous one (xix). It may well be a hymn after a battle, as Psalm xix may well have preceded one. There is, too, much in it that can be applied to our Lord. But " the heart's desire " is an expression that has come to form part of our language.

2. We have so many preferences, wishes, hopes, things we " would like to have "—but not much that is worthy of being called the very heart's desire. What do I *really* want, " in my heart ? " The question may almost terrify us, because we often discover that what we do has only a secondary motive —for instance, to stand well with another ; to escape what we ought to do and dislike doing : the fibres of self-love strike unbelievably deep into us. We begin then by imploring God to purify those unknown depths in our heart, where there may be roots of self-worship, origins of self-delusion, of which we simply do not know the existence.

3. And yet, deeper still, we can trust that we do not *really* want what is, after all, the caricature, the poor parody, of the Good; even when I hunt for secondary things, maybe ultimately *that* is not what I really want. Oh God, grant me *that;* and to ensure my really wanting it, " make my heart like unto Thy Heart! " Be a Heart inside my heart. What I cannot put into words or even thought, be *that* Thy mind, Thy desire, Thine effort, innermost within me.

THE TEMPEST'S HEART

Exaudivi te in abscondito tempestatis. In the hidden heart of the tempest have I heard thy prayer.—Psalm *lxxx.* 8. *Fri., Matins, Noct., iii,* 2.

1. This Psalm looks back to the rescue, first, of Joseph from his Egyptian prison; then, to that of the Israelites from Egypt itself. " The hidden place of the thunder " refers to the storm-clouds that enveloped Sinai when God spoke to Moses. We can consider *our* thunder-storms to consist, first, of our temptations, and then to remember that however fierce and loud they be, God is still at the centre of all things, and even in the temptation—for He never allows a temptation to beset us that is too strong for us.

2. Somewhat as in the middle of a cyclone, there is a kind of " heart of stillness," so in the world's uproar there is a space of silence in which *God* is : sometimes in His goodness He may draw us in there, so that the soul knows herself alone with God and united with Him. This produces at once a great calm and a great strength, for the soul has nothing between itself and the source of all strength; nor need either speak in words to the other—nor even through thoughts. The divine Silence is full of God's Creative Word and we need nothing secondary to that.

3. God is always in our hearts, whether they be calm or tempest-tossed. The practice of speaking to God

within her was dear to St. Teresa; and, after dreadful temptation, St. Catherine of Siena asked God where He had been, and the answer was: " In the very middle of thy heart!" May we practise that withdrawal, by Faith, into our own heart, and there meet God.

●   ●   ●   ●   ●

It is but just that we should recall the last part of the Psalm. Despite all His goodness to the Israelites, they deserted God; they wished they were back in Egypt (read Jeremias vii; it is the most tragic account of Israel's " backsliding " and idolatrous faithlessness. Moses had interceded and obtained grace for the People: here, God says: " Pray not thou for this people, neither lift up cry nor prayer for them neither make intercession for them, for I will not hear thee!"). So God, who does violence to no man's will, " sent them off after their heart's desire " (see p. 300); they follow their own inventions. But " Oh that My People had listened to Me! that Israel had walked in My ways! In a moment—at no cost —would I have humbled their foes. . . . I would have fed them with richest wheat; with honey from the rock would I have sated them!" Recall Our Lord's tears over Jerusalem: " Hadst thou but known, even thou, at least in this thy day . . .!" (Lk. xix. 42) " Hadst *known*, with efficacious knowledge: hadst known, and acted according unto it!" But the Latin states a fact, not a wish. In spite of everything, they turned reluctantly, feebly—yet sufficiently—towards Him; and He fed them with the Bread that contains all manner of sweetness. Our Lord does not refuse Communion even to the sinner who creeps timorously, tentatively, pitifully back to Him.

INTO THE HEART OF GOD

Abscondit me in tabernaculo suo: in die malorum protexit me in abscondito tabernaculi sui. Abscondes

I can check myself by acknowledging that the writer meant, directly, by this that God is an overwhelmingly generous host, who " pours out " (the Hebrew is actually less strong than the Latin) the abundance of His household on to His guests, and gives them lavishly to eat and drink : and that the last words mean that in His favour we shall " see light," *i.e.*, prosper. But short of the mystical and theological interpretations that the Middle Ages put upon these words, we have the perfect right, if not to see the whole doctrine of the Trinity or Incarnation in them, at least to go far beyond a mere material deduction. I have the right to recognise what the words mean to *me*. Certainly the words illuminate themselves and influence me in a particular way. Certainly these verses can alter and enrich and encourage my life. Provided I do not go outside Catholic dogma, I may make the most of them.

Well, I am intoxicated by the " cornucopia " of God's House. By the all-inclusiveness and the lavish out-pouring of Himself through His Catholic Church. Why " intoxicated " ? Because it appears that men who have had too much wine see things in a sort of haze · they are not too clever at distinguishing one thing accurately from the next. Well, I can attend to one gift of the Church, and then another—but they come tumbling out too fast, very soon, for me to be able, or to want, to see each one separately. I turn to Heaven—God is there. I look towards man ; God is there also. I cannot touch one thing within God's Catholic gift, without being swept forthwith away to seeing round it and in it and with it innumerable other truths, rights, graces. I am in a swirl. I say to God : " Not so much! not all at once! " *Ubertas ! Domus Tua !* How pinchbeck, departmental, fragmentary, are the doles of science, art, nationalisms, ethics! The Res Catholica! The *whole* thing—yet the one thing within which, I, a tiny item, can wander around, assimilate this and that, and intermittently get intoxicated with the Whole. It is very likely that I shall keep myself to myself when such accidents happen : but all the same, I shall want to " tell the world," and am checked chiefly by the fear of being ill-mannered or unkind from telling the artist or the reformer how very limited he seems to me.

In lumine Tuo. " In Thy Light shall I see light." " I see light at last! " " Ah! if I'd ever looked at it in *that* light! " You see (i) the complete harmony—not, of course, that you really do, nor will you till you see God face to face ; but you see much more of it than usual, and you see something that is *harmony* and not confusion ; and you see (ii) that it is " light," and not darkness, as a rack would be—for, perfectly well put together as rack might be as a machine, it yet would be ugly and creative of disharmony because of the purpose to which it was to be put. But God did not create the world to be a rack, though that is precisely what our sins often turn it into.

In any case, the fountain of light is God, that is, of the sort of light that really suits the world and eternity. You can have a blaze of electricity that dazzles you or illuminates a patch and actually prevents you seeing more than a few yards down the street, and, of course, absolutely extinguishes the stars and removes all perspective near or distant. Such a light emphasises a very few things to the disadvantage of all the rest. God's light creates such a perspective that, it is true, close-at-hand things may be seen as almost unimportant. On the other hand, it makes them glow from within, which no other kind of light succeeds in doing.

I AM PRAYER!

Ego autem orabam. But I, meanwhile, I prayed.—
Psalm cviii. 4. Sat., None, 1, 2, 3.

1. First, it can be held for good reasons that verses 6 to 19 are the imprecations uttered against the Psalmist

by his enemies : not that imprecations are unknown upon the lips of the inspired writers. Under the torrent of abuse, he begs *God* not to keep silence, but to proclaim that the woes of the Psalmist are permitted by Him, and will not always endure.

2. The text is, in Hebrew, vividly : " But I—I am prayer! " The Psalmist simply becomes a living prayer, Prayer incarnate. You sometimes see people who simply *are* hate, charity, lust, honesty. These qualities express themselves in every line of their face, every attitude and flex of their limbs. The Psalmist wished that his prayer should be much more than what he spoke with his lips. " Saying prayers " is never quite the same as praying. Even in the most reverent vocal prayer, there is an interior spirit which prays beyond the outline of the words.

3. It is possible to reach—not exactly a double consciousness, so that while you are doing your ordinary actions you know that you are *also* praying : but a prayer of the will, so that everything is " willed " towards God : you will that He should inspire what you are doing ; be served by it ; carry it forward as *His*. Were God to wish you actively and positively to pray, He would find no obstacle interposed by you. This would really be because the Holy Spirit, as St. Paul says, is praying in the innermost of your heart, and you are giving Him free outlet. Ask that you may, to the maximum, become Prayer. Towards this, may this poor little book have helped, even from a great distance.

. . . . . .

Our main hope, when suggesting " meditations " on any subject, is that readers may so use what is written as to make a meditation, afterwards, entirely of their own, quite likely discarding the offered ideas and even disliking them. Provided they " feed " upon the inspired Word of God, all is well. They will find that the Psalms

" come alive," and that almost every verse, not only the obviously beautiful ones, can act directly on their souls. Just as it is possible to spend a day, or a week, or even longer, with " St. Paul," or " St. John," at the back of the mind (as they say), so is it possible to spend a " Psalm-week," and to find that in the most varied circumstances or moods, something from the Psalms comes whispering its way up, and encourages, or pacifies, or checks one's acts or thoughts, or deepens one's vision. Hence we seriously ask readers to *work* at the Psalms. Never mind obscurities : they always clear themselves up *sufficiently*. Do not let yourselves be checked by expressions—verbal or " temperamental "—which at first may jar on you. Once you are accustomed to the Psalms, you will find that you automatically make a " translation " of such phrases or moods. So don't be frightened of the Psalms! Take it for granted that there is something in them—for you—and something that you won't get anywhere else. And perhaps especially if you think that you are very " ordinary," and can't cope with sublime sorts of Prayer, well, if you are going to be Priests, you *must* try to cope with the Psalms; and, if you are lay-folks, may God fill you with the wish to try to do so. In the whole of the world's literature, the Psalms are unique, though only by praying them—not by comparing them with other ancient literature, or arguing about their dates and so on—will you discover that uniqueness. The Psalms are a *Catholic Treasure :* make the very most of them : for every one verse that we have used, you will find nine that can, and please God will, become your personal dear possession.

DIXI : NUNC COEPI!